HAHN'S ORAON FOLK-LORE IN THE ORIGINAL

HAHN'S

ORAON FOLK-LORE

IN THE ORIGINAL

A critical text with translations and notes

BY
A. GRIGNARD, S.J.,
of the Catholic Mission of Chota Nagpur.

GYAN

ISBN: 978-81-212-1390-5(HB)

First Published in 1931
Indian Reprint in 2017

Published by

Gyan Publishing House
5, Ansari Road
Daryaganj, New Delhi-110002
Phone: 9811692060
E-mail: books@gyanbooks.com

Cataloging in Publication Data—DK
Courtesy: D.K. Agencies (P) Ltd. <docinfo@dkagencies.com>

Hahn, Ferdinand, author.
Hahn's Oraon folk-lore in the original: a critical text with translations and notes / by A. Grignard (S.J.).
pages cm
Reprint. Originally published: Patna: Superintendent, Government Printing, Bihar and Orissa, 1931.
ISBN 9788121213905 (HB)

1. Oraon (Indic people)—Folklore. 2. Folk literature, Kurukh. 3. Folk literature, Kurukh—Translations into English. 4. Oraon (Indic people)—Social life and customs. I. Grignard, A., translator,, editor. II. Title.

GR305.7.O72H33 2017 DDC 398.20491597 23

FOREWORD.

THE great merit from a linguistic view point of the Oraon legends, as published in 1905 by the late F. Hahn of the G. E. L. Mission, is that they were, in style and wording, manifestly aboriginal. Coming direct from the pen of true-born Oraons, they constituted, and still constitute (it is hoped), in this amended edition, a capital document for all students of the language.

But a critical edition of this interesting and idiomatic folk-lore was very desirable. While the establishing of a critical text need not impair the special value of the collection, it would add much to its facility of comprehension, and assist in the acquisition of the language considerably. In conformity with these views, which were those of the Bihar and Orissa Government, the present reviser has been careful not to improve upon native wording and composition, even when its literature seemed to him a little at fault. And if elsewhere, for reasons of another kind, alterations have appeared imperative, he has carried them out invariably with the assistance or full sanction of an Oraon helper at his side.

This much being premised, it may be freely admitted that, if all reforms in word-spelling and all substitutions of plain nouns for accumulated demonstrative pronouns were deemed 'alterations,' the latter might well seem legion. The whole truth is that, in Hahn's publication, the editing rule that other people's texts should be left 'untouched by hand' had been sadly overdone. Haphazard and inconsistent spellings, long words cut up into likely bits, occasional short words combined into one solid term of a just size, expositive sentences sporting a note of interrogation in their middle, or made otherwise unintelligible to even native eyes (though not always to the native ear) : all this seemed to call for a 'handling' of some light sort.

But there were other imperfections. Some tales, and more particularly descriptions of customs and festivals, had a texture so interwoven with afterthoughts and belated additions or restrictions—in short, were so rambling in style,—that they hardly left any neat impression upon a reader's mind. Four or five times in the course of some thirty lines he was penning, the writer had suddenly become aware that a necessary detail had been left out somewhere higher up: he had, then, introduced the complementary information into the fresh matter he was treating of at the moment...The emendation of such texts has naturally required transfers, and some brief welding, besides, of the sentences thus brought into contact.

Finally, four of the tales, rather salacious, had escaped the bowdlerizing vigilance of the reverend Editor. Even such expurgations have been carried out by the present reviser soberly: in two or three places only, a remodelling of a few lines was found indispensable. This, under the guarantee he was working under, was thought by him preferable to a wholesale suppression of the tales, because these happened to be among the richest in idioms.

Translations and notes are another feature of the revised text. Those renderings aim at literality of a sort, and in consequence have often caused a just readable English to be preferred to elegant English. By this means an immense number of footnotes have been dispensed with.

Of the six songs found at the end of Hahn's book only one, but a very fine one, has been retained and translated. Although the rest might turn out—for all the reviser knows—as fine as the sample chosen for reproduction and commentary, it is certain that a full understanding of their lyrism is a very complex and difficult matter. For a serious study of those other songs, the reviser would require choicer help and ampler funds than have been at his disposal.

A. GRIGNARD, S.J.

CONTENTS.

TALES AND STORIES.

INTRODUCTION

A SHORT ACCOUNT OF ORAON CUSTOMS

The Tribe

1. Some notes on the pre-historic whereabouts and doings of the Oraons and Muṅdas, as referred to in the Mahābharatā, will be found in the *Anthropos* Review for 1908.

It may also be mentioned that, according to Oraon traditions, the tribe made a long and happy stay on the banks of the Sone river, in what is to-day the Shahābad district. Many are the heroic legends connected, in particular, with the defence of fort Ruidas (Rohtas). This citadel, an authentic one, is now in ruins ; its purlieu, according to an English descriptive work, is of no less than 29 miles.

2. At some unknown period and from unknown causes, a split seems to have occurred in the tribe. However this may be, we are to-day in presence of three main bodies of Oraons ; the *Nagpurias*, the *Kisāns* and the *Dhankas*.

(*a*) The first-named are spread all over the Chota-Nagpore plateaux, in Sirguja, Jashpur, etc. Many thousands of Nagpuria Oraons are also found in Gangpur, their villages studding the country side by side with Dhankā and Kisān villages.

(*b*) The bulk of the Oraon population of Gangpur, however, is made of Kisāns (in H. ō farmers), often also called, chiefly by themselves, 'Gangpuria Oraons.' This latter appellation is very misleading, since all the three types of Oraons are represented (and by large numbers) in Gangpur. — The Kisāns have been, and some are still, better off in the goods of this world than their neighbours of the same tribe. Moreover the fact that, throughout the country, every fertile spot, every desirable site is occupied by a Kisān village, suggests that the establishment of these people into the Hindoo Kingdom was anterior to the incoming of the Nagpuriās and Dhankās. The lapse of time separating their migratory party from the subsequent ones must have been considerable, since the Kisāns, in addition to unlearning the true sound of the hard Oraon consonant kh (1), have become more decidedly hinduised and corrupt in their morals, and are also distinctly wilder, than their congeners of maybe the next village. A Kisān will not marry into a family of either the Nagpuriā or the Dhankā type.

Kisān Oraons are also found in the Central Provinces, beyond the Gangpur frontier, on a line extending up to Raipur.

(*c*) The Dhankā Oraons are pretty numerous in Gangpur. Their tribal language does not seem, any more than that of the Kisāns, to offer important points of difference from the Nagpuriā or standard Oraon. A few words may be peculiar to them. To the casual observer the chief characteristic of the Dhankas is the metallic ear-ring they are fond of sporting about.

3. It is not unfrequent to meet, in an Oraon-community, other distinctions of minor importance, quite unconnected wit caste prejudices and jealousies. Thus :

(*a*) A small percentage of Oraon tenants claim to be *Addiyar*, i.e. to have sprung from the original settlers who cleared the primeval jungles, and first cultivated the fields still to-day in the possession of their posterity. It is in this particularized sense that the word *Addyas*, or rather its Hindi equivalent 'bhuinhāri' has found its way into, the C.-N. Tenancy Act (2). The being an 'addyas' in this select sense is, of course, proudly worn in the community. It also constitutes a financial asset, since such fields go practically rent-free.

(*b*) Those of the addyā families, whose ancestors, in the hazy period of migrations and village-foundations, exercised priestly office or a mahtoship or a chieftainship, or otherwise acted as leaders, are now called *Khūt*-families, and held in special regard. The common

---

(1) They utter it as an *h* or even (so the Nagpurias will have) as a *g*. Hence the Nagpurias jokingly refer to the self-styling *Gangpuria Oraons* as '*bergā Oraons*,' which stands for 'belkhā Oraons,' i.e. Oraons of the Kingdom. The sting of this strongly resented nickname lies, of course, in the *g*, : which implies that the degenerate Gangpurias, now unable to deliver the true national *kh*-sound, soften it to that wishy-washy guttural. Others prefer to suppose that *berga* means 'mongrel.'

(2) In common Oraon parlance, the word *addī* (ancestral) has a much wider application. *Every* Oraon styles himself in his heart an 'addyas' by reference to some settler of the first ho *Every* Oraon treasures up the name of his ancestral village (though his residence may be 20 or 50 miles away from it), and cherishes the memory of his ancestral fields, though irretrievably passed, by sale or robbery, out of the family. People residing out of their ancestral village are particular, when they can afford it, in carrying the remains of their dead to the *kūnddī* of that village.

run of addyā families possess only one quarter of nobility, whereas these have two. The office and the virtues that led to its bestowal may have long passed out of the lineage : a *khūṭ* the family is, and a *khūṭ* it remains, whereas other families, with similar distinction gained in later times, are not It is not uncommon to find, in a single village, two or three *khūṭ*-families.

(*c*) Families not sprung from the party who first cleared the jungle and broke up the village soil are accounted common citizens (*gauror*). Of course a man who is *gauros* in the village of his residence may be an *addyas* (or, as is also said, a *jeṭh-rayatas*) in another.

(*d*) People of non-Oraon caste are naturally outside of the community, and food, as a rule, is not taken with them. But, apart from this, they are treated with consideration and even kindness. Thus, in addressing a man of one of the menial castes, or in speaking of him in his hearing, one avoids naming that caste. A weaver (*cīkas*) is treated to the courtesy title of *baraīkas* ; a cowherd, potter, oiler to that of *mahto* ; a *Korwā* or *Tūri* to that of--*mājhī* (the equivalent among Mundas of ' mahto ').

The fact that the Oraons of Gangpur eat with the Mundas is remarkable but could hardly be argued from. It is only one more instance of their many departures from customs extant in the rest of the tribe.

The Oraon village

I. An Oraon village (*paddā*) can, as a rule, be descried from far away on the cart-road, by the clusters of trees under which it nestles. As he comes nearer and already sees its roofs, some of them tiled, others covered with thatch and creepers, the visitor will often pass under a stately mango-grove or by a public tank (*pokhārī*), or near the grove reserved for public sacrifices (*sarnā* or *cālā*). If the locality happens to be the seat of a Hindoo landlord (*gollas*), his granary (*bhandārī*) may be seen somewhere on the outskirts of the village : a small building, isolated for fear of fires, but made very strong for fear of thieves. Within memory of old men, there used to stand also, near the entrance of most villages (1), a bachelors' hall and a spinsters' hall (*dhumkuryā* or *jōkh-erpā*). These were large huts, built by the youngsters of the place, to serve at night as dormitories for boys and girls and, at certain times of the day, as a training school in

(1) In the Eastern parts of Chota-Nagpore, at any rate. With the advance of Christianity, these institutions tend now to disappear, even from pagan villages.

which the popular songs, the art of drumming and the steps of jatra-dances were taught. They were, of course, schools of a fearful moral corruption as well.

Oraon villages, when they happen to lie on dead-level ground, become extremely filthy during the rains; houses can only be approached by wading through mires and a one-foot thick layer of mud and cattle droppings. This mud is so soft that even fowls sink into it belly-deep. But, as a rule, the founders of a village have the sense of selecting a site on a ground more or less slopy.

Some villages, the very large ones, are a perfect maze of crooked lanes surrounded outside, and reinforced inside, by low crumbling walls, a very ineffective defence against bears and tigers. So are, for instance, Burha-Kukra near Mandar, and Murma on the road from Dighia to Soso. But most Oraon villages consist of one single lane (*khūri*) of houses on a double line, with here and there smaller rows of habitations straggling out of the alignment. No mud walls to spoil the view.

A nice and rather common feature of an Oraon village are noble old trees with a canopy of spreading-out foliage. Another such feature is the large village-square (*akhṛā*), which serves for panchāyats, dances and other rejoicings. A piece of forest land (*ṭoṛang*), within convenient distance, is attached to almost every village: women go there for dry leaves and other fuel, men for timber and children for their games.

Pure drinking water is a sore point in the places, rather numerous, where there is neither a well nor a tank. Of running brooks (perennial brooks, I mean), there is none anywhere: the soil is too loose and percolating for that. In the least favoured places, drinking water is fetched every morning from hollows at the bottom of the terraced fields. In seasons when even this is wanting, some marshy or spongy ground is pitched upon: an empty cask or a palisade is sunk into it, and the result is a sort of cistern. But the whitish water which oozes into this (a *tūsā*) has a sorry taste, being of course full of matters in decay.

II. With regard to persons, a typical Oraon village is composed —if we leave aside the rank and file of the population—of the following elements:

1. The *mahto*. He is the village headman *de facto*, though not by any right. Properly, he is the local zamindar's Oraon agent for apportioning between the villagers and under variable kinds of

contracts, those fields (*majhias*) that are the zamindar's own property.[1] Originally, and up to the last few decades, there was but one mahto per village. He was paid by the landlord, not with money, but by the free grant of a piece of land (*mahtwāri*), resumable of course at will. His position, it will be readily understood, made him a feared, and consequently, an influential man. He is still so.

It sometimes happens that a mahto's services are remunerated, not with any land specially earmarked as mahtwāri, but by simple exemption from the rent due on his own rayati holding. The latter does not, as is evident, become from this fact a 'mahtwāri' at all, yet the villagers will *honoris causa* call it so. The arrangement is all the more dangerous because a mahtoship often continues in the same family for 50 or 100 years. Formerly, once the true nature of such a mahtoship-contract had fallen into oblivion, the zamindar could, in good or in bad faith, accaparate the holding as mahtwāri land : for this, he had only to appoint a mahto belonging to some other family. He can no longer do this to-day, except on the off-chance that the dispossessed raiyat does not know about the Government land-survey book (*Sarkār-Khatiān*), or somehow will not apply for redress. The presence in a village of *two* mahtos, one in office, the other honorary, is generally the outcome of some old dispute of the kind, in which an ancestor of the latter sued his landlord successfully.

2. The *village-watchman* (*kotwārās* or *diguāras*). He is a sort of constable with no very clear title, and also a gatherer of public moneys, fines, etc. decreed by the panchāyat, in short a general peon at the beck and call of the notables. He spends a part of every night in roaming in and about the village, armed with a bludgeon and accompanied by his mastiff. Every three minutes, he shouts with a powerful and dolent voice : 'Be all at peace', or words to that effect.

3. The *menial castes*. In every village of importance there is to be found, side by side with the aboriginal population, a limited number of Hindoo or hinduized families, who make a livelihood by ministering to various needs of the people. Theirs is a lonely and friendless existence : for with their Oraon neighbours they have no relations, apart from business relations ; and with their own congeners, intimacy is hindered by the trade-caste bar, leaving alone the fact that these fellows are, in point of numbers, but a sprinkling.

---

(1) *See* hereafter p. 16.

Ploughshares are made or tinkered by the blacksmith (*lohras*), pots and tiles are turned and baked by the potter (*kumbhras*), clothes are woven (out of the homespun cotton) by the weaver (*cīkas*). In large and prosperous villages, the whole cattle of the place is entrusted to an experienced cowherd (*mahras*), generally an old man, who ekes out his pay (in milk and ghee) by contracting, with the owner of some unfertile spot, to choose this as *baiṭhān*, for the cattle to rest during the hot hours of the day (1).—Where there is plenty of pasture lands, tanners (*camras*) prepare the skins, cut the leather to straps for the plough, and also manufacture leather amulets for the children to wear. Where the land is advantageously situated for water and shade, an occasional vegetable-grower (*kuīris*) is met with ; he carries his produce to market, or sells it on his own premises. Here and there an itinerant barber (*naūas*) may be found ; he is recognizable by the leather bag containing his implements, always carried on his shoulder. Finally, performing al-o for a large circle of villages, come the professional drummers, trumpeters and musicians (*gosains*) : for a consideration they will consent to enliven weddings, jatras and other feasts.

4. The *naigas* or heathen priest. The most important of his insignia is the shovel basket (*kẽter*), in which are carried the requisites for minor sacrifices. The office is bestowed by election. The people being assembled on the *akhṛā*, the candidates stand in front of the late priest's sacred basket, and vehement incantations are recited until the basket spontaneously flies towards one of the candidates. Examples are quoted of baskets not only choosing their man, but leading him at a brisk pace through the street up to his house, all the while hopping on the ground and *not* held in his hands (2).

Strange as it may seem, the chief duty of the priest is not sacrifice ; preternatural healing comes first. When a man falls sick, when epidemics break out, his it is to discover to which kind of harmful spirits the visitation is due : and, once he has got the clue, to name the witch (*dainbisāhī*) who has set those imps on the sick man, or turned them loose upon the village.

His other duty concerns sacrifices. On the various cases that are submitted to him, he is to indicate when a private sacrifice is really

(1) The *mahras* is also to take the cattle every day to a certain swamp (*chapaṛ*) for bathing and salt-licking : for this swamp has been dug and salted for the purpose at common expense by 5 or 6 villages.

(2) For another procedure in these elections, see Oraon Dict. under *naig-nād*.

needed or advisable, what kind of victim is required (a cock, a goat, a cow or a buffalo), and finally who is to be propitiated. The actual performing of such private sacrifices is *not* his business. In public emergencies, like an outbreak of small-pox, he treats with and enlightens the panchāyat.

As to sacrifices in connection with feasts, and other public sacrifices, he performs them with his own hand if he is a poor man, or should the salvation of a whole village be at stake. If he is well off, and the sacrifice is one of the ordinary calendar, there is nothing to prevent him having the slaying performed by a special servant of his (the *irbus*, lit. slayer). Sacrifices are often offered in the sacred grove (*sarnā*), if the village possesses one.

5. The *deõras* (also called *ojhas*, *matis* and *sokhas*) is the sorcerer. There are perhaps no more than three or four deõras per pergannah, and long journeys are frequently undertaken to consult one who has made a name for himself. His duties, in the case of illnesses, lie much on the same lines as those of the naigas: only he expels the evil spirits by adjurations, whereas the priest possesses *absolute dominion* over them. Witches he can always detect as surely as the naigas. His other work consists in finding out lost objects and healing the sick by incantations. It is he who is called in cases of snake bites, and by his massages and insufflations causes the venom to 'descend', i.e. to turn back the way it came, until it reaches the bite-point, at which it leaves the body. Occasionally he will also, for a consideration, set a harmful spirit after his client's enemies. Every deõras keeps a school of sorcery in his house, and confers degrees according to the number of formulas mastered.

Witches are universally detested, not exactly because of their moral depravity, but because they dabble in things the harm of which they cannot undo. Just as a witch is unable to catch another witch, she cannot save a man on whom she has set a spirit: being an ignorant woman, she knows not how to stop that imp in time. All these things the deõras can do, as he is *pūrā*, i.e. perfect in his art.

The Oraon house

The first thing that strikes one in the appearance of an Oraon house is that its thick mud-walls seem to be, here and there, rather out of plumb. This is due to its mode of construction having been so haphazard and intermittent: a fresh layer of wet clay waiting to be superimposed to the finished portion of the walls until this has become perfectly dry. Moreover, as that clay has been kneaded out of elements not altogether homogeneous, it contracts more in one place than in another: hence a deal of bulging-in and bulging-out. The house is none the less solid, partly owing to its heavy (if rough) roofing; partly because it rests on a perfectly level foundation (*neo*) of hard earth. This earth, in fact, when in a semi-liquid state, was poured on the chosen spot into a sort of square cistern dug out of the original ground, and then left for the Indian sun to dry.

Along the house-frontage (*cālī*), or on its rear (*collā*), there occasionally runs a low verandah resting on rough hewn posts.[1] Most houses consist of just one room which, admitting light only from the entrance and the yawning between walltops and roof, is rather dark. Where there are two apartments, the extra room, called 'the inner room' (*ulā kothrī*), has no opening on the outside, except may be a window-bay (*bhawārī*). These are, one should know, the *penetralia domus*. Strangers, though welcome in the family parlour, are expected never to stray, even on a friendly pretext of inspection, into the recess beyond.

Fowls and the horned cattle are, as a rule, admitted for the night into the house; and they know it. It is a sight, when buffaloes and cows and goats are returning at dusk, to watch from a safe distance the scrimmage at every door in the street. They are confined behind a low palisade which divides the entire depth of the sitting-room. Upon the posts ordinarily a sort of floor made of loose planks has been thrown: the dark recess above (*aṭṭā*) does duty for a garret.

The pig-sty (*kis-kumbā*) is always outside. But the better-off Oraons have also out-of-door pens for the cattle (*kurgī*), for goats (*ērā-kuṛyā*), and even for fowls (*kuslī*). If to these we add one shed (*kuṛyā*) or two, for stowing away the pounding machine or the oil-press, we shall form a fair idea of what an Oraon house and its appurtenances are like.

The furniture is of the most primitive kind. Let us notice first the furnace (*culhā*), a stone and clay fixture, with the set of pots and pans (*kaṭṭū nandā*) accessory to it. At the foot of one wall, we see earthen jars containing corn, or perhaps ricebeer (*boṛe*), or again

(1) Cfr. Oraon Dict., under *koṭṭhā*.

rice-water (*bāsi-amm*). On a scaffolding in a corner, a huge rice-bale (*mōṛā*) of plaited straw makes itself conspicuous.(1) If our time is the after-noon, we may be invited to take our seat on the unwieldy plough; or else, a wooden stool, four inches high, called a *manci* may be offered to us. A few rolled up mats, on which spare clothes are hanging, draw our notice. Old granny's attention at her spinning wheel is not disturbed by our arrival. If an occasion offers, many wonderful knick-knacks of furniture will be extracted, for us to see, out of the most unlikely corners: a hunting bludgeon, a sounding horn, a spear, a child's bow and arrows, a shepherd's flute. When the inmates are wealthy, this can be told at first glance by the unusual display of piled up baskets full of tubers and pulses, or the presence of kettle-drums and tomtoms, or even sometimes of a home-made mandoline (*ektarhā*, *kendrā*). Should our conversation drift on to lawsuits, documents concerning the lease of fields, summons receipts, certificates, etc., will turn up out of a little niche (*pakkhā*) in the wall, from behind the house-lamp (*bilī*), where the bamboo case containing them had been secreted among nutmegs and pepper.

To the rear of the more up-to-date houses, there is a garden (*batgī*). But this is generally a misnomer, as such plots are fuller of weeds than of cucumbers, garlic and chillis. If any fruit-trees at all grow there, these will be, ten to one, a few thirsty and stunted papayas, planted in the utmost disorder, *capācurā*.

Family events

1. *Marriages*. The marriage customs of pagan Oraons are very quaint, and would afford matter for a long chapter. But they have been described so often, and in such detail, that it is useless to cover that ground once more. The only points worthy of being singled out for memory here are: (*a*) that, even for pagan Oraons, marriage is invested with a distinctly religious character; (*b*) that it is essentially performed by the vermilion unction (*sindrī*) which the bridegroom and bride themselves make on each other's forehead; (*c*) that, immediately the young people have become united in wedlock, words are uttered that plainly intimate conjugal indissolubility. The old lady (she *may not* be a widow) who officiates as priestess says to the young man: ' See, so-and-so, this girl N. has now become thy

(1) In some houses, the *mōṛā* is replaced by a grain closet (*kutthī*), receptacle in hard mud built in a corner of the room.

wife. While she is at work and culls trees greens, should she fall from the trees and break her arm or leg, should she become palsied or deaf, should her beauty by any accident be spoiled, thou shalt not desert her. Whatever she cooks for thee, this thou shalt eat, and keep thy peace. And no look shalt thou cast towards any other woman whomsoever.' To the young woman: 'See, so-and-so, this boy N. is thy husband. When at work or hunting in the forest or on the mountain side, should he break his arm or leg, or become palsied, thou shalt not desert him. Whatever he'll bring in, this thou shalt cook and serve before him. And no look shalt thou cast towards any other man whomsoever.' (1)

Of the marriage customs formerly in honour, all that is extant to-day may be summed up thus: (*a*) It is still the boy's or girl's father who fixes the time of the marriage, and chooses his child's partner in life; (*b*) girls are never presented for marriage before they are 15 or 16 years of age, boys are generally older; (*c*) the girl is given a chance of publicly expressing her concurrence or disagreement with the suit, when the boy and his parents pay their official visit to her house, on the conclusion of the preliminary arrangements. In sign of agreement, she hands over to her intended a brasspot-ful of water, which he next places on her head, and then takes down. Her backing out of this ceremony means that she refuses him. Such marks of independence occur at times on the part of girls; and, unfortunately, too often bring down the ire and abuses of both parties on them; (*d*) all the marriages for the current year are made in a body or in three or four large batches, during the month of January: a relic of the time-honoured custom among pagan Oraons of marrying their children in the cold weather, while their garrets are replenished from the recent harvest. (*e*) Young people who have received the nuptial blessing are not, for the matter of that, allowed to live together until after the wedding banquet. Should this meal be unavoidably put off for a fortnight, the newly-married couple won't live as man and wife for a fortnight. This delay, at bottom, proceeds from a regard, not for the meal itself, but for the *vermilion unction*, which is still observed in many places *and customarily takes place on the day of the wedding banquet.*

2. *Births.* The pagan customs in connection with child-birth are still largely prevalent among Christians. Here is a summary of these customs. A mother, from the day of her delivery, is looked upon as defiled (*bechāt*). She is debarred from cooking

(1) See this book, *Oraon Marriage Customs.*

for her household, and may not even touch the vessel where the cooked rice is contained ; her own meals are handed over to her. Neither is she allowed in the place in which the furnace is : if there be only one room, she has to stay in a corner behind a hastily erected partition or screen.—Where, as in parts of the Barway and on the Lohardaga side, the incoming of a baby defiles the entire household, the inconveniences of prolonged uncleanness are felt less severely, the newly delivered woman remaining at liberty to cook as usual, she unclean for the unclean. Only, other people won't eat with them. On the 9th day or thereabout, she goes and purifies in the river or the neighbouring field-cistern (*tūsū*).

This done, the *chathi* ceremony takes place on the same day : a function half familial, half religious, in which the child is given a name. Before a few relatives and friends, the infant's fluffy hair, considered as unclean (*tūrī-cuttī*) is shaven ; names are next proposed (generally grandparents or other ascendants' names), and omens, taken for the purpose of hitting upon a lucky one. After which the company do honour to the meal, all other defilement having been taken away by the *chathi*.

The umbilical chord, when desiccated, is buried in that portion of the common room where the cattle spends the night. For intimating to you that such a village is his native place, an Oraon will tell you unconcernedly : '*Ā paddā nū enghai kuḍḍā gararki ra'ī*'; in that village my navel-string is buried !

3. *Burials.* Pagan Oraons cremate their dead like the Hindoos. Oftener than not this is done immediately after death ; it may also take place, as is practised in Dighia, after the bodies have lain 6 or 8 months in the village graveyard (*masṛā*). In either case, the ashes from the funeral pile are collected in an earthenpot, which is secreted under no great depth of earth close to the house of the bereaved, just below the projection of the tile or thatch-eaves. In January when the rivers practically carry no water, the ashes of all those who have died in the village during the year are transferred in state mid fierce drumming, mournful songs and dances, to the riverside. The beds of the Chota-Nagpore rivers are strewn here and there with floors of rock, into which the perpetually revolving sands and eddies have perforated deep roundish screwy holes, named *kūnḍḍī*. Every family in the village has made one of these *kūnḍḍīs* its own, and this is never interfered with. It is into these holes that the ashes

are poured. The day's whole ceremony goes by the name of *haṛboṛā* lit. bone sinking.

4. One useful and interesting topic connected with burials is that of the Oraon customs which regulate *inheritance and partition*. This question, however, having been exhaustively dealt with by the present writer in Vol. I of the Census for 1911 (Appendix, pp. vii-xi), a simple reference to that work is all that is needed here.

Village life

The above heading does not point to anything like the existence, in Oraon villages, of a 'public life'. The local council of elders (*panchāyat*) and the regional councils (*pācōrā p.*, *barhī p.*) are the only institutions that savour—and yet how vaguely !— of a spirit able to rise above narrow individualism. Even in these assemblies, questions of the greatest importance for the community, such as sanitation, supply of drinking water, mutual assistance, repairs to village roads, improvements in farming and methods of agriculture, are never referred to 'Everyone for himself and God for all' is the Oraon's motto.

By village life, then, we merely understand the accustomed round of works, feasts and pastimes that fill in the days of the peasant during a twelvemonth.

1. *The year's works*. For the grown-up Oraon male, the busiest months are those from April to the middle of September. During the period, *ṭonkā* and *nāl*-lands are to receive three successive ploughings at least, and a complementary dressing, which is given with the hoe. From the first showers that herald the advent of the rains, a nursery ground is to be laid out for raising rice-seedlings in huge quantities, and most of the minor crops are to be sown. The mud-ridges (*āṛi*) which, in the low fields divide one tier from another and, within the same tier, one square from the next, are to be erected; the same will have to be attended to regularly every day through all weathers, in order to regulate the waterflow in and out of each square. Rice seedlings, when ready, are to be transplanted into the low fields, and watched over for days, in order to guard them from the depredations of birds. As the harvest ripens and becomes exposed to all sorts of damage, a log and foliage hut (*kumbā*) shall have to be constructed near the field, and many sleepless nights to be spent in shouting wild animals out of the rising crop.

Housewives have duties somewhat less hard, but which in compensation never relent, year in and year out. Besides the care of the children, brewing ricebeer, cooking and washing for the household, they have every day, from early morn, to collect in baskets and carry out the dung left overnight by the cattle, to fetch water often from a distance, to go to the forest for fuel, viz. dry sticks, dry leaves, etc Market days, which men use as holidays, are doubly tiring for their wives. And whatever time there may remain to the already overworked womanfolk is claimed by a number of minor employments useful for home comfort. The commonest are cotton carding and spinning. mat plaiting, and the expressing of oil, for consumption or other uses, out of a variety of seeds, like mustard, colza, kusum, groundnuts, or out of fruit stones, like the karanj and mahua (*ḍurī*) stones. Of course, the services of women are also required in connection with the transplantation of rice, the weeding of fields, the picking up of mahua flowers and generally the garnering of crops.

II. *The slack season* may be said to start from September, when the rains are slowly drawing to a close, and the only heavy bit of work still in prospect is the October harvest. It is in this happy half of the agricultural year that a thoughtful parent arranges a marriage and sees it through. This is also the season for all able-bodied men to charge up and down the country, in order to refresh acquaintance with old friends, and indulge in boozes. Between two such visits, a few repairs to the house or fences or plough are thrown in as a relaxation. The thatch is also looked into.

Of occupations of a more intellectual kind the Oraon has none, even for these long colder months of comparative leisure. Few letters are received indeed and none at all posted. The only correspondence that may come in is in the shape of receipts, or warrants, or writs of summons. It is this very lack of all mental pursuits that gives rise to the annually recurring craze for visits, and also causes the weekly market-day to loom so large in Oraon village-life, chiefly for the male members of the community. The market-day is for the Oraons what, to the Englishman, his newspaper and club, his post-office, race-course and even stock-exchange would mean if rolled into one.

It is not that regular feast-days are wanting in the Oraon calendar. These need not detain us long, as descriptions of them may be found in many books. They are, in order : (1) The *k͟haḍḍī* festival, on the occasion of the mahua-tree blossoming, about March ; (2) the *Karam* festival in August-September ; (3) The two *jatra* festivals, held one in May, the other after the rice-harvest. It is to be particularly noticed that all festivals are attended with songs and dances, and that these are sometimes loosely referred to as 'jatras'; but *the* Jatras are two special festivals, sorts of rustic balls which, for display of banners, music, general finery and attending crowds, stand unique and are stuck to as national institutions. (4) The harvest season naturally brings in its train many songs and rejoicings, a special festival called *jatiyā* being celebrated in this connection ; (5) the *sohrai* festival, or feast of the cattle, held in October-November ; (6) the 'woman-folk hunting day' (*mukkargahi sendrā*) held every twelfth year in many villages : this probably as a memorial of the gallant defence which, according to Oraon traditions, women in men's clothes made of fort Ruidas against a besieging party of Mohammedans : these had cunningly chosen, for storming the citadel, the night of the *Khaḍḍi* feast, when they were sure every Oraon warrior would be drunk. However this may be, on the festival day, women sally forth in turban and dhoti from their village, and burst in upon any likely village, where a great massacre takes place of fowls, pigs and goats. The women of the plundered community are entitled to return the attention at their earliest convenience. (7) To the above mentioned feasts, all of which are aboriginal in character, should be added the *ind*-festival, offered (in many places) by the village Hindoo landlord to his tenants. The night revels which in some parts take place on these occasions simply baffle description by their overt licentiousness, and should be shunned by every self-respecting Oraon boy or girl, Christian or Pagan.

Among pastimes of a more casual and intermittent recurrence, one may quote the two annual hunts, in which all Oraons, big and small, are very keen to join. The Phagun-hunt is a one-day affair ; but the *bisu*-hunt lasts a fortnight. Again, during the rains, all kinds of fishing-baskets are disposed in the low-fields, which abound with crabs and small fishes. In the hot season, athletic sports (*jadrā*) are practised on the village square ; and at all times of the year, one may meet here and there some swinging contrivance (*rocā*) erected for the young. Wrestling (*kusti*) between young men of the same village or of different villages affords also, on occasions, a much appreciated spectacle.

Public meals, i.e. meals that assemble a number of guests round the same board, are few and far between. Panchāyat counsellors delight to feast on the produce of a fine, or the fees exacted for their trouble when a case has been judged. Neighbours who have helped a man in transplanting his rice, or in hurrying the tillage of his fields before the rains, are recompensed by a good square meal (*pacaṭ, madait*). Finally, an outcast who seeks re-admission among his fellows must pay a meal to the entire village.

Village lands : Customary Crops

1. Village lands are of two main kinds with regard to use and value.

(*a*) Portions free from buildings, forest, roads, streams, etc., and which, from their being nearly level, suit ordinary crops, are called *ṭonkā*, i.e. high ground.

(*b*) Terraced slopes, or slopes deeply dug-in and disposed in tiers, each of which is divided into squares by ridges (*ārī*) with a view to the wet cultivation of rice, are called *nāl,* i e. low fields. The set of squares nearer to the top of a terraced slope benefits less by the rains than those at its bottom. The former are known as *cauṛā*, the latter as *gaḍḍī khail.*

A rayat's holding ordinarily consists of a portion of *nāl* (some of this *caurā*, and the rest *gaḍḍī*) and of a portion of *ṭonkā* ground. It may however, in particular cases, consist of *nāl* only or even of *ṭonkā* only.

2. *Tonkā* lands are roughly measured in kāths. One *kāth* is the area for sowing which one maund of seeds is required. *Nāl* lands are commonly estimated in pawas, one *pawā* being the surface which can be sown over with four uḍḍū-baskets containing each 1¼ maund of paddy. (¹) At that reckoning, *kāth* and *pawā* are no mathematical land-measures : and, as a matter of fact, the measured surfaces vary in the inverse ratio of the fertility of the soil.

3. The overlordship of all village lands, of those just named and of others we are going to name, is vested in the English Government. But for all purposes of rent-recovery from the rayats, the sum total of lands belonging to any particular village are constituted under one trustee, to whom the courtesy title of 'zamindār', landlord (Or. *gollas*) is extended. Hence there are as many zamindaries as there are agricultural villages : and everyone of these landed properties is quite fixed since the C.-N. cadastral survey (*khatiān*) ; the amount of rent, payable on the whole and on each part, has also

(¹) In the Barway this surface goes by the name of *sad.*

thereby been made of easy calculation. The zamindār, for his trouble, receives from the Government certain cultivable lands, which are on that account called *majhias*, from *mājhī* middleman. The other lands, which he holds in trust for the village, form what is known as *rājyas* (Government lands)

The landlord, as a rule, has his majhias-land cultivated by the village-rayats on any contract on which both parties may agree. It is in this connection, and also for the purpose of urging rent payments on rajyas plots, that zamindārs appoint in every big village an Oraon agent of their own, viz. a *mahto*.

4. Privileged lands are of three kinds :

(*a*) Just as the zamindār's majhias is privileged in *two* senses, i.e. free from rent and free from the operation of the law on the right of occupancy, so are certain portions of the rajyas lands. Thus, all patrimonial plots (H. bhuinhāri, Or. *addī khall*), and the three plots set aside by statute for the upkeep of the Pagan priest (*naig-khall*), and the necessities of worship (*nād-khall* and *dalikatārī*), go rent-free, or are liable to no more than a nominal assessment. The same are further privileged inasmuch as, however long one occupant has held them, no right of occupancy accrues to him, in Chota-Nagpore, from the fact.

(*b*) But a rajyas land may also be privileged in the latter sense alone. A *bakast* land, i.e. a land which has been deserted by its tenant, remains the property of *his* village, and is thus debarred from ever conferring a right of occupancy on a *stranger* who came over and cultivated that plot, however subject to rent-payment.

(*c*) *Nāl* lands, newly created by a rayat's industry out of his own *tonkā* portion, or out of any rājyas waste or jungle tract, are semi-privileged, in this sense that they go rent-free for the first three annual crops. Such newly created rice-lands are known as '*korkar*'.

5. A rayat may, with certain restrictions and under formalities prescribed by law, mortgage his plot (*bandhak nannā*), alienate it, or relinquish it. In this last case, if he has given notice of intended relinquishment, a certain latitude is left him for cancelling the step taken. The right every rayat has of 'making korkar' has already been mentioned.

In Chota-Nagpore, all rent is payable in cash, or can be made so on application. Before the settlement, assessments on *ṭonkā* lands were payable in kind (*rakumāt*) and by predial service (H. begāri, Or. *biṭṭhī*).

6. Three distinct ploughings (*carrnā, karnā, tekṛa'ānā*) are generally gone through, preparatory to sowing. If an extra one is given, as is at times done for ṭonkā grounds, this fourth ploughing is, in some places, called *dobra'ānā*.

A. Crops on ṭonkā-lands—On these, various crops are raised, which provide the rayat with food, raiment and oil. The most common of tonkā crops are :

(*a*) *Pandṛū khhes*, an early rice not growing in water : it only requires to be sown as the rains set in. With the produce, the family keeps body and soul together, until the October paddy gets ready for the sickle. *Gurlū*, millet. It helps the poor to eke out the supply, often scanty, of the early rice just mentioned

Jinkhōr, Indian maize ; *jawā*, Indian barley ; *būt*, gram ; *rahaṛ*, the pulse whose grains, when cleared and split in twos, go by the name of 'dāl' ; *māsī* (H. urid) a kind of round jet-black bean, eaten with rice.

(*b*) *Kabsī*, cotton. After it has been cleaned from its seeds cotton is carded by means of the *dhunel*-bow. Carded cotton is called *tūlī* ; but when made into rolls for spinning, it takes the name of *pyūrī*. (See Or. Dict. under *dhun'nā* and *dhaṇdhap*.)

(*c*) Oil-yielding crops are : *Cinabadām*, groundnut ; *tīl*, linseed ; *luṭnī*, mustard. There are three varieties of mustard seeds : in the lutni variety, the seed is extremely minute and the colour that of brick. Oil is also expressed from the kernels of the *karanj*-tree stone, and of the *mahuā*-tree stone (*ḍurī*). The latter oil (*doē isung*) is used for light, and also as a substitute for ghee.

B. Various methods of paddy cultivation in low-fields.—The common and more profitable, but also more laborious, is the transplantation method The *rāl*-fields, in this plan, are not sown over, but receive rice-seedlings (*birā*) which have been prepared on a large scale in a nursery. This operation, called *ro'ā idnā*, is often done with the assistance of the neighbours For a description of it, see Or. Dict. *biṛā*.

Ro'ā khess (lit. planted paddy) is always opposed to all sorts of *cākhkā khess* (sown paddy). If, on account of illnesses, damaged seedlings or early rains, the fields have not been ploughed in time, the rayat makes his paddy sowings in *lewā*, that is in slushy soil. The *nāl*-fields, already sodden with rainwater, are turned over and thoroughly kneaded with a buffalo team and the dragging plank (cāgarkhā), till brought down to the consistence of mortar; this operation is called *khallan lerna, khallan cotor kamnā*. On the glazed surface the paddy seeds, previously sprouted, are then sown. Until the seedlings have got leaves, they must be guarded against the voracity of birds (*lewā haknā*).

Vain beliefs and superstitious observances.

1. *The Oraon mythology*. (*a*) There is a supreme God called *Dharmes*. He is very good and powerful; but whether he created the universe, or merely occupies the first place in it, is not clear. The happiness of the righteous after death will be to live with him; yet homages and sacrifices to him would be meaningless, precisely because he is so good. Unfortunately, he is too high above mankind to trouble himself much about the infinite details of this world's affairs. Except for wars and zamindars, all would be very tolerable here below, were it not that Dharmes's dominions are infested by so many whimsical and mischievous demons (*nād*).

(*b*) For this sablunar world is certainly full of these fiends, male and female. Being left their own way with all that is physical, they cause all sorts of evils, and yet can at times be made to relent by the superior power of the *naigas*, the adjurat ions of sorcerers, or the flattering odour of a sacrifice. The more powerful and less malevolent of those imps concern themselves with the produce of the soil. Such are 'the lady of the grove' (*cālā-paccō*, also called *jhakhrā paccō*): it is to her that the Oraons have to look for plentiful rains; the 'dame of the fields' (*darhā-paccō*): her wrath, only too easy to rouse may yet imperil a harvest which had the blessing of the former deity; the 'dame of the mountains' (*barndā-paccō*); the 'goddess of hunt' (*candī-deo*). (1) Other spirits, of a distinctly malignant character, do not live among us as a rule; they are tied up in some unknown place, whence however they can be occasionally released at the call of a sorcerer or a witch; they then play havoc on the lives of men and beasts, cause an illness, spread epidemics, etc. Of these fiends the best known are the tribes of the *rakts* and *raksī* and the goddess of small-pox (*debi mai*). The *danō-dait*, a fiery and hungry dragon, is rather, it would seem, a bugbear in children stories than an object of serious belief.

(1) About all these so-called deities and other topics in this chapter more details may be read in the Oraon Dictionary, under the headings quoted between brackets.

(c) But, with the Oraons, the borderline is very hazy, which divides demons from disembodied spirits as long as they continue in the unrest stage. Until the *harborā*-ceremony, which takes place only once a year, has come round, the most loving friend or relative, once dead, is no longer to be trusted: for he delights in scaring and tormenting those he has left behind, and behaves more or less like an authentic nād. The spirit of a woman who died in pregnancy is particularly mischievous (see below *curil*).

2. *Sacrifices.*—Female animals are never offered in sacrifice, nor castrated males.

Public sacrifices, performed (as has been said) by the naigas, are rare: three, at most four, annually. The regular ones are the *khaddi* sacrifice in March (1) for obtaining good rains; the *ta'ri* sacrifice in thanksgiving for the harvest, and the annual sacrifice for the common welfare of the village (*paddan khōjnā*). In time of small-pox epidemics, it is laudable to offer an extra sacrifice, viz. to *debi mai*; this is called *paddan kamnā*.

Private sacrifices, performed by the person interested or one of his household, are very numerous; occasions and victims differ according to the naigas' advice and the gravity of cases. For instance, upon the death of a man or woman, the deceased's relatives sacrifice a pig, immediately after they come home from cremating the body; and a bit of the flesh, cut off with a cast-iron blade, is buried near the house door. For further details see above, page 6, n 4.

3. *Other superstitious beliefs and practices.*—Oraons are afraid, especially for their young children, of the withering influence of the evil eye (*najar*). On meeting any suspicious-looking individual, a mother with her child will take a chilli-pod, and make, with this, mummeries round the baby's eyes and forehead, to exercise him (*newca'ānā*).—Anyone who experiences a tingling sensation under the sole of his foot is thereby informed that evil-intentioned persons are just then engaged in running him down or plotting against him.—People on a business journey, e.g. going to a distant village for a marriage proposal, will retrace their steps, should a jackal cross their way or a dead rat or mouse meet their eye.—The spot on which a meal has just been taken must be cleaned and smoothed with

(1) For a detailed account of the *khaddi*-sacrifice, see the book, *Tribal Festivals.* Examples of other public sacrifices special to one part of the country are, on the Lohardaga side, the *asāri* and *hariāri* sacrifices, in connection with rains and rice-transplantation.

cowdung and water; and this practice could hardly be one of tidiness, since it is stuck to even by travellers, when halting anywhere for more than a day; it is called *satnā*.—To prevent lightning from striking a house, a small piece of iron is slipped into the roof thatch. —Snakes may not be mentioned, even by their most generic name, at night or when they have just bitten somebody: at such times, they are referred to as 'ropes' and cords (*ōp*) —Namesakes (*mitā ālar*) do not address each other by names; and females married or not, are not allowed to tell how they are called —A popular belief has it, that witches disguised as wild cats do enter houses at night, lick people till they become bald or full sick, cause the rice put by for the morrow to spoil, etc It is enough to place a bit of charcoal in the way of that cat (*cōrdewā*) to stop its ill-doings.—With regard to all illnesses our flesh is an heir to, indigestions, colic, etc., one example may be given. Let us choose that of 'the poisoned bit' (*bisī*). This is the name either of a hair crumpled into a knot, or of an imperceptible fragment of bone, beforehand poisoned and thrown into the victim's food. For its expulsion, the patient must be laid with his head pointing to the north: a conjurer can then suck the obnoxious bit out of the man's navel. The object, as soon as extracted, spreads round an abominable stench, and is at once thrown into the fire.

But the worst of superstitious practices are, naturally, those connected with the hereafter. As soon as a dead body has been taken out to be carried to the funeral pile on the *masrā*, a stop is made: and the mourners strew the housefloor with fine wood ashes; then, before resuming their journey, lock up the door carefully. As soon as home is reached again after the ceremony, those ashes are scrutinized for footprints of fowls, snakes or cats, or for thread-like marks: from these signs an inference is drawn whether the defunct died a natural death or was cut off by a sprite.—Souls, from the hour of death *until the consignment* of the body-ashes to their final resting-place, still need every day a little rice and meat and pulses and tobacco; they are also uneasy and fretful. Singularly so are the ghosts of women dead in pregnancy. These are most bent on revisiting their old homes; they tickle the living and make them laugh to death. There is only one way of laying a *curil*-ghost: it is to rob it from the load of coal it invariably carries, fancying this coal to be its child.—With after life ideas also are connected those 'fire-spots' *sikā*) which everyone has noticed on the forearms of boys: these burns assure them success in life and admittance into their ancestors society after death. The corresponding superstition for women consists in having straight or zigzaging lines or floral designs tattooed on the forehead, temples or left side of the chin, on the wen (if there is any), on the shoulderblades, chest or feet. All this is considered indispensable for obtaining recognition and necessaries of life in the other world.

A. GRIGNARD, S.J.

ORAON FOLK-LORE

I. Tales and Stories

Bankō Alas. The Simpleton.

Ort jōkhas sasrār kālālagyas dara oṇṭā poṭom nū jokk asmā hō'ālagyas. Kānum kānum tanghai ēkhan kirr īryas[1] dara bujhras ort nannā ālas enganē bar'ālas[2]. Ās ēkhan ānyas : 'Kalā, bhāi, kirrā; enghai sasrār nū kiṛā ,ra'anar ; endran oi'or'? Antile jokk gecchā keras kī onghon kirr īryas[3] ki bācas : 'Īs asman īryas-kī eṛāputtdas'. Aōnge oṇṭan, kullyas-dara, asan ḍahrē nū uiyas kī keras. Jokk hāṛī īkyas khanē, ērdas ā nannas annuhō bar'ālas; anti ānyas : 'Īs embā sāras, aōnge malā kirryas : aur jukk'im ci'on'. Ennē ennētī urmī asman kierin dara ṭempan hō uinūtim keras ; oṇṭā bhagoā nīdī baochrkī rahcā : adin hō mūnjā nū ḍahrē nū uiyas. Āganem puttyā, khanē ērdas nannas malkas. 'Ohrē (bācas) Ī ahṛā-mūkhus oṇṭā bhagoāge engan pachra'ālagyas'.

Akkū gā ās, thotham ra'as khanē, āṛsyas-kī collā tarā kaprkas kuddas.[4] Tang sās sasūras oṇḍar mokkhar ; ā gūṭi āsgahi pāb ērālagyar. Paccō pacgīsin menjā : 'Kukkosge eōgoṭā asmā uiyon'? Pacgis ānyas : 'Eō uiyoi ? oṇṭā dara koo'ā uiyai'. Ennē urmī ba'anan ā bankos menālagyas, Khokhā nū paegis 'jaōdkhaddīsin ērā kāldan' bācas-kī, eṛpantī urkhas. Collā tarā ortosgahi kaprnan[5] ēr khakkhyas kī mikhyas : 'Ne baro, ne baro'? : Inim gā'. Endrnā eṛpā mal kōrckai'? 'Kiorī hō malā ; ckāsē kaon'? Antile urmin tingyas. Khanē sasūras oṇṭā kaṛean ottbras kī bāor'ā ciccas. Ā jōkhas eṛpā ulā kōrcas, dara khedḍ khekkhan nōṛhar-kī ukkyas.

---

[1] He saw behind. *Kirr* is the root of *kirnā*, to turn back.

[2] Colloquial for *bar'ālagdas*.

[3] *Īryas-kī* means '*having seen*'. This extremely common idiom should be studied thoroughly. See Gramm., 285, n 4 and p. 286, n. 5.

[4] Or, Gramm., p. 243, n 7.

[5] Or Gramm., p. 236, n. 52.

Tangsās, eõ asman āsge uiki rabcā urmin ciccā. Munjyas khhane, meñjā : 'Jokk indri'im mokhoi kā hurū' ? Bācas ās : 'Endrā ra'ī, ēn mokhon ? Iūram gā rabcā ; endr ēn baldan'? I katthāti ajgut manjar kī bācar :[1] 'Īs jokk indri'im akhdas'.

Āsgahi ayyā ṛa'anum, bēlas gahi sōnantā chippā khalb kerā[1]; aõnge bēlas deõṛa-bhagtārin eṛ'ā taiyas adin beddāge. Ā paccō belāsin ānyā : 'Eng jaõdkhaddis gā urmī ennē katthan khōb akhdas ; āsīnim menjke'. Paikar ā bhakkuas gusan kerar dara ānyar : 'Gucā ningan bēlas eṛ'ālagdas.' Ās bācas : 'En endrā hõ baldan, babā ! malā kaon'. Ār malā pattācar, backan baṛiyam occar. Bēlas'āsin ānyas. 'Enghai sonāgahi chippan beddoi holē, ningāgē khara baggē baksis ci'on ; backan pōlkai beddā hōlē, gaṛherā ci'on'. Bhakkuas kōllam mañjas dara ullā[2] nēcas. Khanē āsin'onṭā eṛpā nū muccyar kī satthē ullā cicoar.

Annē annē nū khalbas dikdikra'ā dikdikra'ā jiyā nū khōb elcālagyas. Āsgahi nāme Nīndiyā[3] rahcā Ās oṛgas : 'Ēron gā īs ekāsē deõṛai nandas', dara mākham makhadim ā eṛpā gusan keras kī chachem menā helras. Ṭhaukam ābīrim bankos khōbrar khōbrar ānālagyas : 'Akkū nīndyā ! ab to jītē gaṛherā hoī.' Khalbas, tanghai nāmē ho'onan meñjas-dara, cāṭē bācas : 'Anā bhāi, ambke tengā, ambke tēngā ; ningā hõ ci'on'. Bankos menjas : 'Eksan eksan uiki ra'adai'? Ās tingyas : 'Pokhātī nū ṭsajjkan ṛa'adan'. Antile bankos 'tisga'ā ! tisga'ā ! ba'anum, baramba'ā helras. Cōcar, tisgar, menā helrar'. Ās anyas : 'Kalā, pokharī nū ra'ī'. Kerar kī beddā helrar ; anti ṭhaukam khakkhyar. Bēlas ajgut manjas, dara āsin dewān kameas.

—A young man was going to the house of his parents-in-law, and was carrying some cakes in a package. While moving on, he observed his shadow behind him, and thought that another man was coming along with him. He said to the shadow : 'Off with thee, brother, go home ; in my wife's house they are poor : what shall they give thee'?

---

[1] To be stolen, *lit.* to disappear (in) theft.

[2] *Ullā*. See Dict.

[3] *Nīndiyā* is the 3rd pers. sg., neuter gender, of *nīndnā*.—The words which come next are Sadri, for *akku gā ujjnam gaṛherā ra'o*.

He then went on for a little distance, and, seeing once more (that shadow) behind, he said (to himself : 'The fellow has caught sight of my cakes : this is why he tramps after me'! So, opening (the package), he deposited one (cake) there on the road and went on Having proceeded a little further, and noticing that the other was coming along all the same, he said (inwardly) : 'He has found it good and so has not gone back : I shall give him some more'. Thus, from one bit to another, he went on laying down cakes, clothes and even (his) walking stick ; only his loincloth, and nothing else, was left to him : even this in the end he deposited on the road. At this moment the sun disappeared

He then notices that the other man is no longer there 'Halloo,' he said, 'the blackguard was following me for my sole loincloth'.

Now, however, being rank naked, as soon as he reached, he walked (lit. *walks*) to the back of the house to hide himself. His parents-in-law had had their meal ; (but) were (still) expecting him. The old crony said to her husband : 'How many cakes shall I put by for the boy'? The husband said : 'How many thou wilt put by? Reserve one, and a bit more'. All this conversation the simpleton was overhearing. Later on, the old man went out, saying he was going to look for their son-in-law. He caught sight of some one hiding behind the house and called out : 'Who's there? Who's there'?—'Well, I myself'.—'Why not have entered the house'?—No clothes · how should (*lit.* shall) I'? And he related the whole affair. Then his father-in-law took out a loincloth and gave it to him to put on.

The young man went in, and after washing hands and feet sat down. His mother-in-law gave him what she had put by of the cakes for him. When he (had) finished them off, she asked : 'Will you have some more, or will this do'? Says he : 'Thou hast nothing more for me to eat. There was just as much as this, I know this perfectly well'. They were abashed at this retort and said : 'He knows a great deal'.

While (that young man) was staying in the village, a golden cup of the king's was stolen : so the king sent for sorcerers and bhagats to find it back. The old crony said to the king : 'Oh my son-in-law knows a good deal about things of this kind ; question him'. Peons went to the simpleton and said. 'Come along, the king calls thee'. He replied : 'I know nothing at all, good sirs; I shan't go'. They demurred and took him away by force. The king told him : 'If thou findest my golden cup, I shall give thee a splendid remuneration ; but, if thou failest (to do so), I shall give thee the burying-pit'. The simpleton felt aggrieved and asked for time. Then they confined him into a house and allowed him seven days.

All this while the thief, uneasy and chafing, stood in secret frights. His name was 'All-Over'. He thought : 'I must see how this man proceeds about sorcery'; and in the dead of night he went near the house and listened. Just then the simpleton was saying in bitter lament : 'Now it is all over (for me); all alive, the burying-pit'! The thief, hearing himself named, quickly said : 'I say, brother ; don't tell, don't tell; I shall give thee a share'. The simpleton asked : 'Where didst thou put it'? The other replied. I have hidden (*lit.* placed) it in the tank'. Then the simpleton began to rave as if entranced, shouting the while : 'Open ! open'! (People) got up, opened, and plied him with questions. 'Go, he said, it's in the tank'. They went, began to search, and found as they had been told. The king admired (the man's cleverness), and made him prime-minister.

2. *Laṇḍhiyā Kukkos.—The Lazy Boy.*

Oṇṭā raṇḍī paccō rahcā, adigahi tangdas kōhā laṇḍhiyā rahcas. Ās pairī paitī gā ūgtan ceṛ'ar-kī aḍḍō khēdnūtim k͟haḷl tarā kālālagyas, pahẽ biṛdō uiālagyas. Jokk gahṇḍī k͟hōk͟hā, ennẽ uinan hõ ambyas ciccas kī tanghai ullan oṛā piṭnum khep'ū helras.

Ī katthan balnum, āsgahi tangyō khōb sukmār'ālagyā Oṛgalagyā: 'Engdas uiā hõ uidas, ōṛan hõ piṭdas. Ēn āsge asman mekkhon, arā balī nū ṭangon : hole, engdas barā k͟hanem etto'os[1] darā mōk͟hos'. Asman mikkhī, darā ṭāngī ci'ī Tangdas, gohlā bicobrnā beṛā nū, ēṛōṭā oṛā pityasdara ondrasdara bardas, ara munddh asman etta'ādas kī mōk͟hdas. Ār annem sagarkhane nanālagyar.

[1] Will knock it down (with his pallet and bow).

Annūtim cākhnā ullā barcā. Khanē tangyō tangdāsin ānyā : 'Akkū gā cākhna ullā barcā, beṭā ; ōrmar cākh'ālagnar ; gucā, ēn bihnin hō'odan ; cākh'ā kaot'. Anti tangyō uḍḍū nū khessan kummyā.

Ond aḍḍā ārsyar khanē,tangdas nannargahi usskā khall nū bihnin cākhdas . anti khall-urbar mēkhnar ; ' Embai khall nū nē cākhdar, [1] barō ? Emhai khall nū amba cākh'ā' ba'anar. Khanē tangdas tangyon āndas : 'Īd gā khall nambai mallī ayō ; adā ānnū nambai khall ra'ī'. Nannā khall gusan kānar dara ayyan cākhdas. Pahē ā khall urbar hō mēkhnar : 'Husan nē cākhdar harō ? Kalā nimhai khall nū cākh'ā'. Annē annētī uḍḍū nū bihnī munjrā kerā.

Antile tangyō kadrāra, dara tangdasin, oonhā naunā lekh'ā, ānyā : ' Ē beṭā uḍḍun, ḍhēkan pesā-dara,[2] nind'ā '. Ās nindas, khanē tettas ciccas. Anti tangyō ḍhēkātī tangdasin, launum launum khed'a helrā.

Bongnutī bongnutim, ā kukkos ḍangrā-mucur gusan ārsā helras. Tangyō ārin gecchātī mīkhya : ' hūsin dharke ! hūsin dharkē' ! Langrā-mucur a kukkōsin menjar : 'Ā mukkā endr ba'ī, babū' ? bācar. Ās anyas : 'hūsge ḍangrā pottan ci'a, ba'ī' bācas. Khanē ciccar, dara ās phīn bonga helras. Khōkhanū onṭa puttāgahi kōhā lātan khakkhyas : ā lātā nū kōrcas.

Tangyō ārsyā dara ā lātan ḍangtī hanḍra'ā helrā. Ās ā ḍang nū pottan liṭpiṭambācas Khanē tangyō cīkhā helrā : 'Ēn engdasgahi pottan otthorkan ' bācā darā tanghai erpā kerā ; kalpārnum tanghai cūtnā-piṭrī nū cūtyā, dara khandrā kerā. Mākhā bīnī tangdas barcas dara mēkhā helras : 'anai yō, balin tisga'ai' bācas. Tangyō ānya : ' Engage khaddkharrā malkar ; onṭā engdas rahcas[3] : āsin gā, bhunḍū nū hurckan-dara, piṭkan ki āsgahi pottan otthorkan ; engage akkū khaddkharrā malkar' bācā dara malā cōcā.

Khanē tangdas rūsī manjas kī nannā rājī keras, ara onṭā baṛiyas guyā jōkh ra'ā helras. As gusan ra'anum tanghai munddhantā dara

[1] *Lit, who, you fellow, do you sow in our field ?*

[2] *Pesā* is properly an imperative. But as shown by the general construction of the sentence, this imperative has here merely the force of a conjunctive participle. See Grammar, p. 286, n. 6.

[3] I had an only son

bujhr'ā dara nalakh nanā helras, dara tang'ā ujjāpūrtī puñjī nañjas.[1] Ayyantī urkhas khanē, ekannē hēbrkas rahcas, annem nalakh nanjas barcas.[2] Nalakh nannum nannum tán hō̃ urb manā helras; karē karē kōbā khurjī uiyas dara, baggē jō̃khārin uiā helraskī ā heḍḍentā ālargahi majhīnū bēlar lekh'ā mañjas keras.[3]

—There was a widow whose son was very lazy. True, every morning he would go to their field, with the plough on his shoulders chasing the bullocks in front of him; but he used to plough clumsily. Even such ploughing he soon gave up altogether and henceforward spent all day in killing birds (with his pellet bow).

Not knowing this, his mother was only too pleased. 'My son (she was thinking) tills the fields and kills birds. I shall make a cake for him and hang it over the door: when he returns he'll knock it down and eat it'. She bakes the bread and hangs it up. In the evening (*lit.* at unyoking time), the son comes back bringing a couple of birds he has killed; he at once knocks the cake down and eats it. So they did every day.

In this manner the sowing season came round. The mother said to her son: 'The sowing season has come, son; every one is sowing; come, I take the seeds; we are going to sow'. And the mother put a basket of paddy on her head.

Arrived at a certain spot, the son scatters seed over the tilled field of some other people. Its owners shout (to him): What do you throw seeds for in our field, you people? Do not sow in our field'. Says the son to his mother 'Well mother, this is not our field; our field is there, further on'. To the other field they go, and he scatters seed over it. But the owners of it also raise a shout: 'What do you sow there, you people? Go away, sow your own field'. Meanwhile the seeds in the basket had been spent.

Then the mother got angry and, in apparent sweetness, said to her son: 'Son, pick up clods and fill up my basket'. He did so, and helped (the burden) to (his mother's) head. She then began to pursue him, pelting him the while with these clods.

---

[1] *Lit.* made for himself a hoard for livelihood.

[2] See Gramm., p. 149*c*.

[3] Note the plural *bēlar*. Or. Gramm., p. 180, n. 28.

The boy in his flight came near men who were cutting up a dead bullock. From far the mother shouted to them: 'Stop him! stop him'. The knackers asked the boy: 'What does that woman say, boy'? He replied : 'She tells you to give me your bullock's guts'. So they gave them to him, and he resumed his flight. Later he came upon an ant-hill with a big hole in it : he entered into that hole.

On arriving there, the mother began to fumble into the hole with a long stick. Round that stick the boy twisted the bullock's guts. The mother started crying : 'I have disembowelled my son'! She went home, lay down on her rest mat and fell asleep. At night the boy came back and shouted : 'Mother, do open the door'. The mother said : 'I have no children. I had an only son, and, poking into an ant-hill, I have killed and disembowelled him. Now I have no children, said she ; and she did not get up.

Then the son in despair went to another country and took service in a merchant's house. In the course of his stay there, he began to understand his past errors (*lit.* condition) and took to work, and amassed a very fair hoard for himself.

On his leaving (the merchant), he continued to work as he had (now) grown accustomed to do. By dint of exertion he became rich himself, gradually acquired a fortune, and, as he began to keep many servants was looked upon by his neighbours and acquaintances as a sort of king.

3. *Bidrkā Haslī.* *The Recovered Carcanet.*

Ort urbas rahcas, āsgahi sattōjhana kukkōkhaddar rahcar ; ārin ās kundrkā lekh'am pāli pāli binjyas. Āsgahi sannī tangakhedō khokhā mundhbhārēgahi[1] khūb bujhr'ū rahcā. Ād īryā akkū gā kiṛā mañjkam kādam. Mānī mānī, āulantī kiṛā mannum mannum khūb kiṛā manjar kerar. Ārge onā mōkhāge ho malā khakkr'ālagyā khanē, ād ānyā : 'Iyyā gā nambai ujjnā malā kālo. Nām ormat ī rājintī cō'ot kālot : hole nambai ujjnā onnā bagge mano'. Ī katthā ormarge dau laggyā : ār, adigahi ānkā lekh'ā, tambai cirkī ṛiṭrin codar dara kālā helrar.

---

[1] *Lit.* Intelligent of the after and the before.

Kānum kārum undul ōnnā mokhnā munjrā kerā, khanē khūb kīṛā sārā helrar. Sannī khedō ārin ānyā : 'Endran ho ambā khar'ā ; pahē endrā endrā nimāge khakkro'ō, adīnim ondr'ā : nerr, keckā osgā, cotto kā cigālo : mōkhot dara khē' enantī bacohro'ot kaot'. Ār annem nanālāgyar.

Ā punā rāji nū āṛsyar khanē, endr manjā ? Bīṛī bakhṛē ulā, tanghai haslī ṛūnguṭṭhin otthrākī, kūbī gusan em'ā-khajr'ālagyā : ābirī cenkhō adigahi haslin nerr lekh'ā cinnā-bunnan īryā, darā ittyā-kī occā-dara kerā. Adigahi mukkar ekēkā gohar nanjar choṛābā'āge, pahē nē hō ṭollar. Ā cenkhō occā kī, ekātarā abṛā kīṛā ālar rahcar, attaram ṭiḍḍar ciccā. Sannis-tangkhaī īryā dara mankkhyā.

Antile, ennem bācaskı, bēlas caugurdā ḍamuan kōṛtācas : 'Nē nē ā haslin beddor kī ondro'or, ārge pācegoṭang ṭāddā ci'on'. Undul ennē manjā sannis-tangkhaī ciec ondı'ā kerā : ābīī ḍamuan kōṛnan menjā. Khanē : 'Endrgahi ḍamūā kūṛri'ī '? enne ād menjā.[1] Ālar tingyar. Khane ād bācā : 'Ēn biddkan ra'adan'. Abīrim ā ālin bēlas gusan occar. Bēlas menjas : 'Endr nīn enghai bīṛīgahi haslin biddkī ra'adi' ?—Ha'ī.—En ningāge pācegoṭang paddan ci'idan ; enghai haslī ci'ai'. Ād bācā : 'E belāyo, ēn paddā malā beddan. En oṇṭā katthā nē'edan : Sohrai ullāgahi mākhā nū nē ho billī ambnar dagnarnok'ā, aula ēm eklā dag'om'.[2] Bēlas bācas : 'Id gā otthā katthā malli ; ennem nanai'. Sohrai ullā ennem nanjar, dara aḍḍo-mēkkhō mankhā-bhāis, ēṛā-meṛkho guṭṭhi, ūkhın ērā ērā, ekātarā ho malā kerā ; pahē, adigahi billin ērā ēra, saōse rājintā mekkh adigahi eṛpā nū korcā, dara eōdā adigahi eṛpā nū kerā, aōdā adigahīdim manjā. Ennem abṛā ālar munddhantī koṛhe urbar manjar dara tamhai ullā khep'ā helrar.

—There was a householder who had seven sons ; he married them one after the other, in the precise order of their birth. His youngest daughter-in-law was very sagacious. At one time she noticed that the family was in want. In fact, their poverty growing worse and

---

[1] *Lit.* This is the drumming of what (announcement)?

[2] On the night of the cattle-festival (*sohrai*) the animals are given a better feed and taken out garlanded. If any escapes into a neighbour's house, it becomes h's property.

worse as time went on, they became extremely poor. When no means of living was left, she said: (We shall never) prosper here; let us migrate to another clime: at that cost, we'll live in plenty'. The idea pleased them all: so, according to her proposal, they shouldered mats and baggage and made a move. On their journey, their provisions ran short, and great was the hunger they had to endure. The small daughter-in-law said to them: 'Commit no theft; but whatever (eatable) thing comes across your way, bring it (to me): a snake, a dead rat, a mouse or jackal: we shall eat it and escape death'. So they did.

On their arriving into another country, what happened? The queen, after removing her carcanet and beads, was bathing and scouring herself near the well in the royal compound: just then, a kite observed that carcanet flashing like a snake, and with a sweep down carried it off. Her maids raised shouts upon shouts to make (the bird) drop it, but without success. The kite got away with it and dropped it where those poor people were living. The youngest son's wife saw it and put it into her house.

The king then had drums beaten throughout the land, with these words: 'whoever finds that carcanet and brings it back, I shall give him five villages'. One day it happened that the young wife went out to fetch fire, and she heard the beating of a drum. 'What's that drumming for'? she asked. The people told her. She said: 'I have found it'. Immediately they led her to the king. 'Hast thou found my queen's carcanet'? asked the king.—Yes.—I give thee five villages; give me my carcanet'. She said: 'O king, I do not want villages! One favour I do ask: it is that, on the night of the cattle-festival, no one (be allowed to) light a torch (*lit.* a lamp): on that day we alone shall light one'. The king said: 'this is no hard request; do accordingly'. On the festival day, they did so. Bullocks and cows, he and she-buffaloes, goats and sheep, plunged in darkness, made no move until, perceiving her steady light, they—the whole country's cattle—entered her house. Whichever passed her threshold became hers; thus, these people became richer than (ever) before, and spent their days in happiness.

4. Bār'otā Chayā alas.[1] The Protean Man.

Irib paccō pacgīge khādkhairā mal iaboar aõnge, paccō undul ānyā : ān pacgī,lnām khēr pōs'ot. Khēr pūsnum pūsnum, ḍhēr baggē baṛhrā[2] Antile pacgis paccon ṭhak'ā helras dara ānyas. 'Anai paccō, namhai khēi ḍhēr baṛhrā kerā : akkū nām oṇṭā dundū pōs'ot'. Khanē paccō ānyā : 'Eksan īrkai dara, pacgi[3]? —Mahuiang nū gā ra'ī ! accō ; kub'ū madgīgabi khoḍrā nū. Nēlātī ērā oi'ot, paccō ! — Endran ci'ot anti, pacgī ?— Kohā gayan piṭot, paccō'. Iōndā rū mākhābūī cūtyar, dara, bijjvā khanē, pacgis khēran pitvas dara pudgas kī, paccōge cicoas-dara, ānyas : 'Bēs iṛke, paccō, khanē hō'oke : ēn uiā kāklan. Enne ba'anum ās eṛpantī urkhas dara ā khoḍrā nū khandr'āge kōrcas.

Paccō ahṛan nagadkurā iṛyā ki madgī gusan occā dara ānyā : 'Ondai, dundū, ahṛā', ki khoḍrā nū uiyā ciccā. Antile pacgis mokkhas. Khōkhā kū ā ḍhoḍhiontī urkhas kī eṛpā keras dara ānyas : 'Paccō, dundūge ahṛā nitkī ci'ike. Ahṛan bēs iṛke ci'ike, paccō. Ikla'am ambke khēkhel ērai'. I kōgūtī khēr mal munjrā, ā gūṭī paccō ānkā lekh'ā nanjā. Pahē, khēr munjrā khanē, paccō 'ondai, dundū' ba'īkī, khokhel īryā. Pacgīsin īrnum khūb khobrārā, dara 'En ekāsē ī ahṛā-mūkhus[4] guyā ra'on bācā.

Rūsī kālage[5] uḍḍū nū tang āi urmī sanjgi mōkhnā isungguṭṭhin sajjā ciccā : pahē, tetra'ā pulli khanē, nannārin eṛ'a kerā. Iūṛum nū pacgis uḍḍū nū kōreas kī ukkyas Paccō oṇṭā āli ganē kīrryā : īd adin tēttrā ciccā.

Paccō jokk gecchum kerā kī pacgis, uḍḍū ulā, umblas ciccas Ba'ī paccō : 'Ohrē, mahrangle isung tundrā', dara mūhī khekkhā kheḍḍan khas'ā helrā. Antile oṇṭā paddā āṛsyā, ettācā ki īrī gā : pacgis ! Khanē paccō pacgīsin kēbā helrā are khūb cikhyā Iūndam ; pacgis gaue pollā ai eṛpā kirryā.

---

[1] *Lit* The man o'the twelve shapes.

[2] *Lit.* Rearing rearing, (the fowls) increased very numerous. See a similar idiom in the preceding story l. 1

[3] *Lit.* where having seen one (doest thou speak thus, husband ?

[4] *Ahṛā-mūkhus*, rascal *lit.* meat-eater.

[5] *Rūsī*, indignant, in a huff. *Rūsī kānā*, to run away.

Nannā ullā, oṇṭā jatrā laggālagyā khanē, pacgīsin ānı: 'ēn bō̃ jatra ērā kālon'. Pacgis ānyas: 'kalai, paccō'. Adin kālā ciccaskī, ās mākmargan hēcas dara pāgan nanjas. Jatrā nū tān bō̃ keras, dara, ekātarā paccō ra'ī, attrā attrā nāldas ara ḍıṇḍi pāṛdas: 'Pacco mokkhā kanjın pacgis mokkhas ahṛan; tērem rētem, tēren ıētem'. Khōkhānū pacgis adin menjas: 'Paccō, jatrā kirkī; endrau ırkı? —E pacgī, oṇṭā pacgīsin īrkan, ās kukk nū singar manjkas rahcas: enghai mundhbhāre nālālagyas dara ḍıṇḍī pāṛālagyas. Ās gā ning lekh'am etthra'ālagyas. Āsgahi oṇṭā bāgıkan bō̃ pettkan ondrkan'. Khanē ās bācas: 'Enim gā rahackan, paccō. Enghai bāgrkan cī'ai'. Khanē gā alkhā helrā dara bācā: 'En ningane pollon, pacgī; nin bār'oṭā chayā āl taldai'.

—A certain man and his wife having no children, the wife one day said to him. 'I say, husband, let us rear poultry'. The fowls in time became very numerous. The man then played a trick upon his wife and said: 'Wife, our fowls have multiplied to excess: now let us feed an owl (upon a few of them)'. The wife said: 'Where didst thou see an owl, husband'?—'It is in the mahua grove, wife, in the hollow of the crooked mahua. Wife, from to-morrow we shall feed it'.—'And what shall we give it husband'?—'Wife, we shall kill the big capon'. On this they went to sleep, and at dawn the man killed the fowl, plumed it and, handing it to his wife, said: 'Fry it well, my wife, and take it to (the mahua hole): I am going to plough!' Saying so, he left the house and slipped into the hollow tree to have a nap.

The wife fried the meat nicely, carried it to the mahua tree and saying. 'Owl, have some meat', placed the meat into the hollow. Her husband ate it. Later, he got out of his hole, went home and said: 'Wife, give meat to that owl every day. Fry the meat quite to a point, wife. Never look into the bottom (of the hollow)'! As long as the fowls lasted, the wife did as she was bidden. But, when they came to an end, as she was saying 'take this, owl', she peeped at the bottom. Seeing there her husband, she got angry, and said: 'How can I stay longer with this rascal'? With a mind to run away, she packed all her belongings, provisions, oil, etc., into a basket; but, being unable to raise it to her head, she went to call for helpers. At that moment her husband sealed himself into her basket. The wife returned with a woman, who helped her to raise (the burden).

She had got pretty far when her husband in the basket had to urinate. Says the wife: 'Halloo, the mahua oil is spilt'. She rubbed with it her face, hands and feet. She next arrived at a village, put down (her basket) and sees...her husband! Then the wife began to abuse the husband and had a good cry. Enough. she could not get the better of her spouse and returned home.

On another day, as a *jatra* was going on, she said to her husband: 'I too am going to see the jatra'. The husband said: 'Go, my wife'. Having left her depart, he tied antlers to his head and put on a turban. He then went himself to the feast, and, wherever his wife stands, there he (goes and) dances and sings this tune: 'A wife had sour rice-water for herself; her husband ate meat, *la faridondaine, la faridondon*'. Later on, her husband asked her: 'Wife, thou hast gone to the jatra: what didst thou see?—Husband, I saw an old man with a head (very much) adorned: he was dancing in front of me and singing. He looked absolutely like thyself. I have picked up and brought one of his combs'. He then said: 'It was myself, wife. Give me my comb'. Then she laughed and said: 'I am no match for thee, husband; thou art a man of many shapes'!

5. *Khudang-ḍibrū Raskas.* *The Drumming Sportsman.*

Ās iūndā koṛhē raskā rahcas, ōṇḍ mākhā nū sattē paddā bēcālagyas dara tangbai eṛpā mākham bar'ālagyas. Bēcā kālālagyas khanē, khēlan hō̄ tanggane ho'ālagyas, dara akhṛā nū kālarkī ennē assālagyas: dhatung-dang, khudang-ḍibrū: Idim āsgahi ōr rahcā. I kharkhan menarkī jokhar pellar ba'ālagyar: 'Barcas, koi, Khudang-ḍibrus. Gucā, ko, bēcā kālot'. Āra cubbā lekh'ā sapṛārkā urkhālagyar. Bēcnum bēcnum ratyār'ar kālālagyar khanē, ās chachem nan paddā kālālagyas: anti āsgahi kānan hō̄ ballālagyar. Ār ennē oṛgālagyar, ās em sangem bēcnum ra'as, dara rijh ra'ālagyar; bēcā bēcā khaṛdālagyar. Āsin ambar rijh mala laggālagyā. Āsgahi nāme cauguṛdā binḍrā kerā, dara ennem ḍher ullā gūṭi rijhrang manjas.

Abṛā paddā madhentī chauṭhurgahi ḍabrē sobhā rahcā, pahē sattēpūrnā paddā nū āṛsāge Khosrā kaṭṭā manālagyā : aōnge khāṛ nū lau-laṛang jhapeki rahcā. Khosrā nīndālagyā annūhō, otkhāsim kaṭṭālagyas. Onghon ennē manjā ek'am dokhar kerar dara ā lau-laṛangan tāryar ciccar kī tambai eṛpā kerar. Ās gā munddhuntā lekh'am abṛā chau paddā nū biccyas beotācas rijhtācas, khōkhānū Khosrā pakhentā nū kālā helras. Ā lau-laṛang nū argyas-kī assnum pāṛnum bēonum kālālagyas, pahē majhī nū aṛsyas-kī, khaccrā kerā. Ā amm nū khattras : ād bōhābācā dara jokk gecchā occā dara mulkhtācā...

Nannā ullā Khosrā pakhentā jōkhar pellar beddā helrar. 'Endr manjā, ās emhai paddā mala barcas ?'. Beddnum beddnum Khosrā gusan āṛsyar, dara endr ērnar : larang tārkā ra'ī. Anti ār bācar : 'Ek'am mudair ḍāhēti ennē nanjar ! Iyyam khattras keras, ko' ! Khosrā nū beddā helrar kī āsin kecckā biddyar. Cāṛem abṛā sattō paddantā jokhar pellar gusan tengā kerar. Urmī paddantar barcardars, cīkhar-dara, āsin sattō paddantā pellorgahi bāgrkātī bassyar ciccar.

—So keen was he on sport that, in a single night, he would (go and) dance in seven villages and return home before the night was out. On his way to a dance, he used to take his tomtom with him, and, repairing to the village square, he would patter thus : dong ding, ding dong ; such was his prelude. Swains and maidens, hearing the notes, said (to one another) : 'He has come, girl ; (here is) Mr. Dingdong.—Come, boy, let us go and dance' ; and they sallied forth adorned like peacocks. When they became intoxicated with prolonged dancing, he would steal away to another village. They did not notice his departure. They thinking he was still with them made merry ; they danced themselves dead tired. Without him there was no pleasure. His fame spread on all sides and he thus remained a jolly fellow for many a day.

To six of those villages the road was easy, but, in order to reach the seventh, one had to cross the Koel : hence a bridge of Bauhinia creeper had been thrown over the river. Even when the Koel was full, he would cross it alone. Once it happened that some enemies went and incised that creeper (-bridge), and returned home. He, just as before danced and led dances and rejoicings in those six villages, and afterwards turned his steps to the (village) beyond the Koel. Having got on the creeper, he advanced drumming, singing, dancing all the while; but, when he reached the middle part, it snapped. He fell into the water, which carried him off to some distance and drowned him.

On the morrow, the young people of over the Koel started a search. What has happened that he did not come to our village? Their search led them to the Koel, and what do they see, but that the creeper (-bridge) had been cut into? Then they said: 'Some enemies, through jealousy, have done this deed! Here he has fallen, boy'. They searched in the Koel and found him dead. Immediately they went to inform of this the swains and maidens of the seven villages. From everywhere people came, and they amid laments burned him, the girls of the seven villages making of their combs a funeral pyre for him

6. *Paṭi'a'ānā lekh'ā Mukkā.* *The Faithful Wife.*

Ēṛ bhaīr rahcar. Ār pardyar khanē, tām tām rajōt nanjar kī bācar: 'Nē[1] mundh beñjro'or'? Kōhas ba'as: 'Nīn benjr'ā, bhayā'. Sannis ba'as: 'Mundh benjro'on dadā hōle, ek'am tartī bar'on, maṇḍī amm nē'ā ongon; mundā ningāge gecchā gecchā mannā manō'. Kōhas malā mancas khanē, sannīsim mundh benjras. Sannis ek'am tartī bardas hōle, tām mukkā mēt kharā khusmāinum kachnakhnardara ra'anar: pahē kōhas sarmār sarmār endra'ānim nē'edas dārā gecchā gecchā manda'; tangṛisgahi-ālī āsin gecchantī endra'ānim ei'ī.

Ā kōhas tanghai lūran bīskas ōndkas rahcas: sannisgahi āliu sībākhāreas, dara āsin piṭāge ḍahiē beddā helras. Undul āsin ānyas: 'E kō, gucā sendrā kālot'. Khanē irbāirim[2] sendrā kerar. Kōhas ēṛetthan occas kī aṭā okkā keras; sannis gā nākhnūtī khēdnum kōhas

---

[1] *Nē* may always be followed by a verb in the plural, even when one single person is meant. (See Or. Gramm., p. 193, n. 4).

[2] See Or. Gramm., p. 155, 5.

tarā ho'ālagyas. Ḍhēr mākguṭṭhi attrā kerā: annubō malā laudas. Khanē gā sannis bhartācas dara, beḍḍē āṛsyas khanē, kōbas āsin eṛēthti lagcas. Piṭyaskī, āsin khaikā aṭkhātī jhapcas dara eṛpā keras.

Ā ālī menjā: 'Ningṛis,[1] dā hoī, endrge malā bardas? Ās bācas: 'Khōkhā taram rahcas. Ās bardas hōtang'. Jokk gahpdī nū ās eīkhā kalpār'ā cōcas dara bācas: 'Nerr āsin parmyā. Pahē ambai elcai: ēnim gā ningan enghai ālin nanon'. I katthan menarki ād balin muccya-kī ukkī. Ās ba'ā helras: 'Kollai, lolā, biṛī, rigi-cigi, balin, ennege ēn kūl-kiṛā ammonkātī khē'ālagdan'. Ād bācā: 'Dulhasgahi katthāti jiyā sālī[2]', mundā baynālasgahi katthātī kōllam laggī. Ra'ā Akkun jokk ullā āsin basot, bhōjē nanot, huṛāba'ot: anti sagai manot pahē[3]...... Ibrā khōkhānū gā ninghai ra'adan'. Khanē ās mancas.

Bassnā ullā āṛsyā khanē, ād ānyā: 'Tikhil dālī dara jōkhārin beddā. Kālot dara namhai nēgcār lekh'ā nanot oi'ot: hōle āsge hō dau manō dara namāge hō manō pahē Antī sāṛan kamcar; adī manyā kankan khuppyar dara keckāsin ayyā laccar. Cicc dagāge beddnar: malki. Khanē ā ālī bācā: 'Jōkhaṛ khaṛdkar ra'anar; ēn hō cāṛē bar'ā pollon īge ninīm kalke: cāṛē ondr'ā'.

Keras kī ād ijjā dara ennē Dharmes gusan nēcā, khekkhātī kicrigahi nākh gaṇḍan dharcākī: 'E Dharmē, cico ci'ā! E Dharmē, enghain[4] menā! enghai ālasge cico ci'ā'? Ennē nē'a[5] hō nēcā anti, cicc laggyā kerā: laukādim ciccan ciccā. Āganem ā ālī cīkhyā-dara tān hō kōrcā are tang mētas gane cind manjā

—There were two brothers. When grown up to manhood, they deliberated together and said: 'Which of us shall marry first'? The elder said: 'Marry first, brother'. 'Brother, if I marry first', says the younger, 'I shall be entitled, whenever I come home, to ask (my wife) for a meal or a drink (without hindrance): but you (in asking her for the same), you 'll have to stand at a respectful distance'. As the elder did not yield, it was the younger that married first.

---

[1] See O. Grammar p. 15 b.

[2] My soul takes delight in my husband's speech. *Dulhas*, prop. bridegroom, is here a term of endearment.

[3] See Or. Gramm. p. 235, n. 47, b

[4] Possessive pronoun, accusative case See Grammar p. 46.

[5] Grammar p. 280 second half.

Whenever this younger man comes home, he and his wife have long and pleasant conversations, while the big brother asks with a blush for anything (he needs) ; he keeps at a safe distance ; and it is from afar that his brother's wife hands anything over to him.

That elder brother (was a man who) had lost his morals[1] : he coveted the cadet's wife and sought an opportunity for killing him. One day he said to him : ' Come, boy, we'll go out for a hunt '. They went alone. The elder took the bow and kept watch : the younger, in breathless pursuit, was driving (the game) towards him. Many deer took that direction : still (the man) lets fly no arrow. The younger brother wondered, and, as he approached (to see what was the matter), the elder discharged his bow upon him. Having murdered him, he covered (the body) with dry leaves and went home.

The woman inquired : ' Brother, where is thy small brother ' ? He said . ' He has remained behind. He is coming, I suppose '. A moment after, he burst out crying and lamenting and said : ' A snake stung him ; have no fear, however : I shall marry thee.' On hearing this, she closed the door (upon him)[2] and sat down. He began to say : ' Open the door, love, my queen, my beautiful : for I am dying of hunger and thirst '. She answered : ' My husband's voice makes my soul happy, but my brother-in-law's makes it sad. Wait. Some days hence, we shall burn him, give the meal (in his honour) and carry his bones to their resting place : then possibly, we shall marry......After these (ceremonies) I am thine.' To this he assented.

When the day for cremation arrived, she said : ' Fetch rice and dal and servants (i. e. carriers). We'll go and do things according to ceremonial : that will be good for him and for us likewise, I hope '. They built a funeral pyre, heaped wood on top, and placed the dead body upon it. They looked for fire to light (the pyre) : there is none. Then the woman said : ' The carriers are tired ; myself I cannot (go and) come back soon : go thyself and quickly bring fire '. When he had left, she stood up and thus prayed to God, keeping in her

---

[1] *Lit*, had sold out and drunk his common sense.

[2] The man had, according to family etiquette, remained on the threshold of the house.

hands the four corners of her garment : 'O God, give fire ! O God listen to my (prayer) ! Give fire to my husband !' The instant she prayed in this manner, fire caught (to the pyre) : a lightning flash kindled it. Thereupon that woman with a cry stepped into (the fire) and was consumed with her husband.

7. *Mūnd'oṭā Asmā. The Three Cakes.*

Oṇṭā kōhā paddā rahcā : ayyā ort paccō pacgī ra'ālagyar. Pacgis ullā ullā tembā kālālagyas : khess kōdai tīkhlan tembardara ondra'ālāgyas. Āsgahi paccō eṛpā nū ra'ālagyā : pacgisgahi bar'āge ammguṭṭhin ondra'ālagyā, dara kankguṭṭhin beddarkī uyyālagyā. Endr tīkhlan pacgis tembarkī ondra'ālagyas, adin cunjarki maṇḍin bīta'ālagyā : anti irbārim nagad sangem pāti-pāti okkarkī sukhmārnum ōnā mōkhālagyar. Ā paddā nū oṇṭā kōbā bēlas hō rahcas : ā pacgis bēlas guyā hō nitkī-nitkī tembāge kālālagyas.

Undul ā paccō tangpacgisin ānyā : 'E pacgī, asmā mōkhā ṭukkī[1] : kalā, jokk'em ābdā tīkhlan tembke dara ondrke' bācā.— Ha'ī anti, paccō : innā gā ābdā tīkhlan jokkeari nē'on kī ondro'on' bācas, dara tembāge urkhas. Āsge sankā sankā eṛpā nū kōdain ciccar, khessan ciccar, guṛlun ciccar. Timbnum timbnum oṇṭā kōhā eṛpā nū āṛsyas: ālar āsge kōdain ci'inar, adin malā hō'odas. Khanē khessan ci'inar, adin hō malā hō'odas. Khanē ōndkā tīkhlan ci'inar, adin hō malā hō'odas. Khanē dālin ci'inar, ḍhiban ci'inar, abṛan hō malā hō'odas. Ās ābdā tīkhlan beddas : khanē ond muṭṭhīkem ābdā tīkhlan ci'inar. Ās adin ondraski eṛpā barcas.

Annuntile paccō tīkhlan oppā dara guṇḍā kas'ā helrā. Kas'ā manjyā khanē, asman mikkhyā . mūnd auṛkā tīkhilgahi asmā mūnd'oṭā manjā. Asmā mēkhnā gūṭī[2] , tangpacgis kuddā kerkas rahcas.

Barcas khanē, paccō ānī : 'En āṛ'oṭā mōkhon, pacgī ; nīn oṇṭan mōkhoi' ba'ī. Pacgis āndas : 'En tamām kuddan : ēn āṛ'oṭā mōkhon, paccō'. Ennem irbargahi majhī nū khaṭrnā[3] mal ban'ī khanē, gacchrnakhrnar : 'Lagē: irbātim piṭrin bācro'ot-ki cūtot : nē

---

[1] Or. Grammar, p. 94, n. 38.

[2] Do. p. 300, 301.

[3] Or. Dict. khaṭṭnā.

k͟hōk͟hānū cō'or, ārim ēṛ'oṭā asman mōk͟hor' bāenakhrnar. Annuntī asman uyyar, kī cūtyar, dara, begar k͟handrnum hō̃, cūtkar ra'anar. Pacgis tanghāi jiyā nū āndas : 'Paccō munddh cō'ō ; ēn k͟hōk͟hānū cō'on kī ēṛ'oṭā asman mōk͟hon', ara mal cō'das. Paccō hō̃ ānī : En gā malā cō'on, pacgis munddh malā cō'os hōle.' Ennem ār ērānakhrnum ulmūnd gūṭī cūtkar rahcar.

K͟hanē bēlas ā pacgīsin beddā helras : ' Oṇṭā pacgis nitkī nitkī tembā har'ālagyas ; ās ulmūndtī endrnā malā bardas ? endr manjas hoṭang'? Bēlasgahi jō̃k͟har kerar : ā paccō pacgirgahi eṛpā nū ērnar: irbārim piṭri jhaprardara keccā lekh'ā cūtkar ra'anar. Ār belāsīn ānyar : ' Paccō pacgi irbārim tambai eṛpā nū keccka: ra'anar'! K͟hanē bēlas ānyas : ' Kālarki ārgahi eṛpantā kankan bāsan ujhra'arkī sāṛā kam'ā, dara masṛā gusan ceṛ'arkī bō'ardara bassar ci'ā'. Ā jō̃k͟har ḍāṛan murkyar kī ā keckārin ceḍḍar kī masṛa gusan occar. Eṛpan ujhrāoar kī kankguṭṭhin k͟huppyar, kank manyā paccō pacgī irbarīnim laccar. K͟hōk͟hānū cicotī utgyar. Āganem irbārim cicyār-num cō:ar : ' En ēṛ'oṭā mok͟hon' ! Ormā ālar gā elonar-kī bongnar, ' eman mōk͟hor' ba'anardara. K͟hanē ā paccō pacgis bēlas gusan kerar kī tambain tingyar. Bēlas ārin tanghai cālībālī nū uyyas, dara āultī bēlas gusan ra'ā helrar.

—There was a big village : an old man and an old woman were living there. Every day the old man went out a-begging : he brought in paddy, corn, rice given him as alms. His wife stayed at home : for her husband's return she fetched water, oil, etc., and made provision of fuel. What rice he brought her, she pounded and cooked : then the pair, nicely sitting near each other, took their meal with joy. In that village there resided also a great king : the old man used to beg from him as from others every day.

One day the old woman said to her husband : ' Husband, I have a fancy for cakes : go and beg for a little unbleached rice and bring it to me '.—' All right, wife : to-day I will ask for some unbleached rice ' said he, and out he went on his begging tour. In poor houses, they gave him corn, paddy and millet. In the course of his begging, he arrived at a rich house : people offer him corn, he does not accept it. They then offer him paddy : neither this does he accept. They offer him scalded rice : he does not take it either. They offer him dāl, money : he refuses these likewise. He asks for unbleached rice : they give him a fair handful of it. With this he returns home.

Immediately the old crony soaked this rice in water and set about grinding it to flour. This done, she baked cakes : with the three measures of rice three cakes were turned out. While the cakes were baking, her husband had gone out for a stroll.

When he came in, the old creature said : 'I will eat two (of these cakes), husband, thou shalt have one'. Says the old man : 'I am always on the tramp. I shall have two, my wife'. So, a fair sharing between them two being impossible, they enter into a compact : 'Come : each of us will lie down, rolled in (*lit.* covered with) a mat : whichever will rise last shall have the two cakes'. And immediately they put the cakes aside and lie down, unable even to get asleep. The old man says to himself : 'The wife shall rise first and I shall have the two cakes', and he does not get up. The old woman on her side thinks : 'For myself, I shan't get up, until my husband is up'. And thus, watching each other, they remained lying three days.

The king however began to inquire after the old man : 'An old man was coming here to beg every day; what has become of him these three days'? His servants went (to see) : they peep into the house of the old pair ... the two of them, covered with mats, are stretched along like dead. The servants thus reported to the king : 'Both the old man and the old woman are dead in their house'. Then the king said : 'Go and breaking up the wood and bamboo (work) of their house, make of it a funeral pyre; carry (the corpses) to the cremating ground and burn them'. Those servants cut some poles, took the dead on their shoulders and conveyed them to the burning place. They (then) destroyed the house, piled up its wood, and on the wood placed the two (corpses) : they then gave them a touch of the fire ... Instantly they got up screaming : 'I shall eat two'! Of course, all the people in a fright run away saying : 'they are going to devour us'! The old man and woman went to the king and related their story. The king gave them a place in an outhouse of his, and they henceforward lived with the king.

8. *Bokkhō Pāḍes.* *Locust the Pandit.*

Bokkho Pāḍē nāmē ort ālas rahcas; āsgahi paccō hō̃ rahcā, Ār kīṛā rahcar. Āsge lessā-nalakh ucchyā. Ās īryas nē līkh'ā paṛh'ā akhnar, ārge baggē khakkhri'ī, ara ōrmar ārin majhī majhī nannar.[1] Khanē ās hō̃ sikhr'ā biddyas dara tanghai ālin ānyas; Ē paccō, engā jokk'em tīkhil darā sattū kam'aī ci'ai. Ēn sikhr'ā kādan'. Paccō tīkhil dāli sattū urmin musgyā ciccā: pāḍes abṛā kharcāguṭṭhin ceḍḍas kī keras.

Candō ēṛ mūnd gūṭī nantaram rahcas, pahē̃ sikhr'ā pōllas. Khanē, ekestī ekestī ḍhērkhunā patran paccā kāgajguṭṭhin khōṇḍas-kī, eṛpā kirryas. Bīṛī puttbīrī dhundhur manjkantī eṛpā āṛsyas. Paccō mal rahcā: ās khaṭī kīyā ūkhā nū cūtkas ra'as. Paccō barcā dara mikkhyā mokkhā; anti: Pacgisge hō̃ (bācā) onṭā dara koc'ā uyyon: bar'os hōle, mōkhos; makhle ēn pairī mōkhon' bācā. Ibṛan urmin ās mēnālagyas. Ād khandrā khanē, khaṭi kiyyantī eṛpanti chachem urkhdas, dara bālī nū ṭhokkhdas. Ād cōcā, billī ūrcā derā kheḍḍ nōṛhr'āge emm ciccā; nōṛhras kharē, ā asman ciccā. Munjyas khanē menjā: 'Aur jokk' indri'im mōkhoi kā hurū? Ānākirtācas ās: 'Okhō ra'ī anti, ci'oi?'[2] Ād bujhrā: 'Paṛhcaskī teyār manjas'. Khusmār'ā helrā.

Ṭhaukam irb ālar ebarkā gadhan beddālagyar. Paccō ārin cāṛē cāṛē tingyā: 'Emā pacgis gā sagṛiguṭṭhi nanā akhdas'. Khanē āsin menā helrar: 'Erā gā; aṭgar nanā, gadhā ekātarā ra'ī.' Ās ā gadhan ōṇṭā rabṛi khall nū mennan īrkas rahcas. Tanghai puthin begarnum bīrdkas kuddyas[3], dara ānyas: 'Purb dishā kālā: ḍahrē heḍḍēnum rabṛi khall nū menālaggī'. Ār kerar dara khakkhyar. 'Ṭhaukam tengā ongdas"; bācar ki āsgahi ōhma nanjar.

Annū annum bēlasgahi sōnantā pānbaṭā hō̃ ebarā kerā: adin bēlas, em'ā keras-dara, kubī gusan pakhnā kiyā uyyas-kī modhrkas rahcas. Ās Bokkhō pāḍēsin eṛtācas kī añyas: 'Beddoi bōle, ningā kharā baggē annem ci'on.' Bokkhos balnātī elcā helras; pahē̃, nannā

---

[1] Or *mēdanar* ... mix with them. The sense is not: give them the place of honour.

[2] *Lit.* Where is there (anything) for you to give? See. Gramm, p. 230.

[3] He moved turning (the leaves of) the book aimlessly. O. Gramm, p. 268.

ullā, kūbī tarā pāp beddnum beddnum, saīntgahi pakhnā kīyā [1] ā pānbaṭan ṭhaukam īryas: asānum uyyas ciccas. Cāṛē tangbai puthinoccas, bēlas gusan keras dara achat, ghī'in dhūan ara endran endran ondra'ʿāge bācas. Khanē baramba'ā helras, attṛā ittrā bongkas keras, dara 'pakhnā nū ērā' bācas. Bēlas āsin tanghai kōhā mantrī kamcas.

Undul bēlas Bokkhō Pādēsin ānyas: 'Gucā, sendrā kālot. Patran'ērā gā, māk laggō kā malā'? Patran īryas: 'laggō' bācas. Saīntgahi mākan piṭyar.—Eṛpā kirrō bīrī, īrbārim pāti-pāti ghoṛō nū argkar rahcar. Bēlasgahi eōkh nū onṭā bokkhō uṛhyārnum kerā dara ukkyā. Adin bēlas cāṛem dharcas dara muṭṭhcas; anti bācas: 'Tengā. Pānbaṭā pāli nū bēs tingkai. Akkū, enghai muṭṭhī nū endrā ra'i'? Ās akbakkhras keras; āulā gā eka'āsem tingkas rahcas, pahē akkun endr ha'os? 'E belāyō, ānyas, eō ullā ningan phasto'on? akkūn gā Bokkhō pādesgahi jiyā kālō!—'Ṭhaukam tingyas' bācas-kī bēlas ēdas ciccas: onṭā keccā bokkhō! Bēlas Bokkhō pādēsin aur kōhā nanjas darā urmi katthā nū āsti salah hō alagyas.

—There was a man named Locust the Pandit; he had a wife. They were poor. Working on hire was not to his taste. He noticed that people who know how to read and write live in affluence and are welcome everywhere. Desirous himself to study, he said to his wife: 'Wife, make for me a little rice and millet: I am off in search of learning'. His wife made a packet of rice, dāl, millet, etc.; the Pandit put these provisions on his shoulder and went away. He stayed abroad two or three months, but could learn nothing. So, getting together a quantity of almanacs and old deeds, he turned homewards. He reached his house after sunset, as dusk had already fallen. His wife was out: he laid himself under the bed in the dark. His wife came in, baked (cakes) and had her meal; then she said: 'I shall put by one (cake) and a bit (more) for my husband; if he comes, he'll eat it; otherwise I will eat it to-morrow morning'. He was hearing all this. When she had fallen asleep, silently he gets from below the bed out of the house, and then knocks at the door. She got up, revived the fire, gave him water to wash his feet. After he had done, she served him the cake. As he had finished it, she asked: 'Will you have some more?' He retorted

[1] *Lit.* under a chance rock, under a stone which happened to be near.

'As though you had anything more to give'! She thought. 'His reading has made him sharp'. She was delighted.

Just then two people were after an ass, which had got astray. Quickly the wife said to them: 'Our[1] man is a good hand at divinations'. They questioned₂ him: 'Do look up; make a guess as to the whereabouts of the donkey'. He had noticed that donkey grazing in a dāl plantation. In mere show, he rummaged through his book and said: 'Go eastward, (the animal) is grazing in a dāl field by the roadside'. They went and found it. 'He guesses first rate'! they said; and they sung his praises.

About that time, a golden pān-box of the king's was lost: the king, in going to bathe, had put it below a rock near the well, and then forgotten all about it. He sent for Locust the Pandit and told him: 'if you find it, I shall make thy fortune'. Locust, who knew nothing, began to fear. On the next day, however, seeking for flowers near the well, he happened to look under the rock and saw the box: he left it there. At once he took his book, went to the king and called for sorcery requisites, ghee, incense and the rest. He next began talking as in delirium, ran this way and that way and said: 'Go and look under the rock'! The king made him his prime minister.

One day the king said to Locust the Pandit. 'Come, we shall go for a hunt: just look whether we shall have a deer'. The Pandit consulted his almanac: 'we shall', he said, and by good luck they did kill a dear. On their way home, the two were riding side by side. A locust flew against the king's breast and stuck there. The king quickly catching it, closed his fist and said: 'About the pān-box, you guessed right. Now what is there inside my fist'? (The pandit) got confused: on that (other) day he had indeed made a hit through good luck: but what to say now? 'O king, he said, I shan't cheat you any longer. Now, it's all up with the life of Locust the Pandit'! 'He has guessed quite right'! exclaimed the king, and he showed (what was in his hand): a dead locust. The king raised Locust the Pandit to a still higher station, and took advice from him in every affair.

---

1. *Emā* (dative plural of *in*) for *emhai*. This use of the dative case reminds one of the French vulgarism *la femme à Nicolas*.

9. *Kūāras dara Naūas. The Prince and the Barber.*

Ort kūāras dara ort naūas iyār nanjkar rahcar. Undul kūāras bācas : 'Anā, iyār, gucā. Embas onṭā benjru'ū kukoin nannā rāji nū cajjyas : adin ērāge kālot'. Naūas ānyas : 'Ṭhankam ; gucā, kālot'. Kūāras tanghai urmi sapṛārnau attyas dara ghōṛō nū argyas ; naūas tanghai pothan ṭangcas.[1]

Kānum kānum onṭā kōhā pokhārin ṭoṛang nū khakkhyar. Kūāras bācas : 'Anā, iyār, ondā : uṛung ghōṛon dhar'ā ; ēn em'ā kāldan'. Kūāras tanghai kicrīguṭṭhin urmin uyyas dara em'ā keras. Annū naūas tang iyārasgahi kicrin attyas kī ghōṛō nū argyas kī keras, tanghai pothan asānim ambyas-ki. Kūāras bar'ō biri bhartācas,[2] pabē endr nanos ? Naūagahi kicrin attyas dara pothan tangcas, kī : 'Khokkh'ā, iyār ! khokkh'a, iyār, ! ba'anum calr'ā helras.

Naūas, ghōṛō argkā bārī, munddh āṛsyas Kukoigahi tangyō tambas āsin jaōdkhaddiō bācar kī parcbācar kī mankkhyar. Ās gā jōkhārin bācas : khōkhānū enghai cerwādāras bar'ālagdas, paghā ās gusan ra'ī ; ās āṛsos hole, ghāsi khoyāge taikē ! Ā khattas barcas khanē, cicyār'ā helras : 'En gā jaōdkhaddin ! ēn jaōdkhaddin ! jōkhar āsin ānyar : 'Kalā, cerwādārā ! ning urbasgahi ghōṛōge ghāsi khoyā !

Khōkhānū kukoigahi tangyō tambas deoṛā bhagtārin eddar, ibṛā āṛ jaōkhāddīrin bicar nanāge : pabē ār akbakkhrar kerar dara pollar. Khanē ā ujgō kūāras ānyas : 'Īs Dharmesgahi ciccā bār ra'adas hōle, ī deōṛargahi lipdī nū, mancī, saṭr'ai kalai' ! Annem manjā. Ālar ā naūāsinim ānyar : 'Nīnim ēra. endrgē ennē manjā' Khanē ās bācas : 'Mancī, ēn Dharmesgahi cicckā bār maldan hole, chutr'ai kalai'! Mancī annuntile chuṭṭrā kerā. Aulantim ā ujgō kūarāsim jaōdkhaddī manjas, dara naūāsin ujjnam gaṛherā ciccar.

—A prince and a barber had sworn friendship to each other. One day the prince said : Come, friend : my father has chosen me a bride in another country : we shall go and see her.' The barber said : 'Very well, let us go'. The prince put on his best apparel and mounted a steed ; the barber hung his tool-wallet from his shoulder.

---

[1] He hung (on his shoulder).

[2] Wondered, from bharta'ānā.

On their way through a forest they found a large tank. The prince said : 'I say, friend, take the (bridle), keep the horse a few moments; I am going to bathe'. And, undressing, the prince went off for a bath. Meanwhile the barber put on his friend's clothes and rode off, leaving there his tool-wallet. On his return the prince wondered ; but what could he do ? He put on the barber's clothes, threw the tools on his shoulder and walked on shouting : 'Wait, friend ! wait friend' !

The barber, being mounted, arrived first. The girl's parents, mistaking him for their son-in-law, came out to meet him and received him in their house. He moreover told the servants : 'My syce is following; he has a tether with him; when he arrives, you shall send him to mow grass (for the horse)'. The unfortunate man, on coming up, started shouting : 'I am the bridegroom ! I am the bridegroom !' The servants said to him 'Be off, syce ! go and mow forage for thy master's horse.

In the sequel, the bride's parents called in sorcerers to decide between these two sons-in-law; but the sorcerers got confused and could do nothing. The true prince then said : 'If this fellow be her god-given bridegroom, you stools stick to the rears of these sorcerers' ! It happened so. The assistants said to (him who was) the real barber : 'You yourself explain (*lit.* see) why this should have happened.' This man said : 'You stools, if I am not her god-given bridegroom, fall off'! Immediately the stools got loose. Henceforward the true prince was acknowledged as (*lit.* became) bridegroom, and they buried alive that barber.

10. *Aghnu Kumbhras'.* *Aghnu the Potter.*[1]

Oṇṭā paddā nū ort bēlas rahoas. Ā paddānum Aghnu nāmē ort kumbhras hō̃ rahcas, āsgahi ālī ērāge khōb dau rahcā. Ā bēlasgahi tangdas, adi gane rityārkas rahoas-dara, jiyā nū āndas : 'I kumbhrāsin ek'am paṇḍhē piṭṭāokan hōle, adın īnim uyyon'. Aghnus, akkhas-dara, jiyā nū ānā helsas : 'Ikla'am āsin enghai

[1] This story is particularly rich in illustrations of that capital idiom by which the Oraon language converts any *finite tense* into the corresponding *participle*. See Grammar, p. 283—287.

eṛpa nū khakkhon hōle, 'piṭā khaecon.' Undul aṛīguṭṭhin bhaōṛī kutta'ā keras [1], dara barnum barnum ūkhyā. Aulā bēlasgahi tangdāsin tanghai eṛpā nū khakkhyas dara lau'ā helras : launū launū piṭā hō khaecyas. Ās ā māṛan oṇṭā kuṛrisgahi baṭgī nū occas dara, pacrī heḍḍē nū attrā-uttrā ṭempā gaḍḍas-kī, ijtācas [2] kī keras.

Kuṛris, 'khanjpāguṭṭhin khaṛnar' bācas-kī, mākham baṭgī tarā urkhas : pacrī gusan ijjkā āl īryas, dara, 'khalbar taluar' bācas-kī, soṭṭā trū laucas : atti ā māṛā khaltr'ā khacoyā. Ērdas gā is bēlasgahi tangdas taldas ! Khanē gā ajgut elcā helras. Cāṛem Aghnu kumbhras gusan keras dara chachem urmī katthan tingyas. Aghnus ā kuṛris gustī ḍhibā occas kī ānyas : 'Nēkan hō ambke tengā : ēn isin hebṛā hō'odan', bācas. Antile ā keccā alāsin mahal gusan occas, dara, ekā eṛpā nū bīṛī cūtālagyā, asan keras-dara, ā bēl-kukkosgahi cāltī [3] 'tisga'ai, tisga'ai' ! bācas-kī mekhā helras. Bīṛī mēkhnan menjā, pahē bujhrā : 'Īs, sagar mākhā khilḍi-kasbir gusan rahcas-dara, akkun barcas kī mēkhdas' bācā, kī malā tisgācā. Khanē ā kumbhras onghon mīkhyas kī ānyas : 'Balin tisga'ai ; makhle ēn isan ṭangro'on-kī [4] khē'on'! bācas. Anti ā keccā bēl-kukkōsin khēser nū phasrī nanjas kī ṭangcas dara tanghai eṛpā keras.

Bijjyā khane, mahlantā ālar ormar ajgut cīkhā olkhā helrar. Ābīrim kumbhras, lō, khoṭorkā aṛīguṭṭhin ceḍḍas-kī, aṛī bīsnā nangutī [5] barcas. Cīkhnāguṭṭhin menjas-kī. 'Endr manjā, endr manjā'? bācas.—Tingyar : 'Bēlasgahi tangdas ṭangras kī keccas' Khanē gā Aghnus hō, tanghai cirkhin kacṛācas-kī, cīkhā helras. Pahē bēlas ānyas : 'Ālas keccāsim [6], eō kalpār'or ? kalā, bassar ci'ā.'

Ālar keccāsin adhar ceḍḍar kī occar, adhar kankguṭṭhin ceṛ'ā kummā helrar. Ār ganem ā kumbhras hō cīkhā cīkhā kank occas. Sarhā kamcar dara, māṛan ayyā ladcar-kī,- ormar jokk gecchā kerar kī ukkyar.

---

[1] To carry about, *lit.* to carry on a (hawking) tour.

[2] *Lit.* and, having driven sticks into the wall on either side (of the corpse), he caused (the latter) to stand (against the wall).

[3] *Lit* with the voice of that royal boy.

[4] Reflexive form of *ṭangnā*. Having hanged myself, I shall die.

[5] Under the pretence of.

[6] Or. Grammar, p. O. page 268, *c*

Ā maṣṭāgahi kiyyantā khōkhel türckā .türckā rahcā, ād kumbhrasgahi eṛpā heḍḍē rahcā aōnge. Aghnus eṛpā kānā lekh'ā manjas, pahē astlem abṛā lātan kōrcas kī sarhā kīyam gūṭī chachem ēṛyas. Ekābiri cice laggālagyā, ābīrin mēkhā belras: 'Adhā bēlkhan Aghnū kumbhrasge ci'ike'. Ormar menjar kī sarkh'ā helrar; tām tām ānyar; 'Menā gā, endr ba'as'? Nē ne bācar: 'Jiya paltār'ālaggī'! Onghon ōṇṭim cāl menjrā. 'Adhā belkhan Aghnū kumbhrasge ci'ike; makhle ōrmar eng lekh'am manor'.

Masṛantā nēgcar nanjar kī santan pettar khanē, bēlāsin tengā kerar: 'Ennē ennē gā lalus ānyas'. Bēlas Aghnūsin eṛ'ā tayyas Ās tanghai eṛpā heḍḍē dhapdhapra'ā kaṭṭū nandā kōṛāge lakkas- ra'as. 'Gucā, bēlas eṛ'ālagdas; akkū gā nīnim bēl manoi' bācar. Ās, malpattu'ū dara ajgut manur lekh'ā tangan ēdnum [1], keras. Belāsin ānyas: 'Babā, ēn ekā ōrtan [2] anti, engā rājī khakkro'ō dara calāb'ā ongon? Ībagge dewān mōsōḍi ra'anar: ārin uyyā'. Bēlas ānākirtācas: 'Ningāgem ci'idan: engdas tānim sāṛsā mañyā ninghai nāmē nanjas'.

—In a certain village there was a king. In the same village there was a potter called Aghnu, whose wife was goodlooking. The king's son, who had misbehaved with her, got (*lit.* gets) into his head that, if he killed the potter, he would have the wife. Aghnu, knowing this, determined that, should he ever catch the man in the house, he (Aghnu) would kill him outright. One day he left to carry earthenware about for sale, and in coming back was overtaken by the night. That day he found the prince in the house and began laying about him: in doing so, he killed him. He carried the corpse into the close of a market-gardener, rested it against the wall causing it to remain erect by sticks driven, right and left of it, into the wall.

The market-gardener, thinking that his fruits were being stolen, went out into his garden in the dark, saw a human form standing against the wall and, imagining it was the thieves, dealt out a blow with his stick: the corpse fell to the ground. To his surprise he recognizes the king's son! then, indeed, he took great fright. He

[1] *Lit.* behaving as (do) incredulous people. Or. Grammar, p. 180, n. 26.

[2] Or. Grammar, p. 164.

at once went to Aghnu the potter and related to him the whole story. Aghnu took money from the market-gardener and said: 'Say nothing to anybody; I am going to take him away and dispose of him.' He then carried the dead man near the palace and, going to the house in which the prince's wife was sleeping, he mimicked the prince's voice and shouted. 'Open! open'! The princess heard the shouts, but thought: 'The fellow comes and shouts after spending the night with harlots'; and she did not open. Once more the potter shouted: 'Open the door, or I shall hang myself on this spot'. He next passed a noose round the neck of the dead prince and hanged him, and went home.

At dawn, there was weeping and lament through the whole palace. The potter himself, under the pretext of selling earthenware, turned up with a load of cracked pots. As he heard the wailings: 'What has happened? what has happened'? he said. They told him: 'The king's son has hanged himself and is dead'. Aghnu, dashing his load to the ground, began to cry with the others. But the king said: 'Dead is the man; what's the use of bewailing? go and burn him'.

A party of the people carried off the dead man; another party took wood in their arms or on their heads. The potter, always crying, carried his own load of logs with the others. They made a funeral pyre, and, having placed the corpse upon it, withdrew to some distance and sat down

The subsoil of that cremating ground was pierced with galleries: for it was close to the potter's house. Aghnu made a show of retiring to his house, but, from it, he entered those galleries and secretly got up to the spot just below the funeral pyre. While the fire was catching, he shouted: 'You shall give half the kingdom to Aghnu the potter'! All heard this and were thrown in wonder; they said to one another: 'Why, hear, what does he say'? Some said: 'He is coming back to life'. Once more the same voice was heard: 'You shall give half the kingdom to Aghnu the potter, or else all of you shall share my fate'!

The cremating ceremony over and the skeleton (bones) having been picked up, they went to tell the king: 'thus and thus has your darling spoken'. The king sent for Aghnu. He was close to his house beating earth and engaged in turning out pots and pans. 'Come, they said; the king wants thee; thou shall now be a king' He went with a show of incredulity and great wonder. He said to the king: 'Lord, who am I, pray to have a kingdom and be able to govern it? You have so many ministers and officials: appoint them.' The king replied: 'It is to thee that I make that gift: my son himself on his funeral pyre has named thee'.

11. *Kecckasgahi āl-piṭnā. The Dead Man who turned a Murderer.*

Ort paegis dara paecōgahi k͟haddar kecckar rahcar: nattibagar ḍoṭ'ō rahcar. Pacgis, gōllas ganē biṭṭhī kānum, khi'ū dara kecckā Hindurgahi nēgcār nannan Gangā gusan īryas: oṇṭā māṛāgahi bohārnan hō̃ āsānim īryas. Tanghai paddā nū kirryas k͟hanē, ās tangpaceon ānyas: 'Ān paccō, ēn khē'on hōle, engan ambke bassā: pahē̃ K͟hosrā k͟hāṛ nīndō hōle, ayyā bohāba'āke ci'ike'. Enne cirdī nū bācas; Māghe barcā k͟hanē, nāṛī trū keccas keras.

Paccō āsgahi ānkan jiyā nū uikā rahcā. Tang nattībagārin bācā: Anā, k͟haddarō, nimbas bācas: engan ambke bassā dara māṛā, engan k͟hāṛ nū tukke. Endr ba'adar'? Ār bācar: 'Uyyaı'[1]. Uyyāge ād āsin biṛnā nū, khandhā[2] aṭṭācā-kī, laccā ciçcā. Asārnum, cēp possādara, K͟hosra nīndyā. K͟hanē ād kecckāsin kummyā dara luisluisra'ā hō'ā helrā. Āsgahi k͟hekkhā khayyā-kī konkō manjkī rahcā. Ād āsin eōk͟h nū[3] kummyā kī tamānim gecchā occā, kī, darangā nū ijjā-dara, hebṛā helrā. Hebṛō bīrī, āsgahi k͟hekkhā adigahi k͟hēsran tō̃rcā dara amm nū tiḍḍā ... K͟hanē paccō: 'Bicchra'ā bicchra'ā, ba'adan; malā mendai?' mīkhyā. Anti sangem bohārar kerar.

—An old man and an old woman had lost their children; only grandchildren were left to them. The old man, in a fatigue journey with his landlord, witnessed the ceremonies done near the Ganges in connection with dying and dead Hindoos; there also, he saw a corpse

---

[1] *Lit.* reserve it, put it by (meanwhile). In February and March, rivers carry no sufficient water to carry away a corpse.

[2] *Khandhā* a partition. Understand here a closed up and roofless screen, *adjoining* the house.

[3] Eõk͟h the chest *of the corpse.*

(thrown in and) carried off by the waters. On his return to the village, he told his wife: 'I say, wife, when I die, don't burn me, when the Koel will be full, throw me in, to be carried away'. He was speaking thus at the harvest; when spring came, he died of a fever.

The old woman had kept in mind his recommendation. She said to her grandchildren 'Children, your (grand-)father has ordered me neither to burn nor bury him, but to throw him into the river. What is your advice'? They said 'Put the corpse to wait.' For this she had a small apartment constructed (adjoining the house), and she put the dead man upon it in the sun. In June, with the rains, the Koel became full. She raised the dead man on to her head and carried him off at a jog-trot. His arms in drying up had become crooked. She carried him very far, his breast resting upon her head; then, standing upon a high bank (of the river), proceeded to throw him in. In this act, his arms caught her neck and caused her to fall into the waters. Then the old creature: 'Let go! let go, I say! don't you hear'? she shouted. And they drifted away in company.

12. *Irb sagṛi nanur.* *The Two Critics.*

Oṇṭā ālas maṇḍīgahi sagṛī nanus[1] rahcas, ara nannas mukkāgahi sagṛī nanus rahcas: ār iyār manjar dara rājī ērā kuddāge urkhar. Kōhāle paddā nū barcar dara bēlasgahi k͟hāṭnā-eṛpā nū kerar. Ḍērāgahi k͟hāpus ārin menjas: 'Nim nū endr gun ra'ī? dara ekāgusan kādar'? Ār bācar: 'Ēn mukkā-chatār'ū ra'adan. Ēn maṇḍīchaṭār'ū ra'adan'.

Ā bhaṇḍāris ullā ullā ōrmā pāhiyargahi sekrā nanālagyas, urbas gusan hō'ālagyas dara tengālagyas: 'Iōndā ālar ōnd ser unur, ara iōndā ālar sattūgahi mūk͟hur, ara iōndā ālar alkhṛāgahi, ara iōnda ālar dūdhīgahi; ara iōndar cār anī, iōndar rupayā, iōndar pāce rupayā unur mūk͟hur ra'anar'. Aulā ās sekrā hō'ō bīrī, belāsin idin hō bācas: 'Innā irb ālar barokar ra'anar; ennē ennē argahi hunar' Bēlas bācas: 'Kōṛēdim; ārin eṛ'ā; en ārge ci'on'.

Anti, kōṛē-kōṛē mōk͟hnā-onnā amk͟hi-maṇḍī saprātacas dara bīta'āge pēsas khaṭ'ūrin. Urmī biccā k͟hanē, ārin onāge eḍḍas dara

[1] *Sagṛi nannā*, prop. 'to guess', means here *to be an expert in*, *a connoisseur*.

ārin ānyas : 'Nimhai manē lekh'ā mōkhā, asman dara iṛkan'. Mōkhāge ukkyar; pahē, ā maṇḍī sagṛī nannagahi mūī nū asmāgahi chābak barcā khanē, as ambyas dara cōcas. Bēlas ārin eḍḍas dara ortosin menjas: Uṛueninga'ā mūk-ūndī mokhkai'? 'Malā, bācas; masṛāgahi khall ra'ī[1], dara adigahi cind dara kuilā aṇḍcā : aōnge mal ōndkan'. Khōkhā nū ā khessgahi aḍḍan ēdtācas : māuim annem rahcā. Ittī belas bācas : 'Ṭhaukaṃ ra'ī singhai hunar'.

Anti 'nīn gā mukkā sagṛi nanū ra'adai? Ningāge mane lekh,ā mukkā mal khakkhri'ī'? Ā nannā ālas bācas: 'Nē hō engan benjā pollo'. Bēlas ānyas : 'Enghai rajīdim ra'ī dara cōndā alārin beñjkan: ningan pollon'? Bēlas jātgahi kukoin biddyas dara ā sagṛi nannsge ēdas ciccas. Ās bācas : 'Idī gane gamkārnā trū mūī uyyāge aḍḍā malā khakkro'ō biṛputtā. Ēṛā dūdhī idigahi baitī ajgut cā'ī.' Bēlas ā kukoigahi tangyō tamban eḍḍas dara meñjas : 'Idin ekāse nanjkar-kī pardkar?[2] Khane ār tingyar : 'Īd lellā rahcā ābiri, tangyōge nāṛī kōrcā, dīdhū battyā khanē ēṛā-dudhī trū pōskam'. Idin menarkī bēlas ēkā ēkā ajgut manjas, dara irbarge kōhā kōhā nalakh tanghai rāji nū ciccas.

— A certain man had weird powers to judge of rice, and another man to judge of persons of the sex: they struck a friendship and sallied out to see the world. On their arrival at a big village they repaired to the king's cooking house. The intendant of the compound inquired : 'What are your talents? and where do you go'? They said : 'I am a clairvoyant about women. I am a clairvoyant in the matter of cooked rice.'

The intendant used to keep accounts every day about the guests' (expenses); he would take (his sheet) to his master and give all details : 'So many have eaten one ser (of rice), so many one ser of semolina, so many one ser of parched corn, so many have had one ser of milk; they have eaten or drunk, so many for four annas, so many for a rupee, so many for five rupees'. After stating his accounts for that day, he added : 'Two men have arrived : such and

---

[1] *Lit.* the field (on which the rice was grown) is made of a (diseased) cremating ground. *Aṇḍna*, to spread throughout evenly, to pervade.

[2] *Lit.* How doing did you rear her?

such are their specialities '. The king said : ' Very well; call them in : I shall make them a gift'.

So he commanded his chefs to prepare and cook an excellent meal of curry and rice. The cooking done, he called those people and said : ' Eat to your heart's content, rice-cakes and fried things '. They sat down to their meal; but, when the flavour of those rice-cakes entered the nostrils of the rice expert, he left them and rose up (to go). The king sent for them and asked from the first : ' Hast thou eaten heartily and (tucked in) knee-deep ' ? ' No he said, that rice was grown on a former cremating ground, the ash and coal of which it has absorbed : so I didn't eat '. Subsequently he caused that rice-field to be shown to (himself). The king said : ' Thy skill is of the correct sort '.

Then : ' As to thee, thou art a fastidious judge of women ? Thou findest none to thy fancy '? That man answered : ' No one will be able to find a wife for me '. The king said : ' I have a *kingdom* and I have married so many people ; shan't I be able to establish thee '? The king sought out a girl of (that man's) caste, and showed her to him. The expert said : ' With this girl, for that stench of hers, I shan't know where to put my nose all day long ! A smell of goat's milk issues from her mouth '! The king called the girl's parents and inquired : ' On what did you rear her '? They said : ' When she was a baby, her mother suffered from fever and her milk was stopped : so we nourished (the child) with goat-milk '. On hearing this, the king wondered very much, and he gave high places in his government to both those men.

18. *Lūrakh'ā Kukkos.* *The Sharpwitted Boy.*

Oṇṭā kukkosgahi tangyō tambà mal rahcar; tang ajjī ṛoṭ'ō rahcā, ād andbrī rahcā. Irb ālar, ā paddāgaui ḍahrē īknum īknum, ā kukkōsin īryar kī tām tām kacnakkhrar : 'Ī kukkos gā khob calākī etthrdas, dara āsgahi khekkhā, khēser, khebdā sōnā rūpātī jhabrārkā ra'ī ; lagē, āsin ṭhak'ot.'[1] Khanē ā eṛpā nū kōrcar kī bācar : ' Ēm ī kukkosgahi māmūbagam taldam '. Tang ajjī endran āsin cinbō ?

---

[1] *Thaknā* (1) to deceive ; (2) to entice away.

Undul ulēṛ rahcar, khōkhānū ānyar : 'Ān ayō, akkū kāldan ; bhagnāsin eṛpa ara tangtācībagārin ērāge taike'. Ād manā nanjā, pahē ār mala mancar ; khōkhānū ād tayyā.

Paddā hedde gā āsin kōṛem occar, endran bō malā ceṛtācar. Pahē kōṛhem gecchā rahcar khanē, āsīnim urmī poṭom jhapin ceṛtācar, dara tām khokhā nū dhīrem ēknar. Ār āsin ānyar : 'Nīn jhapin ikla'am bō ambke tisga'ā, ayyā nerr ra'ī'. Elkhrnā bērā manjā khanē, āsge kīṛā khōb laggā helrā. Ā ālar khōkhā nū ḍhēr gecchan ra'anar īge, kukkos, ōnd aḍḍā keras-dara. jhapin tisga'ādas kī ērdas gā ayyū alkhṛā gullē ra'ī : khanē ukkyas kī kūl uṛcningha'ā mokkhas. Urmin munjyas khanē, ār āṛsyar ; ārin ānyas : 'Māmū nerr gā jhapintī urkhā dara idī puttāgahi lātā mī kōrcā kerā'. Ār kadrārar ; pahē endr nanor ?

Kānum kānum onṭa paddā gusan āṛsyar ; khanē abṛā ālar ā kukkosin ānyar : 'Ē bhagnā, kalā : ī paddā nū ninghai balan bīsā'. Ās paddā tarā keras : ār gecchantī īrim biocyar[1]. Ā paddā nū tillyar kulhū natagta'ālagyar[2]. Kukkos ārin ānyas : 'Nīm ekāsē ālar taldar? aḍḍōti gā kulhū malā natagta'ānar ; āl gā uinar'! Ār bācar : 'Eksan āl beddom-dara, kulhū natagta'om ? Kukkos bācas : 'Ēn irb ālārin ci'idan, khēndor'?—'Ci'ā se ; endrge malā khēndom' ? Tangmāmūbagar āsin balā bīsāge taikar rahcar : ās ārīnim bīsā helras !...Mullī manjur manjā khanē, ā kukkos mīkhyas : 'Māmū ! Gucā menāge ! Bīsage ba'adar kā malā ? Ērā, māmū, irbārim[3] bīson kā'? Ār mīkhyar : 'Ha'ī, bīsā'! Onghon ānyas : 'Ērā, māmū, irbjhanārim bīson kā'? Ār ānyar : 'Ha'ī ha'ī gā : irbarīnim bīsā'. Khanē ās rupayan nēcas ; khōkhānū ā irbārin heddem eḍḍas kī dhartācas ciccas.

Anti tān paddā kirrā helras. Āsge ṭoṛang ṭoṛang barnā manjā. Majhā-majhī ṭoṛang nū onṭa meṛhō urkhā dara ās gane arbānakhra'ā helrā ; āsgahi rupayā chanāchit manjā. Saīnt nū ort ālas ghoṛō nū argardara asan āṛsyas ; ijjas kī ā arbānakhrnan ērā helras. Kukkos

---

[1] See Or. Grammar p 89, n. 31.

[2] *Lit.* Were having their oilmill drawn (round, by bullocks).

[3] Pronominal forms, uch as *irbar*, and lower down *irbjhanar*, are used sometimes, though incorrectly, in reference to animals and inanimate things.

bācas : 'Gucchr'ā, gucchr'ā ! ēn meṛhon rupiyā erkhta'ālagdan. Ningāge hō̃ erkhta'ā tukkī[1], hole, rupiyan enghai khōṇḍ'ā kī gamhā nū hē'arkī barā '!. Ās annem nanjas. Kukkos oṇṭā rupiyan meṛhōgahi erkh-cuppī nū mulgas dara ā ghoṛō-urbāsin meṛhon dhartācas ciccas. Anti tān ghoṛō nū argyas dara calā bongtācas. Ā nannā ālas ḍhēr gahṛī gūtī ā meṛhon igaṛ-jigaṛ nanjas : baṛetekan oṇṭā rupiyā urkhā...Khanē ās : 'Endr ? (bācas), akkū ēn ghoṛōgahi mulli hō'on'. Pahē tā̃nō laucas, nannā oṇṭā hō̃ mal urkhā.

Ā kukkos oṇṭā khāṛ gusan ḍabre nū barcas ; ittyas kī miṭhāī mōkhā helras. Asānim dhūbiar hō̃ kicrī nō̃ṛhālagyar. Ār āsgahi mōkhnan ērālagyar khanē, ās ānyas : 'Endran ērdar ? nimhai paddā nū pē̃ṭhgahi lūṭ manjkī ra'ī, baldar '? Khanē ā dhūbiar bācar : 'Anā babū, emhai kicrin ērke tanī : ēm hō̃ ho'ā kādam ! Ārin kālā ciccas. Tanghai nāme tingkas rahcas ' Cerō dupabār'. Ās urmī bēs bēs kicrin khōṇḍas kī ghoṛō nū argas darā calā occas. Khōkhānū dhūbiar gōhar nanjar : ' Erā harō, ērā harō ! emhai kicrin Cero-dupahāras occas keras '! Alar ārin ānyar : ' Cerō dupahārta katthan innā nīm gohar nandar '? A dhūbiargahi katthan nē hō̃ malā pattācar.

Hāṛī keras kī oṇṭā khāṛ gusan ā̃ṛsyas : adigahi baṛhī kōhā rahcā. Asānim oṇṭā paccō dara tangnattī ijjkar rahcar, baṛhī kaṭṭā pōlnātī. Khanē ā kukkos ānyas : ' E paccō, ningnattin kaṛta'ādan, khōkhānū ningan hō̃ kaṛto'on ' ara nāmen tingyas : ' Eṛpā jaō̃dkhaddis '. Ā paccō ānyā : ' Bēs, beṭā, kaṛta'ā'. Kaṛtācas, dara uṛung bongtācas, ā paccon elgta'āge[2]. Paccō gohar nanjā : ' Era, khaddarō, ērā khaddaro ! Eṛpā jaō̃dkhaddis engnattin ho'ālagdas '! Alar ānyar. An paccō, ās ning jaō̃dkhaddisim ; endrge gōhar nandi ? Khokhānū ā kukkos kirryas dara ā pacoon hō̃ kaṛṭācas.

Tanghai eṛpā ā̃ṛsyas khanē, tanghai urmi rupayan ondras-kī, adin tangajjige ēdas, dara ekā ekā hāl ās manyā manjā tingyas.

—There was an orphan boy ; he had only his grandmother, who was blind. Two men, passing through the village, saw that boy and said between them : ' This boy seems very clever ; and his hands, neck and ears are adorned with gold and silver ; let us entice him

---

[1] Or. Gramm., p. 92, n. 38.

[2] Or Gramm., p. 10,a.

away'. So they stepped into his house and said: 'We are the (maternal) uncles of this boy'. How could the grandmother make out their faces? They stayed a day or two, and then said: 'Mother, we are now leaving; allow our nephew to come and see o. house and his aunts'. She declined to do so, but they insisted; fina she let the boy go. (As long as they remained) near the village, they treated the boy well, and gave him no load to carry. But, when they got far off, they loaded him with everything, packets and bamboo-box, they themselves walking behind at an easy pace They (had) told him: 'Never open the bamboo-box; there is a snake inside'! In the early afternoon, he became very hungry. As these men were a long way behind, the boy, withdrawing to a (secluded) spot opens the box and sees there parched rice and treacle: he sat down and took a full meal. When he had cleared off the whole of it, (the two men) came up; he told them: 'Uncles, the snake has got out of the box, and entered into a hole of this ant-hill'. They got angry, but what could they do?

In their journey they passed near a village. The men said to the boy: 'Nephew, go and sell thy bracelets in this village'! He went towards the village; they remained looking on from a distance. In that village men of the Tēli caste were expressing oil. The boy said to them: 'You, what sort of (queer) people are you? One does not turn an oilmill with bullock power: one uses men for that'. They replied: 'Where shall we get men for the work'? The boy said: 'I offer you two men; will you buy them'? 'Give them by all means; why should we not buy them'? His uncles had sent him to sell his bracelets: it was themselves that he was undertaking to sell!...The price being agreed upon, the boy shouted: 'Uncles, come (nearer) that you may hear. Do you want me to conclude the sale? I say, uncles: shall I sell both'? They shouted (back): 'Yes, sell away'. Once more he asked: 'I say, uncles, are the two to be sold off'? They answered: 'Yes, yes, no doubt; sell both'. The boy asked for the money; he then called on the two men to come quite near, and had them seized upon.

He then retraced his steps towards his village. He had (for this) to pass through a dense forest. In the deep of that wood a bear turned up and fell to a hand-to-hand struggle with him : his rupees got scattered. By luck a man on horseback passed there : he stopped and gazed at the combat. The boy said : 'Off with thee, off with thee! I am forcing this bear to release itself of (those) rupees. If thou wantest to extract some thyself, get mine together, tie them up in (my) shoulder-cloth, and come here'. The other man did so. The boy slipped one rupee into the bear's fundament and delivered the animal to the horseman. He next mounted on the horse and put it to a gallop. The other fellow tackled the bear in every possible manner : with great pain one rupee got out...Then : 'Halloo (he said) : now I shall recover the cost of (my horse'. But however much he beat (the bear), no other rupee came out.

The boy came near a river ; he alighted and ate some sweets. Dhobies were washing clothes near by. As they stared at his picnic, he said : 'What do you look at ? in your village hāt a loot is taking place'. Said the dhobies : 'Youngster, keep watch on our clothes for a short time ; we too are off for some booty'. He let them go. He had given out his name as Yesternoon. Collecting all the best clothes, he rode away with them. Later on the dhobies raised an alarm : 'Behold, behold ! Yesternoon has got off with our clothes' ! People said : 'Why make a commotion to-day about a yesternoon affair' ? The people did not believe them.

Further he met a river which was in high flood. On its banks stood an old woman and her granddaughter, unable to cross. The boy said : 'Mother, I take thy granddaughter across ; afterwards I shall take thee also' ; and he gave his name as Son-in-law. The old woman said : 'All right, son, do so'. On the other bank he gave a little gallop (to the girl), in order to frighten the old creature The latter raised a shout : 'Behold friends ! behold ! Son-in-law is abducting my grandchild' ! The people said (to her) : 'Mother, why ! he is your son-in-law ; what do you shout for' ? Soon (however) the boy returned and took the old crony across also.

When he reached home with all his rupees, he showed them to his grandmother and related to her all his adventures.

14. *Sindrī dara Benjā.* *Vermilion and Marriage.*

Cārjhan[1] ālar, sannī nū bīcnum bīcnum, iyār nanjkar rahcar Ortos jāt nū sindrībīsus rahcas; ortos jōlhas, ortos kankchul'us, ortos sōnar-jātyas rahcas. Onghon ennē bācar: 'Bhairō, nām gucā[2]: nannā rājī nalakh nanā kālot! Ār, ennē salbā manjar-kī, tang'ā tang'ā kambaṛan dharcar kī urkhar Ḍhērim ullāgahi ḍabrē īkyar-dara, ṭoṛang nū āṛsyar. Onṭē kōhā tatkhāgahi mūlī nū ōnd mākhā khepnā manjā. Ā tatkhātī jokk geochā (ṭoṛangtā manngutthī kittardara[3], khāika jhurī khatrkātī[3], ḍhinkī manālagyā. Khanē tām tām ānyar: 'Isan ṭoṛang ṛa'ī: namā pālī pālī khāpnā ra'ō'.

Antī manḍī onarkī bācar: 'Bhāi kanchul'ū, ningā isan ōr nannā ra'ī; endrge, nīn hēbrkai be'edai.' Khanē ās bācas 'Cūtā'. Ar cūtyar. Adhā-idhī mākhā manjā khanē, ās bācas: 'Eō ukkan ra'on[4]'. Kislan occas dara kankan dharcas dara chulnum chulnum ālīgahi muṭṭhan kamcas. Anti adin ijtācas dara ānyas: 'Co'ā, bha'ī sonār'.—Ās cōcas dara khāpā helras khanē, attrā ittrā īrnum, ā ālin īryas; khanē bācas: 'Id singrāckā-malka[5] ijjkī ra'ī: ēn adige attnā pundurnā kam'on'. Ābīrim pasrā nanjas[6], dara khēserge ara khebdāge ara khekkhāge ara kheḍḍge ara cuṭṭige a'tācas. Ā khōkhā nū jōlhāsin cōdas.—Jōlhas ālin īryas-ki bācas: 'Adige urmī ra'ī, pahē kicrī mallā'. Cāṛē sarābācas kī lunḍī tāṛcas dara kicrin issyas[7]; anti kūrtācas, dara sindrībīsūsin ānyas: 'Co'ā, ninghai pālī kirryā'.—Sindrībīsus cōcas ki khāpā helras. Ḍhērim ukkyas kī ond aḍḍā raspasrnā menjas. Iryas-kī bācas: 'Urmī gā ra'ī. pāhē kapṛē nū sindrī mallā'. Kīyyan otthras dara adigahi kapṛē nū sindrī tūdyas. Khanē ād ujjā. Āganem bijjyā kerā.

---

[1] Or. Gramm., p. 30, c.

[2] This use of *gucā* with *nām* is worthy of notice.

[3] The *ḍhinki*, is a seesaw contrivance for pounding; it is moved by a pedal. This detail accounts for the goldsmith being able in a forest to blow his furnace.

[4] A question equivalent to a negation.

[5] *Malka*, not being. *Singrācka-malka*, un-adorned.

[6] *Pasrā*, bellows and chafing-dish of an ironsmelter or gold smith. But *pasrā nanā* means to work the bellows, and thus to smelt.

[7] From *essnā*. Grammar, p. 11, n. 23.

Ormar oŏcar, dara kankchul'ū kukkos āndas : 'Idin ēn uyyon, ēn kamackan'. Jōlhā kukkos ba'as : 'Ēn kicrin is-kan-kī ciockan, idin ēn benjro'on'. Sonār kukkos ānyas : 'Ēn singār 'nanjtāckan, ēn benjro'on.' Sindrībīsus bācas : 'Ēr sindrī tūdkan ; ēn benjrkan ; enghai ālī nē bō'ō?' Ennem laggānakhrnā manjā. Khōkhānū bācar. 'Kōṛēdim, ek'am manānek'ā, gucā : istē kālot! Dabrē nū ontā bhagtāsin khakkhyar : āsin raibaṛī nantācar. Ortos ba'as. 'kamackan' nannas ba'as : 'kūrtāckan'; nannas ba'as 'attāckan'. Bhagtas bācas : 'Nē adigahi kaṛṛē nū sindrī ciccā āsim adigahi ālas' talyas'. Ā cārō iyārar bāṛi kerar-kī uṛung tarkārim rahcar ; khōkhānū onghon laggānakhra'ā helrar. Ābirī onṭā Dharmes lekh'ā khaddāsin khakkhyar : āsin raibaṛī nantācar. Ās bācas : 'Āsim adi mētas, nekhai khekkhātī sindrī occā. Kamcas,[1] ās tambas ; attācas, ās bhāis ; kundrtācas, ās tangkakas talyas'. Khanē ār neokhyar : sindrībīsusgahi ālī manjā kerā.

—Four men, from early acquaintance at the dances, had sworn mutual friendship. They were, by caste, one a vermilion hawker, another a weaver, a third a wood-carver and the last a goldsmith. They said one day : 'Brothers, let us go : we shall look for work in another clime'. Having settled this, they took their respective tools and sallied forth. After many a day's march they arrived in a forest. One night had to be spent under a large mango-tree. Close to the spot the trees of that wood being in advanced decay, a (natural) *ḍhinki* had been formed by the fall of dry branches. They said between them : 'We are here in a wood ; we shall have to keep watch by turn'!

The meal being over, they said : 'Brother carver, you will have to begin : for you are accustomed (to late sittings)'. 'Lie down', he replied ; and they did so. When the night had fully set in : 'I shan't sit (idle)', he thought. He took his chisel, seized a piece of wood ; and, carving away, he evolved a womanly form. He put her (there) on her feet and said. 'Get up, brother goldsmith'!—The latter rose and, as he was beginning his watch, looking about, he caught sight of that woman and said : 'She

---

[1] [Ekā ortos] kamcas, ās tambas [taldas]. Grammar, p. 293, n. 14.

stands there unadorned : I shall make gewgaws for her '. Immediately he set to work with bellows and chafing-dish, and bedecked (the statue with trinkets) on the neck, ears, hands, feet and hair He next roused the weaver.—The weaver, at the sight of the woman, said: ' Nothing is wanting, but clothes '. He at once made ready, counted up the threads (for a *sārī*) and wove a garment : he rolled it round her and said to the vermilion hawker : ' Get up, thy turn has come' ! —The vermilion retailer rose and began his watch. Long he remained seated, when he heard a rustling[1] somewhere. Looking (round) he said : ' Quite complete, but no vermilion (yet) on the forehead ! ' He took out his box, and anointed her forehead with vermilion. She then became alive, and thereupon the day broke.

They all got up, and the carver said : ' She will be my wife, I have made her ' ! ' I ' says the weaver, ' gave her clothes woven by myself ; I shall have her '. The goldsmith said : ' She owes me these ornaments : I will marry her '. The vermilion seller said : ' I have anointed her with vermilion, I have married her ; who will take my wife from me' ? Thus a quarrel arose. At one time they said : ' Very well, be this as it may, come, let us be off.' On the road they met a holy man and took him as arbiter. ' I made her ' says one. ' I clothed her ' says another. ' I bedizened her ' says a third one. The holy man replied : ' He alone that put the vermilion on her head is her husband'. The four friends pursued their journey and for some time kept quiet, then once more fell to quarrelling. Thereupon they met with a youth (of) god-like (beauty) : they set him as arbiter. He said : ' He alone is her husband, from whose hand she received the unction. He that made her is her father ; he that clothed her is her brother ; he that gave trinkets to her is her uncle. ' They bowed their heads and she became the wife of the vermilion hawker.

15. *Ort Kukkos dara āsgahi Bandrā.* *A Boy and his Monkey.*

Ort āli rahcā, adige lauchār mannā ullā āṛskī rahcā. Annum ād khārrā ondra'āge ṭoṛang kerā. Biddyā khanē, tētram pull ..kh an mēkhā helrā : ' Barā, nīk'im ibṛāge rā'adar hole ! Tēt'ar ciā'[2] ! Engā

[1] The *sārī* around the statue was flapping in a gush of breeze.

[2] Or. '*tettā cī'ā*'.

śukoi manō hōle, pōs'āge ci'on; ara kukkō manos hole, sangī jōṛ'on'! Pahē ā aḍḍā bēgar āltēl rahcā. Oṇṭā Lakṛā urkhā dara tētcā. Aālī khuarran ondrā-kī eṛpā kirryā.

Jokk ullā khōkhānū nebbnā manjā: kukkō-khaddim manjā. Nitkī Lakṛā ērā kālī dara ānī: 'Okhō, pacoō? pardyas kā argas[1]'? Ād ba'ī: 'argas; akkun gā bōlō bōlō lagdas'. Annē annem kukkos jokk pardyas dara oṇtā lūrakh'ū bandran pōs'ā helras: adigahi nāmē Jhunkū pinjyas. Mundā ā Lakṛāge bhēṭim malā ci'idas, 'engan mōkhō' ba'arkī. Lakṛā eṛpā bar'ī hōle, as ṭonkā kādas; bhēl ṭonkā kālī hōle, ās eṛpā bardas. Uiā kādas khanē hō̃, bandran hō'odas-kī kādas. Ekābīrī Lakṛā khall kālī, ās gā ātrī-gaḍḍī nū cūtdas dara khaikā aṭkhātī jhaprkas ta'as, dara Bandrā kaṛbā nū ukkī: 'Nau rē! tātā rē'! ba'ī. Annem undul Lakṛā heddē barcā kī menjā: 'Nin? urbas endr keras'? Jhunkū-bandrā ānyā: 'Ās eṛpā nū jharā-bōṛ'ē ōnos kā uiā bar'os[2]? Hāṛī manā! aḍḍō ilcī[3]. Makhlē usangin īcon kī kapṛēn lau'on; palkro'ō kālō'! Lakṛā ilcī-dara kālī...Nann ullā, ā kukkos bandran occas-dara iñjō piṭā keras, dara ōṇṭe tauā nū cice hō̃ occas. Bandrā ganē iñjōn kuṛdas mōkhdas. Aulā hō̃ Lakṛā barcā dara ās nukhras. Lakṛa Jhunkun ānyā: 'Endran mōkhdai, bhāī? engā hō̃ ci'ā'. Bandrā bācā: 'Hū kieri tarā ambā kalā, muṭā; maṇḍīguṭṭhī ra'ī: emsia'ā ongoi'. Ennem Lakṛā kukkōsintī geechā manī; khōkhānū ba'ī: 'Engā hō̃ ci'ā, lē; endran mōkhdai'? Khanē Bandrā jokk jokk sannī coppō-iñjō ciecā, 'khannan minkhā kī angla'ā' ba'arkī...Lakṛā ā katthan pattācā dara khannan minkhyā-kī anglā. Copkārkī rahcā[4] khanē, Jhunkū sārhin dharcā, kī idigahi pannā cice nū maṇḍkā rahcā, adin gaṛgaṛra'ā otthrā kī Lakṛāgahi bāī nū sajjā. Āganem tang urbāsin ānā helrā: 'Co'ā dadā, co'ā dadā! muṭāsin sādhkan, dadā'! Ās cōcas kī Lakṛan mugrā trū passas-kī piṭyas. Ennem Jhunkū Rāi Muṭasgahi baiti tangurbāsin baechābācā.

L.—There was a woman whose term for childbirth had (nearly) arrived. She went to fetch bamboo-saplings in the forest. Her provision

---

[1] Dict. arg(nā).

[2] [I put it to you:] will he be, at this time of day, drinking beer [at home], or is he likely to [come and] plough? The inference is: Of course, he is now at home.

[3] From elcnā Gramm., p. 11, n. 23.

[4] *Copkārnā*, to grow accustomed or inured to danger, i.e., to lose the safeguarding fear of it.

made, she was unable to raise (the basket) to her head. She then shouted : 'Come (and help), anybody hereabout ! Put (this basket) on to my head ! If (my offspring) turn to be a girl, I'll give her (to thee) in marriage ; if a boy, I'll make him thy chum '! But there was not a living soul in that place. A Tiger turned up and raised (the basket) to the (woman's) head. She went home with the bamboo-saplings.

A few days later came her deliverance : she did bring forth a boy. Every day the Tiger goes to see and says to her : 'Where (is he), goodwife ? Is he not grown up yet '? She says : 'Not yet : so far he is a mere baby'. In time the boy grew up a little ; he began (to keep and) tend a monkey which was very clever : he gave it the name of Small-bells. But to the Tiger he allows no interview, knowing it would devour him. If the Tiger comes to his house, out he goes into the open ; if it goes into the open, in he comes to the house. Even when he goes to plough (his mother's fields), he takes his monkey with him. When the Tiger repairs to these fields, he lies down in a furrow under dry leaves : (then) the Monkey sits upon the plough-handle, shouting (to the bullocks) : 'Right ho ! Left ho ! ' Thus, one day, the Tiger came and asked : 'Where has thy master gone to ' ? Small-bells the monkey said : '(Doest thou imagine that) he isn't drinking beer at home ! shall he come here and plough ? Off with thee, the bullocks are afraid. Or else I take out the coulter and smash thy head : will it split '! The Tiger withdraws in a fright ..Another day, the boy with his monkey went out to fish ; he also took a pot with fire. In company with the monkey, he bakes fishes and eats them. On that day again the Tiger came, and the boy hid himself. The Tiger said to Small-bells : 'What does thou eat, brother ? Give a little to me also '. The monkey said : 'Do not step towards yonder bundle, thou ear-cropped ; (my) rice things are there : thou might defile them '. The Tiger thus withdrew from what was really the boy ; and said : 'Give me a little, friend ; what does thou eat '? The monkey gave him a small crawfish or two, saying : 'Close the eyes and open the mouth !' The Tiger obeyed : with closed eyes he opened his mouth. When he was (thus) off his guard, Small-bells seized the ploughshaft, whose iron (-end) was buried in the fire and, suddenly taking it out, thrust it into the Tiger's mouth. At the same time he said to his master: 'Get up, big brother! Get up, big brother! I have given his account to Ear-cropped, big brother'! He got up and by hammering (the Tiger's head) with his mallet killed him. Thus did Sir Small-bells save his master from the Tiger's mouth.

16. *Nūkhur-nūkhur Bēcnā.* *Hide and Seek.*

Oṇṭā ṭeṭengā dara lakṛā iyārī lagābāoā. Iribge nūkhur-nūkhur bēcā tukkyā: dara, sannī sannī pardkā paṭṛā nū mūkūndī khoppā rahcā, ayyam bēcāge kerā Ṭeṭengā munddh tanghai khannan munḍhrā: khane lakṛā nūkhr'ā kerā Pahē, lakṛā kūhā hūṇḍḍū-lē ra'ī khanē, mūkūndī khoppā nū ekāsē nūkhro'ō? Khoppā gusan kerā dara mūkhliddrā. Annuntī ṭeṭengā, 'Kokrō̃y-cō̃e'! bācā-ki, kerā dara lakṛāgahi khebdan dharcā dara ānyā: 'Biddkan gā, iyār', bācā. Khanē lakṛā: 'Onghon nūkhrnā ra'ī, iyār' bācā. Pārmūnd nūkhr'āge cajjkar rahcar. Eō̃ dhaō̃ lakṛā kapr'ā kerā, aō̃ dhaō̃ ṭeṭengā adin biddyā.

Annuntī lakṛādim tanghai khannan munḍhrā. Ohrē! ṭeṭengā, paksā nū nūkhr'ā kerā khanē, lakṛā kharkhnan raspasrnan menjā; ara 'kokrō̃y-cō̃e' bācā-kī paksā nū kapp iryā khanē[1], ṭhaukam biddyā! Ennem onghon lakṛā khann munḍhrā. Khanē ṭeṭengā kerā ki tombā nū argyā. Lakṛā paksā nū kappā kuddī...Ād ṭeṭengā tarā ḍikkan nanjā khanē, ṭeṭengā adigahi ḍikkā nū kōreā kerā! Khanē lakṛā attrā ittrā bongā helrā Ort langṛas saīntnū khakkhras: bongā pollas khanē, ās gusan kerā, ki āsintī ṭeṭengan otthortācā[2].

—A lizard and a tiger struck a friendship. The fancy took them of playing at hide-and-seek, and they went further to a coppice of very small growth with thickets not higher than the knee. The lizard closed its eyes first and the tiger went to hide. But, as a tiger is a big burly fellow, how could he hide in a knee-deep underwood? He repaired to one bush and knelt down. Next the lizard, shouting

---

[1] *Kappnā* to tap, to strike with the open hand. *Kapp irnā*, to tap tentatively. See Or. Dictionary, *irnā*, 8.

[2] Causal form of *otthornā*, *to take out.*

'cock-a-doodle-do' started (on his search), seized the tiger by the ear and said : 'There, I have found thee, friend'. The tiger : 'I have to hide once more, friend', he said. They had agreed to hide (each) twice or thrice (before changing roles). As often as the tiger hid the lizard found him.

Then it was for the tiger to shut his eyes Alas ! when the lizard went to hide among the dry leaves, the tiger heard the rustle, and when, with a shout 'cock-a-doodle-do', he went to tap tentatively among the leaves, he found (the lizard) right enough... ! The tiger once more closed his eyes ; then the lizard went and climbed upon a small eminence. The tiger turns here and there, tapping the dry leaves... When he presented his hindquarters to the lizard, the latter got inside ! The tiger began to run (wildly) hither and thither. By luck a cripple was met (on the road) : being unable (from pain) to run further, the tiger went to him and had the lizard taken out.

17. *Kukkos dara Bachu. The Boy and the Unicorn.*

Oṇṭā Lipī-ōṛā rahcā, adigahi nākh'oṭeng khadd rahcā : mundhtā Lakṛā, dosar Nerr, tisar Bachū[1], khōkhantā Ālas. Urmī khadd pardyā khanem, tangyō Lakṛan ānyā : 'Nīn ṭoṛang nū urmī lakṛāgahi bēl manā kalai'; Nerran ānyā : 'Nīn pokhārī-rājī nū urmī nerrgahi bēl manāge kalai'. Bachū dara Ālāsin ānyā : 'Nim irbārim eksa'an kālor, asānim nimhai ujjnā ōnnā baggē manō : pahē ikla'am hō ambke chiṇḍra'ā'! Ṭangyōgahi ānkā lekh'ā ibṛā urmī kerā.

Kānum kānum Ālas dara Bachū oṇṭā bāndhā āṛyar, ayyā bēl-khaddar em'ālagyar : ijjas-kī ērā belras. 'Endran ērdai, bachū-khāpū'?—Ās 'nimbai emnā mulkhnan ērdan' bācas.— 'Nīn hō sange bēcoi'?— 'Ha'ī, bēcon'.— 'Anti (ānyar) ēm mulu-khdam, nīn ēman beddā. Beddoi hole, ēm ningā ingṛin[2] ci'om ; pahē em ningan beddom hōle, ninghai bachun hō'om'. Ār mulkhā belrar : ārin ās, eō dhaō mulkhyar, aō dhaō biddyas. Antile āsgahi

---

[1] *Bachū*, a fabulous animal represented as having only one horn : it is said to be of great ferocity.

[2] *Ingṛī*, though etymologically derived from *eng-ṛī* (my sister), means '*our sister*' equally well. *Cf.* below : *ningṛige*, about *your sister*.

ṛālī biṛdyā : mulkhyas : tān bachū āsin ḍuryācā. Amm ūlā ūlā keras kī nantarā urkhas. Ennem ek'am ek'am dhaõ manjā : bēl-khaddar oṇṭē hõ beddā pollar.

Hārcar-kī eṛpā kerar, dara khaṭī nū cūtyar, dara amm maṇḍin ambyar ciccar. Tangyō tambas ārin menjar : 'Nīm endrge maṇḍī amm malā ōndar mōkhdar'? Ār ānyar : 'Em bachūkhāpus gusan ingṛin gaclhrkam ; adin ci'or hōle, ōnom'. Tangyō tambas ānyar : 'Co'ā beṭā : ningṛīge jokk tibā malā. Ek'am kukoin singro'ot ki hō'ot dara ās gane benjot ci'ot'. Benjā ullā, nannā kukoin gahnā gīrātī[1] jhabrācar dara ḍhēr dau kicrin attācar ; tangdan gullēguṭṭhin khassar-kī mar khkā kicrin kūrtācar ; khōkhānū irbārin ā bachū-khāpus gusan ondrar. Tangdā manyā tinglī bhankār'ī ; pahē ā nannā kukoin lēl-mukkar cāorti dhuk'ālagnar. Bachū tanghai khāpūsin ānkī rahcā : 'Nēk manyā tinglī bhankār'ō dara marakhkā kicrī ra'ō, adigahi khekkhānim[2] dharke' ; ās annem nanjas. Bīṛī bēlas iryar-kī kōllam manā helrar : annuhõ, tangdāgahi conhāti, āsin tam gusānim uynāgahi nangū nanjar.

Jokk ullā khōkhā, bēlas tanghai dewānar gusan salhā ho'ā helras, ekāsē ī bachū-khāpusin piṭā ongon? Ār bācar. 'Toṛang nū lakṛā dudhin ondra'āge taike ; lakṛā āsin mōkhō. ninghaī khadd bacohro'ō'. Bēlas ārgahi ānkā lekh'ā nanjas. Bachu-khāpus cīkhnum cīkhnum tharan occas-kī keras ; āṛsyas khanē endrau ērdas? Asan baggē lakṛā panc nū khondrkā ra'ī, dara, āsin īryā-kī, āsin mōkhāge lomcomra'ā hilri'ī. Pahē āsgahi kōhā dadā Lakṛā hõ asan rahcā. Ād āsin īryā kī khob khusmārā. Koṛē kōṛem urmī menjā[3] dara ānyā : 'Bhayā, nīn endr barckai'? Ās bācas : 'Dadā, nim gā sukh nū ra'adar, emāge khōb dukh manī. Bēlas engan lakṛā dudhin beddā taiyas ; ād eksan khakkhr'ō'? Lakṛā ānyā : 'Sankā jokk tibā ambke nanā : tō bagge cāṛ manō, aõ ci'on.' Enne ba'arkī ek'am khadmākhō lakṛāgahi dudhin bīntacā, dara oṇṭā lakṛan ceṛtācā[4]. Bachū-khāpūsin hõ oṇṭā nū argācā kī bēlas gusan taiyā ciccā. Ibṛā lakṛā mahal gusan āṛsyā-kī garjār'ā helrā, attī ormar assrnum assrnum

[1] *Gahnā-gīrā*, jingle for : 'all kind of jewels'.

[2] For adigahim khekkan. See Or. Gramm., p. 277, *c*.

[3] *Lit.* to inquire if everything is well.

[4] Causal form of *ceṛnā*.

bongar. Bēlas mīkhyas: 'Gecoham ra'ā ci'ā! ningāge[1] adhā rāju dabēj ci'on'! Antile bachu-khāpus ā irb lakṛan kirtācas ciccas.

Jokk ullā kerā, kī āsin onghon bēlas pokhārintā puṇḍrī-pūp ondra'ā taiyas, ekayyā kōhā kōhā nerr rahcā. Asan ender ērdas: ajgaṛ ajgaṛ nerr beḍrā beḍrā ra'ī ara parmāge lomcomri'ī. Pahē, heddē āṛsyas-kī, īryas tangdadas-Nerr hō ayyam ra'as. Ās kukkōsin ānyas: 'Sankā, jokk tihā amba nanā: ningā ēbaggē pūpgahi cāṛ laggō, ābagge ēn ondrto'on ci'on.' Khōṇḍas kī ā pūpan oṇṭā nerr ceḍḍā. Kukkos tān oṇṭā nerr nū argyas kī mahal kirryas Mahlantar kharā elcā helrar. Ās ānyas: 'Ond chaṭkā lawā iṛyarkī ci'ā: hōle endr hō malā manō'. Āsgahi ānkā lekh'ā iṛyar kī chitcar ciccar: nerr pettā, mokkhā dara tangā aḍḍā nū kirryā kerā.

Khōkhānū bēlas tihā nanjas 'īsgahi bachūnuṃ urmī bhēd ra'ī: adin piṭot'. Kukkōsin ānyas: 'Lagē, ninghai bachun dara hāthin lāucnā khrto'ot'. Bachū tang urbāsin ānyas: 'Ambā elcā, bhayā; en jīt'on'. Hāthin singcācar-kī ondrar kh abachū adigahi kūlan ennē kussyā attī bidgr'ā bidgr'ā kerā.

Munjā nū bēlas ānyas: 'Ninghai bachūge pannātī[2] laṛnā manō'! Ās alkhbnum barcas kī tingyas. Khanē bachū ānyā: 'Bhayyā, akkū gā engā khē'enā manō. Nīn akkuntim punā aṛin, punā ḍabnan beddar uyyā. Ēn khē'on hole[3], urmī khēsou ahṛan khoclan abṛā nū sajjke kī uṭke ci'ike'. Bachū laṛnum laṛnum pannā nū iōndā bajrārā, attī adigahi kukk palkrā kerā.. Khanē gā ālar ajgut riryār'ā helrar. Kukkos cikhā cikhā khēson ahṛan dara khoolan abṛā aṛigūṭṭhī nū sajjas kī mundhcas: abṛā ūlā ūlā, urmī bhaōrō dumbā dara tīnī manjā. Jokk ullā khōkhānū ḍhēr baggē telengar jummrar kī bēl-kukoin bacoāge barcar. Khanē ā kukkos abṛā aṛin calkhas ciccas: bhaōrō dumbā tīnī urkbardara ārgahi mēd nū rīndyā dara utgā helrā. Ormar, āsgahi kheḍḍ nū khattra'ā khattr'ā mīkhyar: 'Manāba'ā, bachūkhāpū, manāba'ā: ningāge bēl-kukoin ci'idam; nīnim sōee rājigahi bēl akkuntim manā ra'ā'. Khanē ās manābācas, dara āulanti rājīgahi bēl manjas.

---

[1] I shall give thee...for (my daughter's) dowry.

[2] *Pannāti*, with sword, F. 'avec le fer'.

[3] *Hole* means either *if* or *when*.

—There was a Lark which had four children: the first was a Tiger, the second a Snake, the third a Unicorn and the last a Man. When they came of age, the mother said to the Tiger: 'Go to the woods and be king of the feline tribe'. She said to the Snake: 'Go to the lake country and rule over the reptiles'. To the Unicorn and the Man she said: 'You two, wherever you go, you shall live in plenty: only, never get separated' All of them betook themselves to the places assigned by their mother.

In their journey the Man and the Unicorn came to a dam near which some young princes were bathing: he stopped and watched them. 'What art thou looking at, unicorn-keeper'?—'I look at your bathing and diving' he said.—'Wilt thou play with us'?—'I will'.—'Then (they said) we dive, find us. If thou succeedest, we'll give thee our youngest sister (in marriage); but if we find thee, we'll have thy unicorn'. They dived, and as often as they did, he found them. Then his turn came: he dived, followed by the unicorn; he plunged into deep, deep water, and came out at an unexpected (*lit* another) point. This was done repeatedly: the young princes could not find him even once.

They went home beaten, lay down on their cots and refused all food. Their parents asked them: 'Why don't you eat and drink'? They said: 'We have promised our little sister to the unicorn-keeper; if you give her, we shall eat'. The parents said: 'Get up, sons: do not worry about your little sister. We will trick up any (other) girl and marry her to him'. On the wedding day, they bedecked another girl with trinkets and jewels, and attired her in fine clothes; their own daughter they besmeared with molasses and wrapped in dirty linen; and they brought both of them to the unicorn-keeper. Round about their daughter flies are buzzing and humming, while royal ladies with a yak-tail are fanning the other girl. The unicorn had warned his master: 'The girl near whom flies will be buzzing and who will be clad in soiled linen is the one whose hand you must take'. So he did. The king and queen felt despondent at the sight; however, out of love for their daughter, they made a pretence of welcoming him to their house.

Some time after, the king had a counsel with his ministers as to how he could kill that unicorn-keeper. They said : 'Send him to the forest to fetch tiger-milk ; the tigress will devour him, and your daughter will get free '. The king took their advice. The unicorn-keeper all in tears took a plate and started (on his errand). On reaching, what does he see! A number of tigers are there assembled in council, and, at the sight of him, smack their lips. But his big brother the Tiger was there also. The latter greatly rejoiced at seeing (again) the boy. He made all sort of kind inquiries and said : 'Little brother, what's thy errand'? The boy said, Big brother, you are (all) happy (here) : but we (*I and the unicorn*) are in a sore plight. The king has sent me to fetch tiger's milk : where is that to be got'? The tiger said : 'Little man, do not worry, I shall give thee as much of it as need will be '. Speaking thus, he had one suckling tigress milked, and loaded (the milk) on one tiger. He put the unicorn-keeper upon another and sent them (back) to the king. These, on arriving at the palace, set up (so mighty) a roar that everyone cleared off in a tremble. The king shouted : 'Do keep away! I shall give thee half my kingdom for dowry'! The boy then dismissed the two tigers.

A few days later, the king sent him to fetch pundrī-flowers near a lake where there were very large snakes. What does the boy see there? awfully big snakes sprawling about, licking their lips to sting him. But, when he came near, he found that his big brother the Snake too was there. He said to the boy : 'Little man, don't worry ; I shall have as many of those flowers taken there as need-will be '. He collected the flowers, and one snake carried them. The boy himself mounted another (snake) and returned to the palace. The palace people had a great fright. He told them : 'Have a big round basket of maize roasted and give it : then no harm will be done '. They accordingly fried maize and cast it about. The snakes picked it up and fed on it, then made back for their abode.

Subsequently the king bethought himself that the whole secret lay in the boy's unicorn, and (said) : let us kill it. He said to the boy : 'Come, we shall make thy unicorn fight with an elephant'

The unicorn told his master: 'Be not afraid, little brother; I shall win'. They caparisoned and brought the elephant: the unicorn butted so hard at its belly that it was ripped open, quite clean.

Finally the king said: 'Thy unicorn shall have to face (*lit.* fight against) the sword'. The boy came laughing (to his unicorn) and told him the news. The unicorn answered: 'Little brother, this time I shall have to die. Immediately procure a number of new pots with new lids. Within them, when I die, drop all the blood, flesh and bones; and shut them up well'. In the course of the fight, the unicorn dashed against the sword with such violence that its head got split...Thereupon the crowd raised shouts of triumph. The boy, with many sobs, deposited blood, flesh and bones into the pots, which he stopped: their contents turned to hornets, wasps and bees. A short time later, a large army assembled and came to carry away the princess by force. The boy opened the pots; hornets, wasps and bees, getting out, spread upon the men's bodies and stung them. All, falling to the boy's knees, shouted: 'Call them back, unicorn keeper, call them back: we give up the princess to thee; from this instant be and remain king of the whole country'. He then called the bees back and from that day reigned upon the land.

18. *Jhunkā Pāḍē. Small-bells the Pandit.*

Ort ālas aḍḍō khēndā pēṭh keras. Khindyas-kī kirrālagyas, ḍahrēnum bīṛī puttyā kerā khanē, ās ba'ā helras: 'Punā aḍḍō ra'ī; bīṛī puttyā...Ēn mundhbhāre onṭā ṭōlā nū bhar mākhā ra'on; bijjō hōle, kaon' Ās aḍḍon onṭā kulbū nū khuṭcas dara tān heddentā chaprī nū cūtyas. Pairī bīrī aḍḍon kollālagyas āganem, kulbū-urbas īryas-kī ānā helras: 'Anā bhāi, endrnā aḍḍon kōldai'? Ās ānyas: 'Bhāi, cērō pēṭh nū khindkan; puttyā, aōnge isānim rahackan'. Kulbū-urbas ānā bindas: 'Anā hō lucā, ī aḍḍō enghai talī: ī kulbūdim dhannācā'! —'Malā gā, ēn cērō khindkan.'—'Malā; enghai kulbūdim dhannācā. Endr ēn baldan? Paddantā ālarin menā sē'. Aḍḍō-urbas paddantārin panc badcas; ār ōrmar ānyar: 'Malā; isgahi kulbūdim dhannācā'.

Khattā ālas ṭoṛang nū keras nannā panc bad'āge. Beddnum beddnum oṇṭā bandran khakkhyas dara tanghai urmī katthan tingyas. Jhunkū Pāḍē ānyā : 'Ha'ī, nīn sendrā bardai kī eng manyā allan dekhdekhba'oi! Kalā, ēn malā bardan'. Ā ālas khōb nihōra nanjas khanē, Jhunkū Pāḍē ānyā : 'Kalā se : phalnā ullā ālarin khōṇḍkai ra'ake. Ēn kaon kī tengon .ci'on'. Ās ā paddan kirryas kī, neḍḍā ullā nū, bharā baggē pancārin khōṇḍas. Ār ōrmar Jhunkū Pāḍēgahi pāb ērā helrar...Ūbēr gahṇḍī nū Jhunkū Pāḍē jhalangjhulungra'ā jhulurnūtī bar'ālaggī. Adin īryāsim-kī kulhū-urbas kadrārnum bācas : 'Lagē, Pāḍē Sāheb, ābīrintim[1] ningan ērdam : nīn baram malā bardai'! Jhunkū Pāḍē ānyā : 'Ē barō barālakkan, oṇṭā pokhārī nū cicc laggyā, iñjō ullyā : adīnim[2] pesa pesā mokkhan'. Kulhū-urbas ānyas : 'Menā, bhāirō : endr ikla'am pokhāni nū cicc-lakkan īrkar kā menjkar ra'adar'? Jhunkū Pāḍē āganem ānyā : 'Menā, bhāirō, ikla'am kulhūgahi aḍḍō-dhanuākan īrkar kā menjkar ra'adar'? Khōkhānū aḍḍō-urbas tarā kırr birdnum : 'Kalā, ninghain kollarkī hō'ā; bhalā, ēn ērdan ne ningan chek'ō'! Ā ālas aḍḍoṇ kullyas kī hō'a helras : ōrmar angal angal ērā helrar, baokan nē hō āsin chek'ā pollar.

—A man went to the market to buy bullocks. He was returning with his purchase when the sun went down. He thereupon thought : 'These are new bullocks ; the sun has set.. I shall spend the night in the hamlet just in front of me ; and at dawn I shall go on'. He tied his bullocks to an oilmill and himself went to sleep under an open shed close by. In the morning, he was untying the bullocks, when the master of the mill, catching sight of him, spoke thus : 'I say, friend, what do you loosen the bullocks for'? He said : 'Friend, I bought them yesterday at the market ; night coming on, I have staid here'. The mill master retorted : 'Thou villain, these bullocks belong to me : it is this oilmill that has hatched them'!—'No, indeed ; I purchased them yesterday'!—'Away ; they are the calving

[1] *Abīrintim*, lit. from that time from a time indefinitely long.

[2] For the reason just given, *ād* is used here in a plural sense, for *abṛad*. See Or. Gramm., p. 42, n. 10.

of my oilmill. Don't I know it? Just ask the men of the village'. The master of the bullocks took the villagers as arbiters; they all said: 'Shut up; it was this man's oilmill which hatched them'.

The unfortunate man went to the forest to procure another arbitration. In his search he met a monkey and related to him the whole affair. Small-bells the Pandit answered: 'Yes, yes: thou comest here on a hunt and art going to let thy dog loose after me! Off with thee, I don't come'. The man entreating him very much, Small-bells the Pandit said: 'Well, go; assemble those (same) men on such a day. I shall go and give sentence'! The man returned to the village, and on the appointed day got together a crowd of arbiters. All of them were waiting for Small-bells the Pandit.

After a long while, he arrives swinging himself (from the tree-tops), waddling and skipping about. As soon as he saw him, the mill master said with impatience: 'Come, Pandit Saheb, we are looking for you from ever so long: you never do arrive'! Small-bells the Pandit said: 'Well, friends, as I was on the way fire caught to a tank; the fishes were burnt: I picked them all up and made a meal on them'! Said the mill master: 'Hear that, friends: did you ever see, or hear of a tank being in conflagration'? Small-bells the Pandit said quickly: 'Hear this, friends: did you ever see, or hear of, an oilmill hatching bullocks'? Then, turning to the owner of the bullocks: 'Go, untie what is thine and take it away. And I am watching here who'll dare to stop thee'! The man untied his bullocks and took them away. All looked at him with an open mouth, but no one could prevent him.

19. *Liṭṭbirī Kukkos.* *Little Tom-o' My-Thumb.*

Ort sannī sannī kukkos rahcas: āsge Liṭṭbirī[1] nāmē rahcā. Ās Khakh'ṇḍāpur[2] Birindāban ṭoṛang nū kālarkī ḍahrē ebsas, dara ayyam ra'a helras. Oṇṭē hō altēlar mal rahcar: pahē ṭoṛangtā mankhā khara baggē rahcā. Ās elonāti manngahi ḍhoḍhrō nū kōrckas ra'ālagyas. Undul mankhā menā mōkhā kerā khanē, ās urkhdas, mankhā-khaddan

[1] A proper name seemingly derived from *liṭyā-oṛā*. See Dict.

[2] The monkeys' capital in the Ramayānā is *Kisk-khandhā*. Near this town there was a forest infested with monkeys (*Bandrā-ban*).

nõṛdas mūjdas. Mankhaguṭṭhi barcā, dara, nūṛkan īryā-kī, menjā : 'Ānā beṭā, nē niman emtācā mūjyā '? Khaddguṭṭhi ānyā : 'Ēm āsin tengom holē, nīm āsin kussā piṭor. Mankhā anyā : 'Malā piṭom, beṭā, tengā'. Khaddguṭṭhi, kiryā mōkhtācā-dara, ānyā : 'I mann nū ort āl-khaddas ra'as : āsim eman sewā nandas'. Mankhā āsin mannantī urkh'āge ānyā dara āsin conkhā ṭāṭā helrā. Aulantī ās nitkī dudhī bīnā bīnā mōkhā helras dara abṛā mankhā āsgāhidim[1] manjā. Ās khob saõngyā manjas keras ; āsgahi cuṭṭi hō sōnā lekh'ā bilca helrā. Mankhā āsge tiryō biddya ciccā : ās ā tiryōtim ennē ba'ā ba'ā mēkhālagyas : 'Dangē, dangē ; baṇḍī bhaīsā sing lage, ḍār ṭūṭē ; khurī khūnde, pathal phūṭe'. Khanē abṛā urmī mankhā menarkī ekasantī'im ās tarā kirrālagyā. Undul ās khāṛ nū emā keras dara, khajro'ō bīrī, āsgahi oṇṭā cuṭṭī caḍrā kerā : as adin aṭkhā nū ṭipcas dara khāṛ nū ambyas ciccas. Kiyyā tarā bēl-kukoikhaddar emālagyar : ār adin īryar dara ānā helrar : 'Ahāy, khaddyō, endrā bar'ālaggī ? Barē : adin dhar'ot'. Aṭkhan dharcar dara kullyar-kī ērnar gā : oṇṭā sonāgahi cuṭṭī ! Ās adin mahal ondrar kī ! ēlāsin ānyar : 'I cuṭṭīgahi ālasin[2] beddoi hōle, ēm maṇḍī amm ōnoir ; makhlē malā'. Bēlas cauguṛdī beddāge tayyas, pahē nē hō pollar beddā Khōkhānū oṇṭā khākhā bācā : 'Ēn gā beddon'. Ād Khakh'ṇḍāpur Birindāban ṭoṛang urbyārā kī Liṭibirisgahi dudhī-bhaṇḍā nū ukkyā. Ās 'kahū rē' ! bācas-kī khākhā tarā tanghai tiryon lebdācas. Khākhā cāṛem ā tiryon pettā dara bāṛī kerā-kī ukkyā. Ās khēd'ā keras khanē, hāṛī occā. Annē annēnum mahal gūṭī ondrā dara asan tiḍḍā ciccā. Bēlasgahi ālar pettar : ās kōrcas-kī tiryon nēcas. Ār, āsgahi sōnantā cuṭṭin īryar-kī, bācar : 'Iyyam ra'ā, bēl-kukoin ningā ci'om'. Ās ānyas : 'Enghai kharā baggē mankhā ra'ī, abṛan ekāsē ambon' ?— 'Abṛan hō isan ondr'ā' !—'Eksan mankkhon' ? Khanē ār ajgāṛ kōhā aḍḍā nū kurkhī hēcar. Antile ās tiriyon otthras dara ūr'ā helras : 'Dangē, dangē ; baṇḍī bhaīsā sing lagē, ḍār ṭūṭē ; khurī khūndē, pathal phūṭē.' Dara, adin gecchantī menā menā abṛā mankhā, khadd dara buṛbī urmī ḍuryārā kī sāesōera'ā bar'ā helrā.

[1] When equivalent to *mine*, *thine*, *theirs*, etc., a possessive pronoun may be emphasized. Or. Gramm., p. 277,c.

[2] See Or. Gramm., p. 168,b.

—There was a very small boy whose name was Tom-o'my-thumb. He lost his way in the Birindāban forest, near Khakhndāpur and took residence (in the wood). Human beings there were none, but a great many wild buffaloes. Through fear of these he used to remain crouched in the hollow of a tree. One day, the buffaloes having gone away to graze, he comes out, washes and scrubs the baby-buffaloes. When the big ones returned, noticing the wash, they asked: 'Sons, who bathed and washed you'? The young ones said: 'Should we tell you his name, you would butt him to death.' The buffaloes said: 'No, sons, we won't kill him; tell us.' The young ones, after exacting an oath, said: 'Within this tree there is a child: it is he who looks after us'. The buffaloes told him to come out, and began kissing and licking him. From that day he fed on milk which he used to draw every morning, and he was the owner of the buffaloes. He became very robust; his very hair used to shine like gold. The buffaloes procured a flute for him; he would, blowing it, sing thus: 'Dangē, dangē: if the short-tailed buffalo strikes with the horn, the branch will break; if he stamps with the hoof, the stone will split'. And, hearing this, all those buffaloes would, from any (far away) quarter, return to him.

One day, as he had gone to bathe in the river, and was scrubbing (his head), one hair of his got plucked out: he wrapped it in a leaf and let it down the stream. Lower down, (some) young princesses were bathing; they saw (the floating leaf) and said: 'There, there! sisters, what is coming up? Come, let us catch it'. They caught the leaf, opened it and see (what?): a golden hair! They took it to the palace and said to the king: 'If you find out the man to whom this hair belongs, we will eat and drink; otherwise, we don't'. The king sent on a search all round, but no one could find. Finally a crow said: '*I* shall find. He flew to the Birindāban forest near Khakhndāpur, and alighted upon Tom-o' my-thumb's milking-pot. 'Away', he shouted, throwing his flute (at the bird). The crow quickly picked up the flute, went further and stopped. When he gave it the chase, further on did it carry (the flute). From spot to spot (the bird) took the flute up to the palace and dropped it there. The king's people picked it up: he went in and claimed his flute. They, at the sight of his golden hair, said: 'Stay here, we shall give thee the king's daughter (in marriage)'—He said: 'I have many many buffaloes: how can I abandon them'?—'Bring them too here.'—'Where shall I stable them'? They then fenced in a large cattle-pen. He drew out his flute and began to blow it: 'Dangē, dangē; if the short-tailed buffalo strikes with the horn, the branch will break; if he stamps with the hoof, the stone will split'. And, hearing (the tune) from afar, all those buffaloes, young and old, followed one another and came in sniffing and snorting.

20. *Mūnd'oṭa Haskaṭ kōṛē Mannā. Three Marvellous Cures.*

Ort andhras ara ort kubṛas rahcas. Kubṛas oṇṭē hō̃ ēkā pollālagyas, andhras oṇṭē hō̃ ērā pollālagyas. Kubṛas ānyas: 'Engan ghoṛō-arga'ā; hōle ēn ḍabrē ēd'on'. Andhras mancas. Annem kuddā ujjālagyar

Undul ār tembnum tembnum oṇṭā mahal gusan āṛsyar Bēlasgahi oṇṭā pardkā tangoā rahcā, adigahi mūndgoṭang dudhī rahcā. Dhēr cān munddh, ād kukoim rahcā ābīrī, 'endrge ennē manālaggī'? bācas-kī, bēlas panditguṭṭhyārin eḍḍkas dara menjkas rahcas. Ār ānkar rahcar: 'Īd dau mallī; idin piṭar oi'ā; makhlē nīn khē'oi.' Bēlas conbātī malā piṭkas rahcas, 'nīk'im hō'or' ba'arkī. Backan nē hō̃ hō'ā malā biddyar. Ennem, ā irbar timbur barcar khanē, bēlas tangdan kubṛasge ciccas. Ār occar kī kerar.

Ond aḍḍā ṭoṛang nū ḍērā nanjar darā khaṭ'ā helrar. Bēlkukoi dara kubṛas ukkar rahcar; andhras cicc ūr'ālagyas. Urnum ūrnum mojkhā khann nū kōrcā, dara ās khannan niṛigra'ā helras: āganem āsgahi khannantā jalā khaccrā: ās ērā helras. Khanē bācas: 'Akkū gā ī kukoin ēnim uyyon: īsin piṭon'. Bācas-dara, kubṛāsin lau'ā kōṛā helras. Launum launum kubṛā gusan ennē lathcas, āsgahi kubṛā ujgārā kerā. Idin īryā, bēl-kukoi 'Ohrē kubṛā, ohrē kubṛā' ba'anum, eōkhan kōṛra'ā helrā: āganem adigahī oṇṭā dudhī kōrcā kerā. Antile gā, īryar-kī ormat kōṛē manjkat, bēlas gusan kirryar kī tamhai urmī katthan tingyar. Bēlas, haikaṭ manjas-kī, andhrasge hō̃ nantarti khaī biddyas dara ārin khadd lekh'ā uyyas.

—There were a blind man and a hunchback. The hunchback could not walk at all; the blind man could not see, even a little. Thhunchback said: 'Take me astraddle: I will show thee the way'. The blind man complied. Thus going about, they made a living.

One day, on their begging tour, they arrived at a palace. The king had a grown-up daughter with three breasts. Years before, when she was young, the king, wondering at the cause of the development, had called in and questioned pandits; they had told him: 'This is no good; kill her or you shall die'. Love had prevented the king from doing so. 'Some one will take her', he had thought. But nobody (had) wanted her So, when these two beggars came, he married her to the hunchback. They left in her company.

At one spot in the forest they halted to cook a meal. The princess and the hunchback were seated: the blind man was blowing the fire. In the process, smoke entered his eyes and he rubbed them: thereupon the scales on his eyes were pulled off, and he began to see. He then thought: 'Now forsooth, it is I who'll have the girl; I shall kill this fellow'. Saying so he started laying about the hunchback. While thus engaged, he kicked him so much on his hump that it got straightened. Seeing (the fight), the princess shouted 'Poor hunchback, poor hunchback'! and she belaboured her chest (with hard knocks): one of her breasts went in. And then, realizing that they all were healed, they returned to the king and told him of these happenings. The king, surprised, procured a wife for the blind man too, and kept them near him like children of his own.

21. *Oṇṭa haskat Kendrā* *The Enchanted Mandoline.*

Oṇṭā eṛpā nū mūnd kōhā bhāir rahcar; ā mūndartī sannī ort bhiyas dara bhiyā hō̃ rahcar. Ā sannī maī ōrmar khatrī khat'ālagyā. Undul ād amkhi iṛt'āge aṛkhā mōcālagyā khanē, tanghai anglin mōcrā[1], dara bācā: 'I khēson eksan cīcro'on? engdadābagar ēror hōle, endr khēsō[2] ba'or. Ennē malā. Ēn aṛkhānum cīcro'on'. Ara ād aṛkhānum cīcrā. Ā amkhin taugdābagar mokkhar khanē, ajgut embālagyā aoṅge, adin menā heliar. 'Ān koi, innā amkhī nū endran sajjki'? Ād ānyā. 'Endran hō̃ gā malā' Malam patta'ānar khanē, tingyā ciocā: 'Anglin mōcrkan dara aṛkhānum

[1] *Mōcnā*, to cut; *Mocrnā*, to cut (oneself). Likewise *cīcnā*, to rub off; *cīcrnā*, to rub off (a stain made by oneself)

[2] If they notice a bloodstain (on my clothes or on the wall), they'll ask (reproachfully): what is that blood?

cicrkan'. Ār tām tām kacnakhra'ā helrar: 'Bhāirō, idigahi khēsō ī-kōṛhē[1] embālaggī, hōle gā ahṛā adkō koṛhem laggō'! Antile kōhar ṭhakcar-kī adin ṭoṛang tarā oocar; asan oṇṭā macā kamcar dara, punā kicrin kūrtācar-kī, adin oktācar, dara gecchanti adi manyā/ eṛeth-cārti inj'ā helrar. Kōhar gā, salhā nanjar-dara, baṛiyam pantarā cengcar. Ekāsē cōkhornakhrkar[2] rahcar, annē annem injcar Sannisgahi pālī manjā khanē, ānyar: 'Bēs lan'ā, kāṛā: makhle ningānim lau'om kī pitom'. Ās elonātī mānim injcas: cār kukoigahi majhī khōkhā tarā laggyā... Ād keccā kerā.

Antile tangdadābagar ānā helrar: 'Lagē, kāṛā, mōca; nin gā piṭkai ciookai'. Mūcyas khanē, ānyas: 'Kank mallā, dadābagārō'. Ār bācar: 'Nīnim piṭkai; kank kādai kā'? Bēgar ēp āsin taiyar: kank biddyas-kī, cīkhdas. Āganem oṇṭā nerr barcā kī menja: 'Endrnā cīkhdai'? Ās urmī tingyas; khanē nerr ānyā: 'Ēn ninghai kank nū pojjordan: engan hō'oke dara alghem nike ci'ike'. Ās annem nanjas kī kankan ondras. Khōkhānū īryar gā amm hō mallā Asan oṇṭā sattē[3] uṇḍhū manjkā aṛī khakkhrā: idi ganc kukkōsin taiyar. Ās tūsā gusan keras kī cīkhdas. Oṇṭā mūkhā menā helrā: 'Endrnā cīkhdai'? Ās tanghai urmī katthan tingyas. Mūkhā bācā 'Injō darā kakṛō piṭā'. Piṭyas khanē, bācā: 'Ninghai aṛīgahi uṇḍhū nū[4] gā ēn okkdan: engan hō'oke dara alghem hō'oke ci'ike. Ningdadābagar ahṛā mōkhor hōle, nīn injon mōkhke; dara khoclan cab'or hōle kakṛon cabke'. Ās ānkā lekh'ā nanjas. Urmin iṛyas khaṭṭyas. Mundā kōhar ahṛā mōkhnar khanē, ās injon mōkhdas; khoclan cabnar khanē, kakṛon cabdas. Tanghai bantā ahṛan dara khoclan oṇṭā puttā nū sajjas.

Ā puttanti bās kundyā. Ḍher ullā khōkhā, ā ujgom[5] oṇṭā jūgyas ēkālagyas khanē ā bāsantī oṇṭā cāl urkhar mindrā[6]: 'Īd gā bhayasgahi iddkā bās'. Jūgyas bujhras: 'Īd gā kendrā kau'āge dau

---

[1] ī-kōṛhē, lit. so greatly as this.

[2] Cōkhnakhrnā, to follow one another; *fig.* used here of the order of birth.

[3] *Sattē*, seven; but here *a number of*, or *some, several*.

[4] *Uṇḍhū* is a plural. The frog will adjust its limbs and fingers to stop all the holes.

[5] See Or. Dict. *ujgō*.

[6] Causal of *mennā*. See Or. Gramm., p. 97, n. 50.

ban'ō'. Ās ā bāsan occas kī kendran kamoas Anti kōhasgahi eṛpā-num tembā keras. Ā cāl ba'ā helrā : 'Ambai kharkhai, ambai kharkhai, kendrā : īd gā dokhasgahi eṛpā talī'. Annē annem ā nannā irib kōhargahi eṛpā gusan bāeā. Khōkhānū ā jūgyas sannisgahi eṛpā nū bō̃ keras ; khanē ba'ī : 'Kharkhai kharkhai, kendrā : īd gā bhaiyasgahi eṛpā'. Sannis, menjas-kī, jūgyasge arkhī-jharā ciccas kī onkhtācas : khanē ā kendran nuḍḍas kī nannā kendran āsge ciccas. Khōkhānu ā kendran ek'ambirī tān assdas khanē, tangṛidim goṭṭam urkhī.

Undul āsgahi tangdadābagar āsin ba'ā barcar : 'Innā gā, ningbai eṛpā nū emāge maṇḍī bīta'ā, ekāgūtī uiom.' Aulā tangṛīdim bītācā. Ār gōhlā bicohrar-kī barcar khanē, tangṛī ūlā tarā khollā khollā uyyī, tangṛis ārge ho'ā ho'ā ci'idas. Khōkhānū sannis bō̃ onāge ukkyas. Adhā ōndas khanē, ād jhakmakhra'ā bilcnūtim birkha'āge urkhā ! Kōhar ajgut manjar-kī utān khattr'ā helrar.

—A family was composed of three big brothers, one small brother and one small sister. This little girl used to cook for them all. One day, chopping vegetables to make curry, she cut her finger, and thought : 'Where shall I wipe off this blood ? If my brothers see it (wiped upon anything), they'll be displeased. Not so. I will wipe it on the very vegetables'. She did rub it off upon the greens When her brothers partook of that curry, as it tasted so sweet, they asked her : 'Girl, what didst thou put to-day in the curry' ? 'Nothing', she replied. As they did not believe her a bit, she said : 'I cut my finger, and rubbed the blood upon the leaves'. They reasoned among themselves : 'Brothers, if this girl's blood is so sweet, how greater a relish would her flesh be' ! Then (those three) elders decoyed her into a wood ; there they raised a platform and, wrapping her in a new garment, seated her (on-high), and from a distance began to discharge arrows at her. The elders, who had consulted among themselves, purposely shot beside (the target). All had their shot one after another, in their order of birth. When the youngest's turn came, they told him : 'Shoot true, thou bungler ; or we shall beat and kill thee'. Through fear, he took a true aim : the arrow stuck in the girl's back about the waist. And she died.

The elders then said: 'Come, bungler, cut her up: for thou hast killed her'. He, having done so, said: 'Brothers, there is no fuel'. They replied: 'thou thyself hast killed her: be off to get fuel'! They had sent him without a strap (to tie round his fagot): when he has found the wood, he weeps (helpless). Thereupon a snake came and asked: 'Why doest thou weep'? He related his story, and the snake said: 'I shall coil round thy wood: thou carry me, and do put me down gently'. He did so and brought the fuel.

They afterwards found they had no water. A pot with a number of holes in it was found on the spot: with this the boy was sent for water. He goes to a spring and weeps (again, helpless). A frog inquired: 'why doest thou weep'? He related his whole story. The frog said 'catch some fishes and crabs'. When he had done this she said: 'Well, I seat myself upon the holes in thy pot; carry me and put me down gently. When thy brothers eat of the flesh, thou shalt eat fish; when they munch the bones, thou shalt munch crabs'. He acted accordingly. He cooked and fried the whole (body). Only, when his big brothers eat of the flesh, he eats fish; when they crush bones between their teeth, he crushes crabs between his. His own share of the flesh and bones he buried into an anthill.

(Now) from that anthill there sprang a bamboo-tree. A long time after all this, as a jōgī was passing that side, a voice was heard issuing from within the bamboo-tree: 'this is the little brother's bamboo'. The jōgī thought: 'This tree will be just the thing for a mandoline'. He took that bamboo and made a mandoline with it. He then went to beg at the house of the eldest brother. The voice began to say: 'Don't ring, don't ring, o mandoline: this is a culprit's house'. It repeated the same at the houses of the other two elders. Later on, the jōgī went to the little man's house; the voice here said: 'Ring, ring, o mandoline: this is the small brother's house'! The little man, hearing this, made the jōgī drunk with beer and spirits, hid away his mandoline and gave him another. And, from that day, when(ever) he himself played on that mandoline, his little sister used to come out in her full size,

One day his brothers came to tell him : 'To-day, cook for us in thy house, while we are out ploughing'. On that day it was the little sister who made the cooking. When, their bullocks unyoked, (the elders) came in, she, within (a recess of the house), ladles out (the meal) into the plates : her little brother carries the plates to them. Then the little man sat down for his own meal. When he had half got through it, she, arrayed in a queen's dress and blazing with light, came into the open to give him a second helping. The elders fell on their backs from sheer astonishment.

29. *Ort Ḍhiḍhras* *The Ogre.*

Ort ālas ajgut urb rahcas. Ās ullā mākhā arkhī jharā nū mulukhka ra'ālagyas ; tanghai ālī jõkharti nalakh nanta'ālagyā. Ekā ortos engdas, adin hõ mõdhras. Tanghai ālī undul, jharā lacoādara, jõkhārin ōnta'ālagyā Tanghai ālasin ānyā : 'Ekā ortas ningdas sabī akhdai hōle, ī saṛkhin pesoi kī ningdasge ci'oi. Saṛkhin pettas dara tarkutintim ērā helras, pahẽ lakh'ā pōllas. Ā ālī tangdāsin ānyā : 'Ērā, beṭā, nimbasge pesar ci'ā'. Ās ciccas Ā urbas īryas, akkū gā engdas jõkh manjas ; anti undul āsge khai beddāge ukhas

Ās onṭā gūnjan dharcas, ledrā jhappras dara kharā baggẽ rupiyā occas. Onṭā geccbā paddā nū āṛsyas khanẽ ōnd aḍḍā tūsā-ḍahrẽ nū ukkas ra'as. Kukoikhaddar amm hō'ā barnar khanẽ, gūnjan ēddas dara ārin eṛdas. Ort kukoi ā gunj gane tulcā.[1] Adigahi khōkhā keras dara eṛpā gusan ukkyas. Kukoigahi tangyō tambas, āsin timbus ba'anar-kī, malā kacnakhrnar Ārin ānyas : 'Āne urbnī urbāyo, ēn ningdā bārẽnū kacnakhra'ā barckan'. Ār ānyar : 'Endr nīn emāge ḍalī ci'a ongoi ?' Ās bācas : 'ci'on.' Ār onṭā kẽtran ciccar : 'Ondā (bācar) ; kõṛan nind'ā.' Ās bācas : 'Kẽtran endr ci'idar ? baugin sẽ ci'ā' Annū baggẽ ḍhibā tundyas. Ond kẽter nindā khaccyā Āsge khedḍ-amm[2] ciccar, onḍar mokkhar, dara ās calras. Pahẽ ḍahrẽ nū saṭhsaṭhanā keccas keras. Ḍhẽr ullā nū mendrā. 'Nimbas keccas ; phalnā paddā phalnā eṛpā nū ḍalīḍhiban ciccas'.

---

[1] *Lit.* she tallied with the red flower, viz. in brightness of complexion.

[2] *Kheḍḍ amm ci'inā* denotes agreement to a marriage proposal. The same honorific treatment as extended to a common guest is *kheḍḍ nõṛnā*.

Āsgahi tangdas kundrkantī ḍhiḍhras[1] rabcas. Ennē hāl menarkī, ās tanghai urmī dhankurjin nunkhyas ciccas, dara ā paddā tarā keras. Eṛpā eṛpā kuddas dara mendas : 'Engan jōkh uyyor'? Ā tanghai pāhi-manjkā kanyāgahi eṛpa nū hō keras : 'Engan jōkh uyyor'? Ār gā āsin ballālagyar. Munddh ānyar : 'I dhadhus endr nalakh nanos'? Khōkhānū āsin khēr khed'āge uyyar. Jōkhar, ninā-khalltī bar'ōbīrī 'guchr'ā ḍahrentī, dhadhū' ba'anar-kī, lathnum kōrnar urkhnar. Undul tang urbāsin ānyas : 'Engā ek'annem[2] 'khall gacchr'ar ci'ā'. Ās menjas : 'Nīn endr uiā ongoi, dhadhū'? Ās bācas · 'Uion gā'! Ond aḍḍā ajgut kōhā marcā rahcā : idin urbas āsge gacchras ciccas.

Ās nitkī ōnd gohlā baggē lanḍī aḍḍon hō'odas dara tanghai khall tarā kādas. Ḍahrē nū onṭā khuṭan gaḍḍas[3] dara ānyas : 'Engāge nē manḍī ondro'or, ārim munddh ī khuṭan ṭhokkē, antile hō'okē[4]'. Urbasgahi ānkā lekh'ā, tangdādim nitkī manḍī hu'ī. Undul malā ṭhokcā : gecchantī īrī ā khallnum ajgāṛ taggē jōkhar uāge lakkar ra'anar, tān sōnāgahi ḍhiluā nū jhukurdas .. Ād khōkhā kirryā kī khuṭan ṭhokcā : āganem ās jōkhārin ormārin, gohlā aḍḍon, kuḍḍī ugtā pagsin nunkhyas dara otkhāsim ā lanḍī aḍḍōtī uidas. Manḍin ciccā dara idin nēkan hō malā tingyā.

Urbas undul ḍhiḍhrasgahi khallan ērā keras. Ērdas gā khall guṛguṛū usskā khoṭṭkā ra'ī. Barcas-kī tanghai nannā jōkhārin kōbā helras : 'Ās otkhāsim ekā lekh'ā khallan ussas! nīm ekāse nalakh nandar'? Ā jōkhar adkō korhem ḍhiḍhras mañyā kadrōr'ā helrar.

Backan ā kukoi, āsgahi bheddan akkhā-dara, tangyō tambas gusan ānā helrā : 'En ḍhiḍhras gusan ra on'. Ār ānyar : 'Ān beṭī, ās gusan endr īrkī ra'oi?[5] Ningāge bēs sobhā jaōdkhaddī beddom ci'om' Ād malā pattāoā, backan onghon ānyā : 'Malā; ēn ās gusan ra'on'.

---

[1] *Dhiḍhras* means either (1) a big-bellied fellow; or (2) an 'ogre', i.e. one who has the uncanny power of swallowing up and disgorging at will furniture, people, etc., without inconvenience to them or to himself.

[2] *Ek'annem*, lit. in any manner; i.e. under any condition, as a personal favour or on lease.

[3] From this spot the field was already in sight, but details could only be distinguished with difficulty.

[4] *Thokkē, hōoke.* Imperative future, 3rd person plural.

[5] Construct : 'Endr īrkī, (atti) ās gusan ra'ā biddī? See expressions exactly similar on p. 24 l. 24, 25, and p. 43, l. 18.

Khanē adin ḍbiḍhras ganem beñjyar car. irbārim tambai khall beddē ra'ālagyar. Undul ās, munddh lekh'ā, tanghai jōkhārin uglācas dara tān sōnāgahi ḍhiluā nū jhukra'ā helras. Āsgahi ālī cāṛum bongkī kerā dara āsin khimcyā, attī as abṛā urmīn pollas nunkhā....Ād ānyā: Eō ullā nīn ningan ḍhiḍhrā ēd'oi? Akkuntī ambā ḍhiḍhrā manā 'l Āulantim āsgahi jōkhārim nitkī ussar, dara mukkā mēt, bēlar lekh'ā, hāthī nū argā helrar. Nē nē munddh āsin sādh'ālagyar, ās ārin sādh'ā helras dara khōb bitṭhī nanta'ālagyas.

—A man was very rich. He remained buried in his cups day and night; his wife had (all the tillage) work done by servants. He had even forgotten who his son was. One day his wife, having brewed beer, was giving a treat to the servants. She said to her husband: 'If you really know who your son is, pick up this funnel and give it to him'. He picked up the funnel and looked at the whole row of them, but could not make out his son. The wife said to her son: 'Come, son, pick it up for thy father'. He did so. The householder noticed that his son had come of age; so one day he left to find a wife for him.

He plucked a gunja-flower[1], wrapped himself in a ragged shoulder-cloth, and took with him a large sum of money. On his arrival in a far off village, he sat down at a spot on the path to the well. When girls come for water, he shows his gunja-flower and calls them near. One girl (was found whose complexion) tallied with the flower's (colour). He followed her and seated himself near her house. But the girl's parents, mistaking him for a beggar, do not address him. 'Well, Sir, Ma'am. I have come to speak to you about your daughter'. They said: 'Shall you be able to pay a dowry'? He said: 'I shall'. They presented a shovel-basket to him: 'Take' they said, 'fill up one of its corners (with rupees)'. He replied: 'What do you bring a winnowing-basket for? Do bring a square basket'. He poured into it many rupees. The shovel-basket became chokeful with them. They gave him water to wash his feet, had a meal together, then he departed. But on his way (back), he died suddenly. A long time

---

(A red-coloured flower.)

after, the news came (to his son): 'Your father is dead; he had paid a dowry (for you) in such a village and in such a house'

This son of his was, by birth, an ogre. Upon learning that news, he swallowed up his all and repaired to that village. He tramps from house to house asking: 'Will you engage me as a ploughboy'? He went to his betrothed's home also: 'Will you take me as a ploughboy'? They did not know him At first they answered: 'What work will this big-bellied fellow do'? In the end they put him to drive away the fowls. Ploughboys, on their return from the fields, give him kicks each time they come in and go out, saying: 'Get out of the way, thou tun-bellied'. He one day said to his master: 'Let me have a field (for me alone to plough), under any conditions you please'. The master asked: 'What ploughing wilt thou do, fat boy'? He said: 'I will plough, though'! Somewhere there was a big piece of waste land: the master rented this to him.

He every day takes with him a team of very lazy bullocks and goes to his field. He drove a post in the path and recommended: 'Let those who will bring me my meal knock first at this post, then come with the things'. It was the landlord's daughter who, by her father's arrangement, brought that meal every day. Once she did not knock: from afar she sees that a great many servants are busy ploughing that very field, and that he personally sways himself in a golden swing. She retraced her steps and knocked at the post. Immediately he swallowed up all his servants, bullock-teams, hoes, ploughs and yokes, and (there) he is ploughing alone with the (two) lazy bullocks. She gave him his rice and said no word to anyone.

One day the landlord went to see the stout man's field. He sees that the field is ploughed to crumbs, (all clods) broken to powder. On his return he began to scold his servants: 'He, quite alone, what a field he has ploughed! you, what sort of work are you doing'? The servants chafed all the more against the big-bellied man.

The girl however, who knew his secret, started saying to her parents: 'I will marry the stout man'. They said: 'O daughter, what hast thou seen (to want) to marry him? We shall procure a good nice husband (*lit.* son-in-law) for thee'. She refused, and said once more: 'No, I will marry him'. So they married her to the stout man. The two of them lived near their field. One day he, as previously, disgorged his servants and went to swing in the golden swing. His wife quickly ran to him and embraced him, so that he could not swallow up the lot again. She said: 'How long wilt thou continue an ogre? don't be an ogre any longer'! Henceforward his servants alone ploughed the field every day; and they, man and wife, rode on elephants like king and queen. And those who had made him suffer, he made them suffer (in turn), and he exacted much unremunerated service from them.

23.—*Tembu Paccōgahi Khēr*. *The Beggar Woman's Cockerel.*

Oṇṭā raṇḍī-paccō rahcā, ād nitkī tembālagyā. Undul ennē manjā oṇṭā eṛpantā ālarge endrā hō mal rahcā ā paccon ci'āge: annuhō ād malam patti'ī. Ā eṛpantā ālī ānyā: 'Endrā hō malā, paccō; endran ci'on'? Munjā, nū, ā paccō ni'idim ni'ī khanē, eṛpantā urbnī ānyā: 'Oṇṭā khēr-bī gā ra'ī, paccō; jokk endrā hō malā'? Paccō bācā: 'Adinim engā ci'ai sē'. Paccō occā-kī kerā dara bācā: 'Innā malā mōkhon, nēlā mōkhon' bācā, kī uyyā ciccā. Mākhābīrī ā bīyyantī khērkhadd urkhā darā: 'ciū, ciū' ba'ī... Paccō 'endrā gā oīkhī' bācā-kī hī: oṇṭā khērkhadd ra'ī. Khanē 'adin pōs'on' bācā. Tembā tembā undri'ī-dara, adarguṭṭhin khērkhadge ci'ī. Ennem ād pardyā[1] kī cīkhālagyā: 'Kokrōy cōe' ba'ālagyā.

Undul ā khēr paccon ānyā: 'En innā lassā kādan', bācā. Paccō ānyā: 'I khēr ekāsē lassō?' Khēr bācā: 'En eka'āsem lasson', bācā kī kerā. Oṇṭā kōhā urbasgahi khall gusan ārsyā kī alārin menjā: 'Engan khoyāge helāba'or'? Ā ālar ba'anar: 'I khēr-buyā ekāsē khoyō dara idin helāba'ot'? ba'anar. Khēr ānā birdī: 'En khoyon gā; nimāge nalakh caṛ ra'ī kā'? Khanē adin khoyāge helābācar kī tām maṇḍi onāge eṛpā kerar. Ārgahi onar bar'āge, ād khossā kī khalī nū argā.[2] Barcar khanē, ērnar gā khoyāge munjrā, dara arg'āge hō munjrā, dara ā khēr mann mañyā ukkī ra'ī. Adin ānyar: 'Nābom

---

[1] Throughout the story, *khēr*, though referring to a cockerel, stands in the root form, so that its exact English equivalent is *fowl*. Hence, here and elsewhere, the neuter pronoun *ād*. Or. Gramm. p. 161 n. 5.

[2] See Or. Dict. *argnā* (2).

aulā, mullī ho'ā barkē'. Khanē kher ā paccogahi eṛpā kirryā. Paccō khēran ba'ī: 'Lassā kādan' bāckai; okhō mullin ondrkai? Khēr ānyā: 'Nābom āulā mullī ho'ā barke bācar'. Ā ālar nābyar khanē, khērge hāl taiyar; 'Nabālagdaın'. Khēr āṛayā khanē, bācār: 'Okhō,? khēr[1] endran hō̃ mal ondrkai...Endr nū hō'oi'? Ād ānyā: 'Ēn eka'āsem hō'on.' Oṇṭā ḍhēr kōhā khess-kudhā[2] khalī nū rahcā. 'Hū kudhantā khessan enghai khebdā nū sajar ci'ā: eoñdā asan sam'ō, aūndim hō'on, bācā. Ār khusmārnum saja helrar; pahē khalintī khess munjr'ālaggi, annuhō̃ khebdā malā nindī! Khalintā urmī khess munjrā khanē, khēr eṛpā kerā dara khebdantā khessan otthrā. Paccōgahi eṛpā khess trū nīndyā kerā.

Idi khōkhā, paccō ānyā: 'khēr-engdas dau dau nalakh nanjas: akkū gā khēr-engdāsin beñjon ci'on' bācā. Kanyā beddāge kerā; ānā kuddī: 'Khēr engdasge kanyā ci'or'? Ālar annar: 'Hāṛī paccō'l khērkhaddge ekāse kanyā ci'om? ād ekāsē engdan pō's'ō'? Nē hō̃ malā ci'inar. Paccō bārcā-kī eṛpā kirryā. Khēr menjā: 'Ekhō, paccō, kanyā beddāge kirkī? biddkī'? Paccō bācā: 'Nē hō̃ malā ci'inar, khēr-beṭā. Khanē khēr ānākırtācā: 'Kalai paccō; nīn polloi beddā; ēnim beddā kādan'. Ennē bācā kī urkhā dara calra'ā helrā.

Kānum kānum ōnd aḍḍā cigālō khakkhrā dara menjā: 'Endr kādai, iyār'? Khēr ānyā: 'Sasrār kādan, iyār; gucā, nīn kādai hōlē'. Cigālō bācā: 'Kālon ba'adan, iyār; pahē endr nū kālon'? Khēr ānyā: 'Barā, iyār: enghai khebdā nū kōr'ā; enghai sasrār nū bēs bēs onā mokhāge khakkhro'ō'. Kānum kānum ōndgusan lakṛā khakkhrā dara khēran menjā: 'Endr kādai, iyār-khēr'? Khēr ānyā: 'Sasrār kādan, iyār; gucā, kādai hōle; enghai sasrār nū dau dau onā mōkhāge khakkhro'ō'. Lakṛā ānyā: 'Kālāge kaon; pahē, iyār, endr nū kaon'? Khēr ānyā: 'Iyār, kālāge endr jhakdai? enghai khebdā nū kōr'ā'. Ennē ennem, hāṛī hō̃, tīnī dara bhaōrō khakkhrā, muñjā nū Cice dara Amın ibṛā urmī khērgahi khebdā nū kōṛcā kī adigahi sasrār kerā.

Antile ā khēr oṇṭā bēlasgahi paddā nū āṛayā, dara, oṇṭā mecchā simbālī maun rahcā, adigahi aggī nū ukkyā kī ba'ā helrā: 'Kokrōy

---

[1] *Okhō* or *ekhō*, *where?* (with reference to an object presumably in sight, yet unperceived).

[2] Not *kudhā-khess*, because the word *heap* is merely descriptive, and not intended as a measuring unit.

cōe ! Bēlas tangdan ci'idas ka eng ganē arbānaklirdas '? ba'ī. Menjas-kī bēlas tanghai telengārin ānyas : ' Kalā ; hū khēran dhar'arki gullē ḍilingī[1] nū sajar oi'ā, laṭpaṭra'ā khē'ānek'ā. Ār enne nanjar. Baekan khēr tīnī dara bhaōrogutthin ānyā : ' Urkhā, iyārō, onā mokhāge : īdigem gā niman ondrkan : khōb mōkhā onā sē'. Tīnī dumbā bhaōrōguṭṭhi adigahi khebdantī urkhā kī urmī gullen mokkhā ciecā. Pairī bīrī bēlas ānyas : ' Ērā to, haro, khēr kecā kā argī' ?[2] Ērnar gā khēr ujjnam ra'ī dara gullē gā ḍilingī nū malkī'. —Bēlas khisārnum ānyas : ' Puttō bōlē, ēṛā-goēsālī nū sajar ci'ā, ēṛā tirkharkī piṭannek'ā'. Sajjar khanē, khēr cigālon ānyā : ' Urkhā, iyār ; īdigem gā ondrkan'. Khanē cigālō urmī ēṛan dharcā dharcā piṭyā. Pairī bīrī bēlas ānyas : ' Ērā harō, khēr kecā kā malā'. Ērnar gā urmī ēṛā kieckī ra'ī, baekan khēr ujjnam ra'ī.—Antile bēlas ānyas : ' Ēn ā khēr ganē pollon ?[3] Innā gā adin mankhā-goēsālī nū sajar ci'ā : mākhā nū mankhāguṭṭhi adin tirkhō kī pitō ci'ōlim'. Telengar ānkā lekh'ā nanjar ; khanē, khēr ānyā : ' Urkhā, iyār lakṛā onā mōkhāge : idi khatrī gā ningan ondrkan'. Lakṛā urmī mankhan piṭyā carryā dara abṛāgahi khēson cippyā. Pairī bīrī telengar ērnar goēsalī nū khēr utkhīdim[4] ujjnan ra'ī.—Munjā nū bēlas ānyas : ' Īnim piṭon ci'on'. Adin akkūnim khuṭ'arkī mesgā nū jurrta'ar oi'ā'! Khanē telengar khēran mesgā nū khuṭoar kī jurrtāoar. Pahē khēr ānyā : ' Urkhā, iyār Cicc, onā mōkhāge : īdigem gā ondrkan'. Cicc urkhā dara erpā nū laggyā Āganem khēr urhyārā kerā, kī ā simbālī manu mañyā ukkyā dara bacā : ' Korrōy cōe ! bē'as eng ganē arbānakhrdas kā tangdan ci'idas'?

Cīkhnum cīkhnum bēlas mann-aggī tarā mīkhyas : ' Amm ci'ā, khēr urbāyō : tangdan ci'ōnim'! Khanē ād barcā dara tanghai khebdantā amman otthrā : ittī cicc tebbrā kerā. Antile bēlas onṭā mārwan kameas kī tangdan biñjyas ciccas. Khēras ā bēl-kukoin ondras-kī ā timbū paccō guyā kirryas. Paccō īryā-kī khōb khusmārā kī ānyā : ' Engdas khēras gā kanyā biddyas'! bācā

---

[1] A huge basket ordinarily used for stocking corn.

[2] Or. Dict. *arg(na)*,3.

[3] The same idiom occurs twice on pp. 32 and 33.

[4] Or. Dict. *ūokh* see Gramm. p. 11 n. 23, *b*.

—There was an old woman who used to go a-begging every day. Once it happened that the people, in a certain house, had nothing left to give her. But she took no refusal. The housewife told her: 'I have nothing, mother; what can I give'? Finally, as the old woman was insisting, the housewife said: 'There is one egg, mother; nothing more'. The old creature replied: 'Well, give it to me'. She went away with it and thought: 'I won't eat it to-day; I will eat it to-morrow'; and she put it aside. In the night a chicken was hatched out of that egg; it chirped: ciu, ciu! 'What, now, is chirping (there)'? said the woman; she looks: a chicken! She decided to rear it. She fed it on bits of rice grains, which she brought back from her continual begging. So the chicken grew up; it used to shout: 'Cock-a-doodle-do'!

One day that cockerel said to the woman: 'I am off for a turn of work'. She said: 'What turn of work will this cockerel do'? The cockerel departed saying: 'I will work somehow'. As he arrived near the fields of a big landowner, he asked the men: 'Will you employ me for cutting the harvest'? They said: 'How can this blessed cockerel cut a harvest and (how) can we employ him'? The fowl retorted: 'I can, though; are you in need of labour'? They then put it to reap, and they themselves went home for their meal. Before they had eaten and returned, the cockerel had cut the (entire) crop and carried it to the threshing-floor. When they came, they found reaping work and portage work all at an end, and the cockerel perched up a tree. They said to him: 'When we do the threshing, come for your day's work pay'. The cockerel then returned to the old woman's house. She said to him: 'You had said you were off for a day's task: well, have you brought your pay'? The cockerel replied that he had been told to go for this on the threshing day. When those people had the sheaves trodden upon, they sent word: 'We are threshing'. On the cockerel's coming up, they said: 'Well, cockerel, you have brought no (sack)? In what will you carry it'? He said: 'I shall manage that'. On the threshing floor there was a huge heap of paddy. 'Pour of that heap into my ear (he said); I will take what quantity will hold in it'. They began, quite pleased, to fill (the paddy into his ear); but the threshing floor gets being cleared and the ear does not fill up! When all the paddy there had disappeared, the cockerel went home and emptied his ear. The old woman's house became chokeful with paddy.

After this, she said: 'My son the cockerel has done fine work: now forsooth I shall marry my son the cockerel'. She went to look about for a bride; she tramps from place to place: 'Will you give a bride to my son the cockerel'? (But) the people say: 'Get away, old crony! how can we give a bride to a cockerel? How will he support our daughter'? Nobody makes an offer. She went back a failure. The cockerel inquired: 'Mother where's the bride you have gone to fetch? Did you find'? The old woman answered: 'Chicken sonny, no one wants to give'. The cockerel replied: 'Leave it at that, mother; you won't be able to find; I go on the quest myself'. Saying so, he left the house and walked off.

On his way he met a jackal, who asked: 'Where are you going, friend'? The cockerel said: 'I go to my parents-in-law's house; come along, if you choose'. The jackal said: 'I have a mind to go; in what (conveyance)'? The cockerel said: 'Come, friend, enter into my ear; in that house there will be very good things to eat'. At (another) point of the journey, a tiger was met; he asked the fowl: 'Where are you going, friend cockerel'? The cockerel said: 'Friend, to my parents-in-law's; come, if you choose: in that house you shall have an excellent meal'. The tiger said: 'As to the going, I am willing enough; but, friend, in what (conveyance) shall I go'? 'Friend, (the cockerel answered), why worry about that? enter into my ear'. In the same manner, further on, bees and hornets were come across, and finally Fire and Water. All of them entered the cockerel's ear and went to his bride's house.

The cockerel came to a village in which there was a king. He took his station on the top of high cotton-tree which was there, and started: 'Cock-a-doodle do! will the king give me his daughter, or fight with me'? On hearing this, the king commanded to his soldiers: 'Go, catch yonder cockerel, and throw it into the treacle basket, that it may flounder in it to death'. So they did. But the cockerel said to the bees and hornets: 'Come out, friends, to eat and drink; for this is what I have brought you for: so do it well'. Bees, wasps and hornets sallied forth out of his ear and ate up the treacle. In the morning, the king said: 'You people, just see whether the cockerel is not dead yet'. They look: the fowl is alive and no treacle remains in the basket.—Angrily the king said: 'Next evening throw it into the goats' shippon, that it may be trampled to death'. When they had done so, the cockerel said to the jackal: 'Come out, friend: for it was for this that I brought you here'. The jackal caught one goat after another and slaughtered them all. In the morning the king said: 'You men, just see whether the cockerel is dead'. They found all the goats lifeless and the fowl very much alive.—Then the king exclaimed: 'Shan't I be a match for that cockerel? To-day throw it into the buffaloes' stable: they will surely trample life out of him in the night'. The soldiers carried out the order; the cockerel then said: 'Come out, friend tiger, eat and drink: for this, in fact, did I bring you here'. The tiger killed all the buffaloes, tore them to pieces and sucked their blood. In the morning the king's soldiers found the sole cockerel alive in the stable.—Finally the king said: 'I shall kill him myself; this instant, tie him to the roof, hang him! The soldiers made the cockerel fast to the roof and hanged him. But the cockerel said: 'Come out, my friend the Fire, to eat and drink: for this occasion did I bring you thither'. The fire came out and caught to the house. Thereupon the cockerel flew to the cotton-tree, where he stopped and shouted: 'Cook-a-doodle do! will the king fight with me or give me his daughter'?

The king all in tears shouted towards the tree top: 'O for water, my lord the cockerel! I will give you my daughter, certainly'. The cockerel then came up and poured off the Water that was in his ear: with this the fire went out. And the king constructed a wedding-bower and gave away his daughter. The cockerel went back to the beggar woman's house with that princess. The old woman felt over-joyed and exclaimed: 'My son the cockerel has found a bride after all'

24.—*Moghābăck Rājī. The Enchanted land.*

Ort bar̤iyasgahi opṭā tangdas rahcas. Āsin tambas beñjā dyts kiianō, tangdas ānyās: 'Nē engan co'ōbīrī hō, okkōbi hō lau'ā oi'ō, adīaim ēn beñjro'on: ne mālā ci'ū, adin ēn malā beñjro'on' bācas. Antle tambas, ekasan ekasan tanghai arbar-parbar rahcar, ayyā pāb-īd'ūsin taiyas: baokan launā bārē.nū menarkī nē hō tangdan ci'ā malā beddmar. Onṭā ālī, ād ā kukkostī koṛhē akh'ū rahcā, adi gusan khāl kerā khanē, ānyā: 'Ēn ās gusan kālon'bācā. Khanē cāṛe simā-joṛā nanjar ki aūin ā kukkos gane binjyar ciccar. Barāt tartī kirryar-kī, ās ukkyas ābīrim, tanghai ālin lau'āge jūtan otthras. Ād bācā: 'Ra'ā: khokhā gā lau'oim: ninghai arjā ekā manḍī ōnōm, aulā laukē. Akkū gā paccō pacgirgahin[1] ōnālagdan.'

Undul ā kukkos, pairim cō as-kī, baggē aḍḍo nū sanjgīguṭṭhin kadcas dara, mūdīrin occas-kī, bisā khēndāge gēccha rājī turā calra'ā helras. Ā rājī nū āṛsyas khanē, ōnd aḍḍā endian ērdas? Khaikā khāṛ nū onṭā ḍongā kālī bar'ī. Jokk bāṛī kaṭṭyas-kī keras, ḍabrē heddē nū bheṭāngo-khoppan ērdas, adigahi pānjkā bheṭāngo[2] ōnd bittā, dara ibṛāgahi goṭā sauā hāth ra'ī[3]. Ās baikat manjas kī, ekā paddā nū ā rājīntā bēlās rahcas, ayyam keras kī tanghai aḍḍon khuṭcas.

Aulā ā bēlas tanghai telengārin paduagahi canguṛdā sarkhā'age taiyas: 'ērā, nambai paddā nū ek'am tartī nik'īm barcar kī ḍērā nanjkar ra'anar kā malā. Teleugar kerar: ēruar onṭā bāṛīyasgahi ḍhēr ladmī aḍḍō dara mūdīguṭṭhyar ra'anar, āsgahi onṭā ghoṛō hō ra'ī, ād sōnā rūpā trū jhabrāīkā ra'ī. Bēlas menarkī ānyas: 'Kalā, āsin ēra beddan, bācas; neotā ci'ā'. Ār kālaikī ā baṛīyāsin ānyar: Bēlas guyā innā onṭā khēṛ bēcor: ās ennē pēsas ī paddā nū eō ālar, ormar ērāge barnarnek'ā; nē malā ērā beddnar, ār akkūnim enghaī rājintī urkhnarnek'ā' bācas. Khanē ā baṛīyas ānyas: Bēs, ēn hō kālon. Bēlas mayāti eḍḍas khanē, endrnā malā kaor'? Anti makhābīrī ālar mahal nū khob baggē khonḍrar.

Ā khēṛ khokhānā ōrmat bēlas ganē gorgoiā ukkyar. Bēlas ānī helras: 'Ē bhāi, ēn gā ekātarā hō rājī malā kuddkan ra'adan. Nantaram endrā ra'ī mal ra'ī menā tukkī. Nīn gā bisū-khīndū

---

[1] See Or. Gramm p. 46.

[2] *Bheṭāngo* has here a plural sense.

[3] *Hāth* means cubit, and also the width of the four extended fingers.

ālai[1]; nīn gā urmī rājīgahi rāgcaran, anthan akhdai : adin tengā'. Baṛīyas ānyas : 'Ē belāyo, ēn hō baldan. Pahē ninghai rājīnum īṛekan khanē ēṛ'oṭang haikaṭ katthan īrkan'. Khanē bēlas ānyas : 'Endran īrkai'? Bāṛīyas bācas : 'Oṇṭā khāṛ nū khaikā calkur nū ḍongā ēknā īrkan Hīṛī bar.kan khanē, ōnd bittā bhēṭāngo khakkhrā, abṛāgahi goṭā sauā hāthgahi rahcā'. Bēlas ānyas : 'Anā haiō! ennē katthan nīk'm menjkar ra'adar? khaikā calkur nū ḍongāgahi ēknan dara ōnd bitta bheṭāngogahi sauā hāth goṭan nē patto'ō'? Ormar ānā helrar : Īs ṛūrūs taldas; khaikā calkur nū ekāse ḍongā ēkō? dara ōnd bittāgahi bheṭāngo, adigahi goṭā ekāse sauā hāth manō'? Bēlas baṛīyāsin ānyas : 'Ē bhāi, ibṛā katthan engan ēd'oi hole, ēn enghai urmī rājin, dara enghai mahal nū iudri'im ra'ī, ara engdābagārin dara ēn engan hō ningāge bīson ci'on. Makhle, ṛolkai ēd'a hole, ēn ninghai aḍḍon ghoṛon jōkhārin daṛā abṛā sanjgīguṭṭhin ekdā aḍḍō nū bar.kī ra'ī, urmin khakkhon' bācas. Hārā jītā manjnakkhrar; dara, bijjrā khanē, ormar ērāge urkīar Munddh bheṭāngo gusan kerar Endr ērnar? Bheṭāngo pānjkā gā ra'ī, pahē sauā hāthgahi goṭā mallā: bhaṛīyas īryas-kī markhyas keras. Ār ba'anar : 'Polkai ēd'ā; akkū gucā : khaikā calkur nū ḍongā eksan īkī'? Khāṛ gusan kerar : ērnar khāṛ nīndkā ra'ī, amm soēsoēri'ī, adi mañyā ḍongā kālī bar'ī. Anti baṛīyas hārcas keras. Kirryaskī bēlas āsgahi urmī sanjgīguṭṭhin dara jōkhārin dara ghoṛon tang guyā occas : asinim kulhū pīkhtācas.

Ā baṛīyas eṛpā bar'ā hō mal bardas khanē, āsgahi tangāli jiyā nū ānyā : 'Īsin nīk'im ṭhakcar'. Anti ād karēan cōcā[2], oṇṭā ghoṛō nū argyā ki tanghai ālasin beddāge urkhā. A mokhtāckā khāṛ gusan īṛsyā khanē, īrī khaikā calkur nū oṇṭā ḍongā kālī bar'ī. Ād ā ḍongan dharcā kī menjā : 'Enghai kirrnā gūṭī ennem ra'oi kā'? Ḍongā bācā : 'Ra'on gā'. 'Ennem mal ra'oi hōle, ēn bar'on kī ṭang'ētī paikon dāra basson' bācā. Hāṛī keiā kī ōnd bittāgahi pānjkā bheṭango khakkhrā, abṛā nū sauā hāthgahi goṭan īrī. Alī ā bheṭangon[3] ānyā : 'Enghai kirrnā gūṭī ennem ra'or kā'?—

---

[1] Ālai for āl taldas. Or. Gramm. p. 163, n. 6

[2] Karēan co'onā, (of women) to put on a loin-cloth, i.e., a male attire.

[3] Plural sense. These brinjals were marvellous in their having a stone, and moreover a stone twice as long as the whole fruit.

'Ra'om gā'—' Ennem malā ra'or, kirron ki niman kaṛkuṛra'ā caṛ'on'. Idigahī ā ālī, eksan tanghai ālas ḍērā nanjkas rahcas, asānim kerā dara ḍērā nanjā.

Bēlas adin hō khēṛ ērāge neotā ciccas. Ād kerā. Tāmārā khokhānū, ālar gorgorā ukkyar khanē, bēlas adin mēt ba'arkī maññjas: 'Anā bhāi, nīn gā rāji rājī kuddai, aōnge urmī aḍḍantā anthan akhdai Engan hō tengā'. Khanē ād bācā: 'Ninghai rājī nū āṛskan khanē, ē tēlāyo, khob haikat mañjkan. Heddentā khāṛgahi khaikā calkur nū onṭā ḍongā ikī; jokk biṛī-calrkan, ōnd bittāgahi bheṭāngo khakkhrā, abṛāgahi gotā sauā hāth ra'ī' ! Munddh lekh'ā bēlas ānyas: 'Erāto, haro, īsgahi katthan nīk'im patt'or'? Ormar la'ā helrar: 'Īs gā pūru ālar lekh ā kaonakhrdas'. Antile bēlas ānyas: 'Ibrā katthan engan ēd'ar oi'ā : hole, ēn enghai rājin dara urmī khurjin ningāge ci'on' bācas. Ennem hārā jītā mañjar ki ormar bheṭāngon dara ḍongan ērāge kālā helrar. Abṛā bheṭāngo gusan āṛsyar ki ērnar gā ōnd bittāgahi bheṭāngo dara sauā hāthgahi gotā Khāṛ gusan kerar: ērnar gā khaikā calkur nū onṭā ḍongā kalī bar'ī. Anti bēlas hārcas keras A ālī bēlargahi mahlantī tanghai ālasgahi aḍḍon dara urmī sanjgīguṭṭhin dara jōkhārin hō otthrā. Abṛan jōkhārin aḍḍō nū ladtācā. Khokhānū tanghai ālāsin kulhūpikhnā eṛpantī heres'anā natgyā kī otthrā dara ormārin ondra'ā helrā. Kirrnum kirrnum ōnd aḍḍā ukkyar khanē, baṛīyas tang-khain lau'āge jūtān otthras. Backan ād ānyā: 'Ninghai arjackā manḍin ōnon, hole gā lau'oi, gacchrkat be'edat. Akkū gā, urmī ninghai rahcā enghaidim manjkī bi'ī : nīn ekāse lau'oi'? Khanē ās mala laucas dara irbārim conhā tule ra'ā helrar.

—There was a corn dealer who had a son As the father wanted to marry him, the son said : 'I sha'l marry the girl who will allow me to beat her as often as I like ; one who refuses this, I shan't have her'. So the father sent a match-scout among his friends and acquaintances : but, upon hearing of the beating stipulation, no one agreed to give away his daughter. One girl, however, who was a good deal cleverer than the young man, said when the news reached her : 'I will take him'. Preparations were made quickly and the marriage took place On their return from the wedding procession, he no sooner sat down than he took off his shoe to beat his wife. She said : 'Stay ! Later on thou shalt beat me, of course : from the day I will eat rice of thy own earning, do beat me. For the time being, I am living at my parents' expenses'

One day, in the early morning, the young man loaded many bullocks with various goods and, accompanied with drivers, started on a selling and buying tour for a distant country. On reaching a certain spot in that land, what does he see, but a canoe that was plying up and down a dry river bed ! He walked a little further on when, by the roadside, he notices a bush of egg-plants, the ripe fruits of which had the length of one span while their seeds measured three inches ! In great wonder, he betook himself to the village where the king resided and tethered his bullocks.

On the same day the king told off his guards to have a peep round the village. 'See (he said) whether any strangers have come to our place and are halting (for the night)'. The guards went. They see a corn-dealer with plenty of pack-bullocks and bullock-drivers ; the man has a horse and the animal is festooned with silver and gold. On their report the king said : 'Go, I wish to see that man ; invite him'. They went and told the corn-dealer : 'There will be a show to-day (to-night) at the king's, his commands are that every one in the village shall come and witness it ; anyone refusing has to leave the kingdom instantly, says he'. The corn-dealer said : 'Very well, I will go ; if the king has been so kind as to invite me, why shouldn't I' ? So, at night, when the show started, there was a good gathering of people at the palace.

The thing over, all present sat down with the king to pay him their court. The king addressing the corn dealer. 'Brother (he said), I have never travelled. I am curious to hear what things may, or may not, be found in other lands. You are a man of traffic ; you know the customs and marvels of all countries : tell us about them'. The corn-dealer said. 'O king, I myself know nothing. Still when crossing into your dominions, I noticed a thing or two very curious'. 'What did you see'? the king asked. The corn-dealer answered : 'I saw a canoe moving on the dry sand of a river ; then, a little further this side, I met with egg-fruits one span in length, the seeds of which measured three inches across'. The king: 'O friends, I say! did any of you hear of such a thing before? a canoe moving upon dry sand, and one span brinjals having seeds three inches across, who'll believe this'? All said: 'The man is mad; how could a canoe move upon dry sand? and brinjals of one span, how could they contain seeds three inches across'? The king said to the corn-dealer: 'Brother, if you will show me those marvels I shall give you in exchange my whole kingdom and whatever there is in this palace, I shall sell off my daughters and my own self in slavery unto you. On the other hand, if you fail, I shall get your bullocks and horse, your servants and whatever goods have come with your pack-animals'. The wager was made, and, when the day dawned, all started for that place.

They first repaired to the egg-plants. What do they find? The brinjals were ripe enough, but had no seeds three inches across: the corn dealer felt ashamed at the sight. They told him: 'Thou hast failed in thy showing; now come along: where is the canoe moving on dry sand'? They went to the river: they see the banks full, the waters are noisy; on their top a canoe moves along. So the corn merchant lost his wager.

The king on reaching home took to himself the stranger's all, goods and servants and horse: the man himself, he sent to the oil works.

As the corn-merchant was never coming back, his wife said to herself: 'Some people have duped him'. So she put on a male apparel, mounted on a pony and started in search of her husband. Upon reaching that enchanted river, she sees a canoe moving on a bed of dry sand. She caught up that canoe and asked: 'Shalt thou remain as thou art now till I return?' The canoe said: 'I shall'.—If thou doest not, said the woman, I shall come and break thee to splinters with an axe, and burn thee'. She went on and met with ripe egg-fruits one span in length: in them she notices seeds three inches in diameter. The woman said to those brinjals: 'Will you remain as you now are till I return'?—'We shall '.—' If you don't, I shall come back and uproot you to dry up in the sun '. Next the woman went to where her husband had (first) halted, and she made a halt at the same spot.

The king sent an invitation to a show to her also. She went. The spectacle being over, as people sat down to do honour (to the king), the latter, who was taking her for a man, inquired : ' Brother, thou art a traveller and must know the curiosities of every place. Tell us about them'. She said : ' When I crossed over into your dominions, O king, I had a great surprise. At a river near-by, upon the dry sand of its bed, there was a canoe moving up and down. I walked on a little further, and there were brinjals one span long, the seeds of which measured three inches '. Just as before, the king said : ' Well, friends, can anyone of you believe this man's word ? All said : ' He talks like a raving man '. The king then said : ' Show me those things, and I shall give thee my kingdom and all my riches '. So they made a wager, and all sallied forth to see about the brinjals and the canoe. On reaching the former, they indeed see fruits one span in length with seeds three inches across. They go to river, and they do see a canoe plying up and down a bed of dry sand. So the king was worsted. Out of the palace the woman took back her husband's bullocks and goods and servants, and had the animals loaded. She next went to the oil house and snatched her husband out with a good pull, and started for home with all of them.

During the return journey, as they sat down somewhere, the corn merchant took off a shoe to beat his wife[1]. But she said : ' When I shall eat rice of thy own earning, thou shalt beat me : such is our agreement. Now however all that was thine has become mine : how canst thou beat me ' ? So he did not beat her, and they henceforth lived in peace and love.

25.—*Jūgiyasgahi Ektarhā. The Jogi's Mandoline.*[2]

Irb tuar k͟haddar bhayā bahin rahcar. Kukkosgahi tangdaī ekastī'im aṛkā ēṛ-mūnd k͟hess be·idarkī ondra'ālagyā : adin tangṛis

[1] The last touch is as humourous as it was unexpected. It brings back the burden of the story, and ushers in its moral, in a manner most felicitous.

[2] A variant of story n. 21.

khaid'o bīrī khāpālagyas. Undul irbārim khess-khaidnā gussa rahcar : aulā oṇṭā khākhā kīndā panjkan ondrā dara ārgahi khessaitāokā heddē tiddā ciccā. Ār pettar kī khatrnakhr'ā mokkhar : embālagyā khanē, adigahi rājin[1] heddā helrar.

Sattē ṭungrin kaṭṭyar kī ērnar gā ōnd aḍḍā ṭoṛang nū khīrā koṛhē kīndā panjkādim ra'ī : mann mañyā argyar kī kūl uṛueningh'ā mokkhar. Adi khōkhā sannis tangdayyan[2] ānyas : 'Ammonkā laggī, daī ! Khanē ād, satte aõṛā khanjpan cokkhā kī caugurdi le' dācā ; dara tangṛīsin oṇṭā dhodhrō nū nuḍḍā-kī, ekātarā amm kharkhyā attram kālā helrā. Pahē, adigahi malko bīrī, oṇṭā darghā bandra ā aḍḍānum ju nmrā kī ā khaddāsin carryā piṭyā, dara capṭan asānim ambyā kī kerā. Tangdaīge, kīrro bīrī, āsgahi oṇṭe cambī hõ malā khakkhrā. Khokhānū ort jūgiyas ā capṭan biddyas dara ektarhā aḍcas : idin assnum assnum tembā helras.

Ā kukoi cīkhnum olokhnum tang pallā kirrālagyā, ābīrī ort bēl-kukkos adin īryas kī ērnānum noghārkas rahcas. Ās adin bā'as : 'Gucai, enghai mahal nū ra'oī'. Pahē ād ānākirtācā : 'Bēgar punā kicrī dara bēgar sindrī nū ekāse kaon'? Khanē kicrī dara isung sindrin ondrar, dara irbārim negcār lekh'ā beñjrar.

Undul ā jūgiyas tembnum tembnum bēlasgahi mahal keras dara bālī nū ukkyas ki assā pāṛā helras :

Pānī āne gele, didī, rājā rānī bhele :
Ṭimkī-ṭikir bandrā, didī, cīr khālaī !

Bīṛī, ennē pāṛnan menarkī, urkhā, yād nanjā dara bujhur bujhur oīkhā helrā. Antile ād ā ektarban jūgiyastī khindyā kī paṭkācā : khanē ulantim adigahi eberkā ṭungṛis jhakāmakā urkhas ! Ād āsin kheõṛā conkhā helrā. Ās adi guyā rahcas, dara bēlas ā-ge rājī nū pēskā ciccas.

—There were two orphans, brother and sister. (Every day) the sister would scrape together, from where she could, two or three measures of paddy : this, as it was put to dry, her little brother used

[1] See Or. Gramm. p. 168, *b*.

[2] See Or. Dict. *dai*.

to watch over. One day both stood close to this drying spot, when a crow brought a ripe date and dropped it where the corn was spread out. They picked it up and shared it: as it proved delicious, they set about discovering the land from which it came.

After crossing many hills and hillocks, at one place in a forest, they see a large number of dates quite ripe; they climb upon the trees and eat to their heart's content. The little man then said: 'I am thirsty, sister'. She plucked some cupfuls of dates which she hurled about (to the four points of the compass): then secreting her little brother in the hollow of a tree, she started in the direction whence a murmur of running water (had caught her ear). But, while she was away, a band of monkeys collected upon that very spot; they tore the child to pieces, leaving only his skin behind. The girl on her return could find no trace of him. Later on a jogi found that skin and made of it the covering of a mandoline, upon which he used to play while begging.

The girl in great distress was returning to her village when a young prince saw her and was enraptured at the sight. He said: 'Come along, thou shalt stay in my palace'. But she answered: 'How can I go without new clothes or otherwise than as thy wedded wife'? So garments and vermilion were brought, and they were married according to rites.

One day the jogi, in his begging round, went to the palace and seated at the door, started playing and singing:

Thou went to fetch water, sister, and becomest a raja's queen;
Monkeys big and small, sister, tore (me) to pieces.

The queen, on hearing this song, came out and became thoughtful; then gradually realizing (the truth), burst into tears. She bought the mandoline from the jogi and smashed it: out there issued her lost brother, all blazing with light! She embraced and kissed him He remained with her, and the king gave him a command in his dominions.

26.—*Arangbarang Garbararnā.* *A Comedy of Errors.*

Birbal nāme ort ālas rahcas, āsgahi enne bān rahoā, ekābiā ās alkhdas, khanē cep possālagyā. Ond cān ās ikla'am hō mala alkhyas;

attī ā cān ekhāgalī mal manjā. Āsin alkhta'āge ā rājintā bēlas an'āman'ā khēṛ ēttācas : malam bancā khanē, āsin bēlkhantī otthras ciccas.

Khōb ūkhyā khanē, Birbals, ōnd aḍḍā oṇṭā maṭh rahcā, asan ḍērā nanjas : ōnd kōṛā nū cūtyas. Uṛung manjā, ort kusārī-bīsus pēṭhentī kirrālagyas ās, ā maṭhnum āṛsyas, dara ās hō̃ oṇṭā kōṛā nū cūtyas. Gahṛi gahṛī irb timbū ālar, andhrā andbrī, barcar, dara asānim ōnd koṛā nū khandra'ar kerar. Munjā nū ort ālas tanghai gadhan beddnum beddnum ḍahrentī barcas: ās hō̃ oṇṭā kōṛā nū ukkyas. Ennem ā maṭhgahi cāryō kōṛānum ḍahre-īkur rahcar : adin tām nē hō̃ balnar ; ormar oṛgnar, ēnim ṭhaukā ra'adan.

Adhā-idhī mākhā bīrī, andhras tanghai ḍhiban gann'nā helras : adin baggē khakkharkī khud'ū khud'ū alkhdas. Āsgahi paccō menjā: ' Bēsim laggī, pacgī '? Ās ānyas : ' Ē paccō, tīnō tirlōk itthri'ī ' ![1] Āganem gadhā-biddus ejjras dara bācas : ' Tīnō tirlōk itthri'ī hole, ērā to enghai gadhā ekātarā ra'ī' ! Enne kacnakhrnan menjā ki, andhrī rittā elcnum andhrasgahi mūhī nū tanghai soṭṭan haṇḍra'ā helrā ; andhras khisārnum ' natgai, paccō, natgai ' bācas. Abīrim kusārī-bīsus ejjras dara bācas : ' Ne harō, ne harō ? Enghai kusārin nē hō̃ ambke natgā ; urmī ganackā ganackā ra'ī' !

Ibṛā urmī gaṛbaṛarnan Birbals menālagyas dara ijga'ā ijga'ā alkhā helras, alkhnātī liṭliṭā manjas. Āganem ajgut possā. Bijjyā khanē, ār ormar tangā tangā katthan tingyar, ekāse ekāse nū ēn engan oṭkhā[2] ba'arkī isan barckan dara tangā kōṛā nū cūtkan. Birbals hō̃ tanghain tingyas. ' Mal alkhnāge engan bēlas otthras ciccas ; ās engan alkhta'āge an'āman'ā tamāsā hō̃ nantācas : annuhō̃ malam alkhkan... Pahē, harō, innā aīn gā engan alkhtākar '.

—There was a man named Birbal who possessed the uncanny power of bringing down rain whenever he laughed. On a certain year he never laughed once, and that year there was no rainy season. The king of the land had all manner of stage tricks performed to unbend him ; as they did not succeed, he banished the man from his dominions.

---

[1] *Lit.* three worlds, heaven, earth and the infernal regions. Said proverbially, much as we refer to ' the third heaven '.

[2] See Dict. *oṭkhā*.

In the dark of night Birbal stopped at a place where there was a sarai : he laid down in one of its corners. A little while later, a sugarcane merchant, returning from market, arrived at the same sarai, and he likewise stretched himself in a corner. In course of time two mendicants, a blind man and a blind woman, came in, and fell asleep in a (third) corner. Finally a man in search of his donkey turned up from the roads : he in turn squatted down in the (fourth) corner. So, in the four angles of that sarai, there were travellers now: none of them knew of the fact ; everyone thought that just he himself was there.

About midnight time, the blind man took to counting up his money : and finding it a large amount, he chuckled to himself. His wife asked : 'Art though pleased, old man'? 'Wife' he said, 'the three worlds lie open before my eyes'. At this moment the man in search of a donkey awoke and said : " If the three worlds are visible to thee, just look where my donkey can be'. Hearing somebody talk, the blind woman, in sudden fright, poked her stick into the blind man's face ; he, in anger : 'Off with that cane, wife' (he) said, 'off with it'. Thereupon the sugarcane merchant awoke and said 'Who's there ? who's there ? Let none of you have a pull at my canes, they are all counted'.

Birbal was overhearing all this rigmarole conversation and burst into a laugh : he laughed till his sides ached. Instantly there came a heavy downpour. When day dawned, all these people related their stories (to one another); how each, thinking himself alone had come there and got asleep in his own corner. Birbal also told his story. 'My king (he said) had banished me for not laughing ; he had all sort of comic shows got up to make me laugh : yet I never did... But to-day you fellows have made me laugh, indeed'.

27.—*Sendrā nanā Kukkos. The Young Hunter.*

Ort urbasgahi kharā baggē aḍḍō mekkhō gūṛī rahcā : khapāge ort kukkosin jō̃kh uikas rahcas : is ullā ullā ṭoṛang tarā menta'ā ho'ālagyas. Undul oṇṭā ṭeṭengan bajhābācas ; dara piṭā biddyas āganem, ṭeṭengā bācā : 'Engan ambā ; ān ning gusan jō̃kh raon'. Kukkos menjas : 'Idī, bhusṇḍī, nīn endr nalakh nanā ongoi'? Ṭeṭengā bācā : 'ninghai aḍḍon khāpon'. Khanē ās malā piṭyas.

Nannā ullā onghon aḍḍon ṭoṛang tarā oocas ; ṭeṭengā hō̃ ās gane kerā. Ās oṇṭā k͟hoppā nū kaprkas rahcas dara ērā helras ṭeṭengā aḍḍon ekāse k͟hāpō. Ād oṇṭā sakhuā mann nū argyā kī attrā ittrā ērā kuddī : aḍḍō gā menā lakkī ra'ī. Āganem oṇṭā lakṛā ṭoṛangti urkhā dara aḍḍōguṭṭhin dhar'āge haṛbaṛambāokī kuddī. Ṭeṭengā mīk͟hyā : 'Enghai aḍḍon endrge elgta'ādai, hō mutā ? Akkun, kerkan[1] hōle, kukkan k͟hoṭṭon '! Lakṛā, kirr īryā dara, attrā ittra kuddī, munjā nū ba'ī : 'Nē hō̃ mal etthrnar dara[2], nē engan mīk͟hī'? K͟hōk͟hānū ṭeṭengan ṭhaukam īryā k͟hanē : 'Ādim engan mīk͟hi '! bācā ; 'adin elcon ?' kī aḍḍōguṭṭhin onghon haṛbaṛamba'ā helrā. Ṭeṭengā bācā : 'Endr hō̃, mūṭā, ānkan malā mendai ? akkun ettdan, akkūnim piṭā k͟haccon'. Lakṛā adin takṭakī īryā dara bācā : 'Barā to, ettā : enghai oṇṭā pallge hō̃[3] malā k͟hakkhro'oi' ! Ṭeṭengā manngahi gaṛk͟hā gūṭī ittyā darā ijjā. Lakṛā adi tarā anglkī bar'ī āganem, ād adigahi baīnum ḍegoa. Lakṛā 'cab'on' bācā. Pahē cab'ā pollā : ṭeṭengā kūl tarā bong kurckī rahcā dara pottāgutthin parmā helrā. Lakṛā uphṛār'ā kī mūyan nīṛgirkī kuddā helrā. Idin īryas-kī ā kukkos ajgut alkhyas. Lakṛā āsin īryā dara ānyā : 'Engan bacchāba'ā kō ! ninghai jō̃k͟hāsin manāba'ā : eō̃ mākguṭṭhin beddoi, ēn aō̃guṭṭhin ningāge piṭon kī ondro'on'. Khanē kukkos bācas : 'Angla'ai ! Ād anglā : āganem ṭeṭengā baī tartī bongkī urkhā dara mannnā onghon argyā.

Āulantim lakṛā ā kukkosge ullā ullā oṇṭā oṇṭā māk piṭā piṭā undri'ī oi'ī. Ālar, abṛā urmī mākguṭṭhin ērā ērā, ajgut manā helrar, is ekestī innelā ennē māk piṭdas.[4] Pahē kukkos lakṛāgahi piṭnā oi'inan malā tengdas, backan āndas : 'K͟hāpnā tarā k͟hakkhrā ; nē eng khatrī piṭor '? Mānī mānim lakṛā āsin ānkā rahcā : 'Ninghai ṭeṭengāgahi ṭkatthan nē gusan hō̃ ambke tengā ; makhlē engan lajjāba'oi, kī ālar ba'or sannīkunā ṭeṭengā kōhā lakṛan ekāse piṭā ongā ? Ikla'am nīk'im gusan ṭengoi, āulam ēn ningānim piṭon kī mōk͟hon. Ēn sagarkhane sarkha'ā kālon'.

---

[1] Perfect tense with the force of an anticipated Future.

[2] *dara* is used here as a postconjunction and means 'since'. Or. Gramm. p. 263.

[3] Thou wilt not tally with even one tooth of mine.

[4] Pregnant construction : *whence (is this that) he kills ?*

Undul eṛpā nū ā kukkos, ṭeṭengā dara lakṛan jiyā nū bujhur bujhur, rittā ajgut alkhā helras Nannar menjar : 'I abṛāmōkhus endrnā alkhdas'? Ās āndas : 'Nimhai kattbāguṭṭhīnim gā menā menā alkhdan'. Dara ḍhēr gahṛī bonnem alkhnum alkhnum ra'as... Munjā nū bācar : 'Tengā se, hō ; endran ābīrintim [1] ijga'ā ijga'ā alkhdai '? Ās ānyas : 'Enghai alkhnan tengon hōle, innam enghai jiyā kālō'. Ār bācar : 'Nē ningan endr nanō ? kā endrā mōkhō ? Tengā : ningan gā ēm kūl ulā nuḍḍkam ra'om'. Khanē ās bācas : 'Enghai ṭeṭengā onṭā kōhā lakṛan piṭālagyā ? [2] : idīnim alkhdan'. Ār menjar : 'Idīgem mal tengdai '? Ās bācas : 'Tengoi hōle, piṭon kī mōkhon ' ba'ī lakṛā : aṅge malā tengālakkan.' Ār ānākirtācar : 'Ningan majhī nū innā kīd'om, dara balin ūd'om, dara adhā jōh'om : nē isun kōr'ō '? Lakṛā gā mākhā mākhā collā tarā sarkha'ā kālālagyā. Tingyas, āulā ṭhaukam menjā ki kadrārā.

Āukā lekh'ā, ālar ā kukkōsin khaṭī nū kīdar dara tām tīnā ḍebbā kīyyā hō cūtyar. Adhā mākhābīrī, ormar khandrar khanē, lakṛā barcā dara, ormārin alghem kūṭī nanarkī, kukkōsin khaṭi-bārī cōdā kī kumnyā kī bongā kerā. Jokk geochā occā khanē, ās ṭhaukam ejras. Munddh gā ās, akkhas-kī, khōb ileyas ; khōkhānū jiyas ḍhiṭh nanjas dara jiyā jiyā ānā helras. 'mōkhō tā mōkhō : ēn tani tamku san'on kī mōkhon '. Cunnā otthro'ō bīrī, cunauṭī kharkhyā... Lakṛā bācā : 'Endran kharkhdai ? akkū eksan bongoi ? ambke tengā bāckan ; pahē tingkai '! Kukkos ānyas : 'Endran kharkho'on ? āulantā ṭeṭengādim ra'ī '! Lakṛā ajgut ileyā dara okkrā kī-ānyā : 'Ra'ā bhāi, ambke otthra'ā, ambke otthra'ā ; engan jokk geochā bongā oī'ā '... Khanē ās astlem eṛpa kirryas, dara ormar āsgahi bacchtkā nū ajgut manjar.

—A large owner of cattle had it tended by a servant boy who took the herd every day out to the forest for grazing. One day, this boy caught a lizard. As he wanted to kill it, the lizard said. 'Let me go. I shall stay with thee as a servant'. The boy asked : 'Thou, insignificant creature, what work shalt thou be able to do'?

[1] *Abīrintim.* See above p. 80. l. 33.

[2] *Piṭālagyā* is an imperfect *de conatu* :— he nearly killed. See another instance p. 103, l 26.

The lizard said : 'I shall look after thy cattle.' So the boy did not kill it.

On the next day he again took the cattle to the forest ; the lizard went with him. The boy secreted himself behind a bush and began to watch how a lizard can look after cows : (he saw) it run up an oak-tree, and move about to have a peep here and a peep there ; the cattle sure enough was busy grazing. Thereupon a tiger came out of (the depths of) the forest ; he runs to and fro, scattering the cattle in a panic, that he may catch (one of the animals). The lizard shouted : 'Why dost thou frighten my cows, thou ear-cropped ? in a moment, if I come (down), I shall smash thy head'! The tiger, turning round, looks everywhere, comes and goes, and finally says : 'No one is to be seen ; who can be shouting at me'? The next moment, on catching sight of the lizard. 'It's she, he said, who calls ! shall I be afraid of her'? and he once more began to stampede the herd. The lizard said : 'Doesn't thou hear my words, ear-cropped ? here I am coming down, this very moment I'll kill thee outright'. The tiger scanned her and replied : 'Do come down, I shall swallow thee at one gulp'. The lizard descended as low as the foot of the tree and stood there. As the tiger was approaching ; mouth open, she jumped into it. 'I crush thee', thought the tiger. But he could not : the lizard had gone at a run down into the belly and was knawing at the bowels. The tiger was thrown into convulsions, turned on all sides wiping his mouth against the ground. The boy burst laughed at the sight mightily. The tiger noticing him said : 'Save me, o boy ! call back (*lit.* forbid) thy servant : for thee I shall kill as many deer as thou desirest, and bring them to thee'. So the boy ordered : 'Open thy mouth'! The tiger did so : instantly the lizard ran out, and climbed up the tree again.

Henceforth the tiger killed one deer every day and carried it to the boy. People, seeing all those deer, were wondering whence they came from. The boy however does not mention that they were killed by the tiger ; he merely says : 'They were got where I tend the cattle ; who would kill them for me'? The truth was that the tiger had told him : 'Do not relate the story of thy lizard to anybody :

else, thou wilt put me to shame, people not understanding that a tiny lizard could kill a huge tiger. If thou ever relatest the story to anyone, I shall kill and devour thee. I shall go and keep watch on thee (about this matter)'.

One day at home the boy, on recollecting lizard and tiger, suddenly burst into a laughter. The other (servants) asked: 'What does the scoundrel laugh at'? He said: 'Well, I laugh at what you say'. And he goes on laughing and laughing quite a long while... At last, they said: 'Do tell (us), boy; what hast thou been roaring at all this time'? He said: 'If I say why I laugh, it's all over with me this very day'.—'Who' they asked, 'will do harm to thee? who will eat thee up? Speak; we shall hide thee in our bosoms'.—'My lizard nearly killed a big tiger', he said; 'that's all I am laughing for.'—'And thou makest a secret of such a thing'? they asked.—'The tiger (he replied) says that, in case I talk, he'll kill and devour me: so I did not (like to) explain'. They retorted: 'To-night (*lit.* to-day) we shall place thy cot in the midst of us and make the door fast; one half of us shall sit up; who could enter here'? The tiger however came every night and remained on the spy towards the back of the house. On the day the boy talked, the tiger heard him allright and became indignant.

Those men put the boy to sleep on a cot, as they had said, and they themselves lay down on his right and left, and even underneath him. At midnight, when all were asleep, the tiger came and, gently pushing aside the others, he lifted up the boy together with the cot, threw up (the whole thing) on his head and ran off. He had gone some distance when, accidentally, the boy awoke. True, at first, on becoming conscious, he was greatly frightened. Soon (however) he hardened his soul, and he thought: 'If I am devoured, be it so: I am going to crush and have some baccy'. As he was taking lime, the metal box gave a chink. The tiger said: 'What noise art thou making? Whither to fly this time? I had told you not to talk, and thou hast talked'. The boy replied: 'I am making no noise; it's (only) that lizard of the other day'. The tiger took great alarm; he stopped and said: 'Stay, friend, don't take it out, don't take it out! give me a fair start of (that beast), ... Then the boy quietly returned home and everyone there wondered at his escape.

28.—*Cigālō Endrnā Khall-ukkṛī mal Nanī. Why Jackals are no Farmers.*

Eṛ-ṭhaur Cigālō raheā. Mukkā-Cigālō tanghai ālasin ānyā: 'Anā paegī, akkū gā kōṛem beddat mōkhdat, pahē khaddar manor hōle, ekāse pōs'ot? Kalā: mahtos gusan bēskunā ghaṭī-ra'anā[1] khallan gacchrke'.

Mēt-cigālō kerā, mahtōsin ollālagyā dara ānyā: 'Gōṛ laggī,[2], dadā'. Mahtos bācas: 'Bhaiyā, kōṛem ra'ake. Innā gā endr barckai? Sannisgahi eṛpā tarā urmī kōṛem ra'ī'? Cigālō ānyā: 'Dadā, jiyāge kōṛem ra'adam. Pahē ning bāynālīgahi ullā āṛakī ra'ī; aōge ba'ī: Khaddar manor hōle, ekāse pōs'ot? Dadas gusan kalā, jokk'em gaḍḍī-ābō[3] khallan gacchra'ā. Idīgem barckan ra'adan'. Mahtos ānyas. 'Bhaiyā, ī galī ekā khallan ci'on? Ra'ā: ningṛībagar gane bujhurnakhra'ā ci'ā. Kalā, nēlbeñjā gūṭī[4] barke.' Cigālō eṛpā kirryā; mūnd ullā manjā khanē, aur onghon barcā dara menjā: 'Okhō dadā, khaddar ci'āge bācar? Mahtos ānyas: 'Anā ko, mōdhrkan. Nelā barke'.

Nannā ullā mahtos naib kōhā kōhā allāguṭṭhin eṛpā ulā occas dara kicrīti jhapcas ciccas. Cigālō onghon barcā dara menā helrā: 'Khaddar dara nāsgō āulantā katthāgabin endr bācar, dadā'?—'Hīṛī barā, kō; innā menjkan ra'adan'. Cigālō hedde barcā dara ukkyā. Āganem mahtos 'Dekh-rē, Caūrā, Bhaūrā, Tilkā, Lodhā' bācas kī kicrin calkhas ciccas. Abṛā allā khed'ā khed'ā helrā...Cigālō umblā erkhā pītā chernum bongā. Bacchrā kī manḍā nū kōrcā.

Mukkā-Cigālō menjā: 'Endr manjā hō? endr manjā'? Mēt-Cigālō ānākirtācā: 'Kalai, bhusnḍī! ninghai baī gā candō lekh'ā bilcī![5] Īd engan khall gacchra'ā taiyī. enghai jiyā kālālagyā....Khallan nē'edan khanē allan ondras kī eng mañyā

(1) *Ghaṭi*, artificial incline in rice-fields *Ghaṭi-ra'anā* is an adjectival expression, *lit.* (in which) there-is-a-slope.

(2) A common salutation to superiors. *Lit.* (your) leg is being pressed (between my hands).

(3) See Dict. under—*ābo*.

(4) *Gūṭī* is here an adverb and means 'exactly', 'without fail'. Compare with: *Khēr alkhnā gūṭī cō'ot*, we'll get up at cockcrow sharp.

(5) Thy face shines like the moon, *i.e.* thou lookest innocent enough.

lilyācas '! Ad ānyā : 'E hō paogi, nē akh'ā kerā ? Eka'āsem jiyā bacchrā. Asan ambke kirrā. Khaddārin eka'āsem [1] pōs'ot'.

—There were two jackals. Jackal the wife said to her husband . ' I say, husband, at present we do find enough to live upon ; but when we have children, how shall we feed them ? Go to the mahto and rent from him a field with a (gentle) slope '.

Jackal the husband went to the mahto, and saluting him said : 'Embracing thy feet, my big brother'. The mahto said : ' Little brother, keep in good health. And what is thy errand to-day ? Is all well in my cadet's home '? The jackal replied . ' With regard to health we are all right. But thy sister-in-law's term is near : so, says she (to me), when we have children, how shall we feed them ? Go to thy elder brother and rent from him a field with a gentle slope. That is what I have come for'. The mahto said : ' Little brother, at this time of the year what field can I give ? Wait though : let me talk the matter over with my sons (*lit.* thy small brothers). Go, thou shalt come back on the day after to-morrow'. The jackal went home. Three days later, he came back and asked : ' Well, my big brother, did the children opine for the gift '? The mahto said : ' I say, boy, I have forgotten (that business). Please come to-morrow'.

On the morrow the mahto took inside his house four huge dogs and secreted them behind a piece of cloth. The jackal came once more and inquired : ' My big brother, what did the children and my sister-in-law say about the other day's proposal '? ' Come near, boy ; to-day I have consulted with them'. The jackal approached and sat down. Instantly the mahto threw the cloth screen open, shouting : ' At him Chaura, Bhaura, Tilka, Lodha '! The dogs to give chase. Away fled the jackal with loose bowels, and weak bladder and foul winds. But he escaped and got into his hole.

Jackal the wife inquired : ' What is up, man, what is up '? Jackal the husband retorted : ' Get away, thou little gnat ! a fine adviser thou art This (creature) sends me to rent a field, and (as a consequence) I nearly lost my life ; when I apply for a field, the

---

1 By hook or by crook, *lit.* somehow.

mahto sets dogs at me'! She replied: 'Well, husband, who was going to foresee this? Life is safe after all. Do not go back there. We shall bring up our children as we can'.

29.—*Lūrhī dara Calkī. Curry-roller and Broom.*

Ort bēlasgahi sattējhan bīṛir rahcar. Ārgahi majhī nū nēkāge hō khaddar mal rahcar: khokhānū sannīge osrā khaddar manjar, kukkō dara kukoi. Iklā ād nibbyā āulam abṛā nannā bīṛir ḍāhētī irib khaddārin kumbhargaḍḍī nū hibṛyar, dara ārgahi khaṭī nū onṭā lūrhin dara calkin kīdar ciccar; khanē bēlāsin tingyar: 'Idigā, khadd calkī dara lūrhī ra'ī!' Ās gā jiyā-mal-nunjnā ālas malā rahcas., pahē khisāras, dara ā saunī bīṛin malbēs nanā helras, ekattī ād keccā kerā. Adigahi khaddārin gā kumbhras ara paccō tangkhaī occar dara pos'ā helrar.

Jokk pardyar khanē, kumbhras ā kukko ge kankgahi ghōṛon dara kukoi-khaddge kankgahi ōṛā khindyas kī ciccas. Abṛā gandā bēl-mukkar pokhārī nū em'ālagyar khanē, ā khaddar hō pōkhārī taram bēcālagyar. Kukkos āndas: 'Enghai ghoṛō, amm ōnai'! Kukoi ānī: 'Enghai kerkeṭā-khadā[1], amm ōnai'! Bēl-mukkar ānnar: 'Endr kank-ghōṛō amm ōnō? Kā kerkeṭā-khadā amm ōnō'? Ār ānyar: 'Endr ālar lūrhī kā calkī khadd pāknai'? Abṛā bīṛir bujhrar ir ga mānim abṛā khaddārim talnar; bēlas akh'os gā... Aōge ār tām tām salhā nañjar. Amm maṇḍin ambyar ciccar, dara belāsin ānyar: 'Hū khaddargahi khēsō khappom, kōṛā manom'. Bēlas kōllam mañjas, pahē ārin malā manābācas.

Kumbhras ā khattā khaddargahi mēdan pokhārī pinḍī nū manḍyas; khanē ayyantim onṭā laṛang urkhā dara daulē pardyā: adigahi pūp ērāge khōb dau rahcā. Bēl-mukkar ibṛan mējhra'āge sībākhārar dara tokkhāge kerar: khanē gā asthom, tākā nū, onṭā ḍanḍī mendrā:

Pūp, ḍolō ḍolō manai;
Mudairtī bongai bacchra'ai.

---

[1] A bird resembling a big sparrow.

Ar āṛsam pollar. Khōkhānū bēlas hō barcas-dara emcas ki lether ukkyas[1]: ābīrī ās hō abṛā pūpan īryas dara tokkhāge taiyas. Khanē onghon oṇṭā ḍaṇḍī mendrā:

Pūp, kukkan leokh'ai ci'ai;

Bēlastī ambai elcai.

Ennē ba'anum, ā irib khaddar piṇḍintī urkhar: ās gā tambas-gahi tīnā, dara ād ḍebbā khosgā nū ujjā-manjar-kī ukkyar. Bēlas bujbras ibṛā engdābagārim talnar. Cīkhā helras dara abṛā gandā mukkārin piṭṭācas.

—A king had seven wives. All were childless; at length (however) the youngest bore twins, a boy and a girl. On the very day she was delivered, the other queens out of spite exposed the two babies in a potter's pit, and placed a curry-roller and a broom in their cradles; then they said to the king: 'There! 's (only) a broom and a curry-roller'! The king was not a heartless man, but he got angry; and he began to ill-treat the young queen, so much that she died. As to the children the potter and his old wife took them and brought them up.

When they had grown up somewhat, the potter bought a wooden horse for the little boy and a wooden bird for the little girl. As the wicked queens were bathing in the tank, these children were at play upon its banks. Says the boy: 'Have a drink, my horse'. Says the girl: 'My young sparrow, have a drink'. Say the queens: 'Does a wooden horse, or a wooden sparrow drink water'? The children reply: 'Do women bring forth young brooms or young curry-rollers'? The queens gathered that these were the (king's) very children, that he would know of this...So they held a consultation. They ceased to take food and said to the king: 'If we could drink the blood of yonder children, we would be cured'. The king felt sad, but he did not forbid them.

The potter buried the poor children in the tank's embankment; from the spots there issued a creeper, which grew strong and bore magnificent flowers. These the queens coveted to put in (their

(1) *ethēr okhnā*, to sit with the legs crossed Indian fashion as the Budha or as tailors.

hair and dresses), and went to pluck them. At this moment, gentle tune was heard in the wind :

Swing off, swing off, o flowers ;
Avoid the touch of the fiends.

They just failed to reach the flowers. Later on the king too came, and after bathing sat down and crossed his legs. He then likewise noticed the flowers and sent someone to pluck them. Once more a tune was heard :

Do bend your heads, o flowers ;
Have no fear of the king.

And, saying so, the two children came out of the tank's embankment : and, (well) alive, they seated themselves, he on his father's right thigh, and she on the left one. The king understood that these were his children. He began to sob and put those wicked women to death.

30.—*Mandar Akh'u Urbnī.* *The Lady-doctor.*[1]

Ort eṛpantā urbasgahi sattē khaddar rahcar : ormārin biñjyas. Kōhā kheṛōgahi khekkhā nū bangī [2] rahcā : adigahī mañjkātī ōrmar ōnnā mōkhnā arja'ālagyar. Pahē pacgis ullā ullā unkhālagyas : ās maṇḍī hō ōnā pollālagyas, annem sagarkhanē arkhī jharā nū mulkhkas ra'ālagyas. Undul oṇṭā bambhnas barcas ; ṭunkī nū deotan dharcas-kī tembālagyas. Pacgis āsin ānyas : 'Engskheṛō engāge amm maṇḍī malā khaṭ'ī ; nīn gā endr ba'adai' ? Bambhnās jokk'em deōṛāi nanarkī bācas : 'Ninghai kōhā kheṛon otthra'ar ci'ā : ād bisābī ra'ī'. Pacgis ormā khaddārin oktācas, bambhnasgahi ānkan tingyas ; ār bācar : 'Otthra'ā sē'.

Kōhas tanghai ālin khōb cōnhā nanālagyas. Ās adin ānyas : 'Eōndā hō'āge ungdi,[3] aōnda ḍhibā khess tikhil ho'ai'. Ād ōnd bangī ḍhibā bākyā, mañyā āṛkō ābdā tikhil sajjā, dara eṛpantī urkhā ; adigahi tangālas ḍahrē ēd'ā naihar kālā helras. Kānum kānum ḍhērim gecobā kerar. Chindra'ā polnātī ukkyar. Munddh ād āsgahi

[1] From a literary point of view this is perhaps the best story of the book.

[2] See Dict. *bangi*, 3.

[3] From *ongnā* ; likewise, lower down (l. 24 and l. 25), *khurpi* and *puccyā* are of *khorepnā* and *poccnā*. See Gramm. p. 11, n. 23,5.

pēn īryā ; khōkhānū, kūgā helrā khanē, āsgahi tolongan kajjyā-kī cūtyā. Ād khandra'ar kerā khanē, ās jūṛontā kantōtī tolongan mūcyas : astile gucohras dara eṛpā kirryas. Ād ejjrā, abīrī gā ērā ērā eīkhā helrā.

Ād jokk hāṛī kerā, annum bīṛī puttyā. Anti, oṇṭā paṭrā heddē oṇṭā kōhā mannan īryā kī asan cūtāge kerā. Ā mann nū ōṛā-khākhā cūtālagyā. Adhā mākhā manjā khanē, ōṛā ejjrā kī tengrnakhra'ā helrā : 'Ekātarā beddā mōkhā cērō kerkar' ?—'Uttar rājī nū oṇṭā paddā ra'ī, ayyantā bēlasge maldan laggī : āsgahi khebdā khurpī. Khebdā nū pocgō puccyā : abṛan urkhī khanē, pet pet mokkham'. —'Ekāse kōṛē mano āsgahi khādī ?—Nīd'im namhai pīkan hō'or kī āsgahi khebdā nū saj'or, hōle gā koṛē manō'. Ī urmī kacnakhrnan ā ālī meñjā. Cōcā kī jokk khakhā-guhāṛin sōṛā nū ṭipcā dara baugī ulā bākyā, dara ā paddā tarā kālā helrā. Ā paddantā pokhārī nū ek'am ālar em'ālagyar ; ār tām tām kacnakhra'ālagyar, nambai bēlas innā khē'os kā ujjos[1]. Idin meñjā-kī, ād bāca : 'Bēlasgahi endr rōgē' ? Khanē ār tingyar. 'Ān paccō, bācar, endr nalakh nandī ? baugī nū endrā ra'ī' ? Ād bācā : 'Biccī-mandar'. Ār ōnyar : 'Paccō, mandar akhdī ; gucai, eng belāsin ērai'. Khanē ād kerā dara bēlāsin īriyā. Pocgon otthrā kī ā guhāṛin kas'arkī khebdā nū ṭap'ā nanjā. Khanē urmī khorop khēs khayyā. Ond bīṛī nū bēlas cōcas kī maṇḍī mokkhas ōṇḍas. Ā paccon 'baid-ayang' bācas-kī, adige eṛpan, kiorin, onnā mōkhnan urmin ci'ā helras.

Āgalim tangsasrus khōb kīṛā manjas. Leṭṭē maṇḍī [2], aṛkhā-cōkhel hō malā khakkhrā khanē, ās dara khaddar khakhndārkar mōkhā ōnā helrar Urmī munjrā khanē, sattō bhāir sangē sangē kank hō'arkī bīsā kālālagyar : oṇṭā ḍhibā, ḍhibā-ēṛ trū bīsālagyar. Undul ennē manjā kōhas ā āligahi cālī nū [3] ondras. Ād āsin lakhcā, āsgahi kankan khindyā 'dara meñjā : 'Anā paagī, kohṇḍā mōkhoi '?—'Cī, ayang' bācas. Ād kohṇḍā-ḍhiṭuāgahi kīyyā mūcyā-dara, oṇṭā mōhar khirryā-kī[4], uṭṭā dara ciccā. Nannā ullā, onghon

---

[1] Will pass the day '. [2] Cooked rice in which a little *marua* flour has been mixed. It is the meal of poor people. The reddish appearance of the mixture justifies its name, (*lit.* pyrite rice). [3] *Calī*, the three or four feet of open ground immediately in front of a house.

[4] *Khindyā*, from *khōndnā*, *khirryā*, from *kherrnā*.

kank ondras k͟hanē, ād meñjā : 'Anā hō ningbai ālī ra'ī '? Ās bācas : 'Nīn mal kadrār'oi hōle, ēn tengon'. Ād bācā : 'Tengā, mudhū'. Ās anyas : 'Nīnim gā taldī '!.

Abīrim ād isung dara bālkā dara kicrī dara amm otthrā kī tangālasin k͟hajjyā ; anti emtācā dara maṇḍī oicā. Bēlas gusan hāl taiyā : Enghai ālas barcas. K͟hanē bēlas monjrā ci'āge keras Āsin urmī kōṛē gandan meñjas[1] kī irbārin bācas : 'Nīm ayangbang ta'dar, ēm k͟haddam. Emhai nanjkan[2] ōnā ra'ake'. Anti ā ālas tangyon bhāirin, tambāsin hō, ondras ; dara ār ōrmar, mundhtā lekh'ā, ā ālīgahi bangītī kōṛem ujjyar ukkyar.

—A family man had seven sons : he married them all. The elder son's wife (*lit.* the elder d.-in-law) had a lucky hand : owing to this circumstance all (the members of the household) earned their living. But the old man was drunk every day : he had no appetite even for rice, so constantly was he buried in his cups. One day a brahmin turned up ; he used to beg carrying a deity in a small basket. The old man said to him : 'My daughter-in-law does not cook rice or anything for me ; what do you say to that'? After some incantations the mendicant said : 'Send away thy elder daughter-in-law : she is a witch'. The old man held a family council, and reported the brahmin's advice. They said : 'So expel her'.

The eldest son loved his wife dearly. He told her : Take with thee as much money and paddy and rice as thou art able to carry'. She put some money in a basket, and, on the top, one measure of unbleached rice, and left the house ; her husband went out with her in the direction of her parents' house, to show her the way. This walk took them quite a long way off. Then, unable to part with each other, they sat down. She first cleaned his hair ; and next, as she felt drowsy, she lay down upon the end of his loincloth. When she fell asleep he, with his chignon-knife, cut the cloth, then withdrew and returned home. As she awoke, seeing (what had happened), she had a good cry.

---

[1] *Lit.* he questioned him about joys and sorrows, he made him all sorts of kind questions.

[2] One of the meanings of *nannā* is 'to cook'. *Emhai nanjkan*, our own cooking.

She walked on for some distance, when the sun went down. Noticing one lofty tree near a coppice-wood, she retired (below it) for her night rest. There were crows at roost upon that tree. About midnight these birds awoke and began to chatter. 'Where did you go to feed yesterday'?—'There is to the north a village, whose king is ill: his ears are festering. A number of worms have formed in them: whenever one of these showed, we had a peck at it'.—'How can that sore get healed'?—'Should one lay a little of our dung in the ears, they would be cured surely'. The woman was overhearing all this conversation. She got up, dropped a little crow-dung into a leaf-sachet which she put into her basket, and she turned her steps towards that village. Some people were bathing in its tank; they were discussing whether the king would pass the day. Hearing this, she said: 'What ails the king'? They told her. 'Woman, they said, what is thy work? what's there in thy basket'?—'Medicinal roots'[1] she said.—They replied: 'Woman, thou knowest about medicine; come, see our king'. So she went and saw the king. She took the worms out and, making the crow-dung into powder, dropped (a little of it) into the ears. All the purulent matter was thereby desiccated. Within a half day's time the king got up and had a meal. To that woman he gave house, clothes and maintenance, calling her his 'mother-doctor'.

About that time her father-in-law became very poor. When even marua rice and leguminous plants failed, he and his children began to eat sparingly (longing for more). When nothing was left, the seven brothers went about together, carrying fuel-wood for sale: (one faggot) for two pice or one anna. It once happened that the elder brother brought wood at that woman's door. She recognized him, bought his wood and asked: 'Wilt thou have a pumpkin, old man'?—'Give away, mother' he said. She passed a knife below the pumpkin peduncle, slipped in a gold mohar, closed the cut and handed the fruit over to him. On another day, as he was bringing wood, she asked: 'I say man, hast thou a wife'? He answered: 'If you shan't feel offended, I will tell'.—'Tell me, master.'—He said: 'It is yourself.'

[1] Properly 'roots for making yeast'; hence, by extension, medicinal herbs and roots.

Then and there, she brought out oil and saffron and clothes and water, and gave a head-wash to her husband; then she made him bathe and put a meal before him. She sent word to the king: 'My husband has come back'. And the king came over to salute him. He made him all sort of kind inquiries, and said to both: 'You are my father and mother, I am your son. You will stay here and live at my expense'. In time, the man brought over his mother and brothers and even his father; and all of them, as in former days, lived in plenty and happiness, owing to the good luck of that woman.

31.—*Kukoi-k͟haddā dara Bisāhī.* *The Little Girl and the Witch.*

Pācējhan ṭurā k͟haddar rahcar. Kukkor k͟hall-ukhṛīgahi tihānim ballūlagyar. Ār sendrā kālā kālā abṛā mōkhālagyar, dara, endra'ādim manō, annūhō̃ oṇṭē tihā hō̃ mal laggālagyā. Ārgahi oṇṭā sannī tangṛī rahcā: ād eṛpā nū sagarkhanē ra'ālagyā. Undul ennē mañjā sannis oṇṭā dau dauim pūpan mējhras-kī eṛpā bardas. Kōhar āsin bāckar rahcar: 'Ambā mējhra'ā: maī̃ ērō hōle, nam gane bar'ā beddō'. Pahē ās malā ambyas. Kukoi, ā pūpan ērā tapṛem, ānā helrā: 'Idigahi mann eksan k͟hakkhri'ī'? Sannis bācas: 'Eksan ōṛā-k͟hāk͟hā hō̃ malā kai dara ālar āṛsā polnar, asan'. K͟hanē ād bācā: 'Ēn hō̃ asan kālon'.

Nannā ullā, pairim cōcar k͟hanē, ād sangem kālāge tussā-bekkhā[1] helrā. Kōhar malā mancar. Ār sarābācar kī sannisgahi mundh-bhāre hō̃ urkhar. Sannis adigahi kirta'ānā nū tīryas; k͟hok͟hānū adin sangem bar'ā ciccas. Kānum kānum ād ennē k͟hardyā ekattī tanghai muddī dara balan hō'āge pullī; k͟hanē ās ceḍḍas. Akai ṭoṛang nū biṛī puttyā. Kōhar malā k͟hakkhrar k͟hanē, ās ṭoṛang-kandā ark͟hyas dara irbārim mokkhar. Nannā ullā ās ārin beddāge tangṛin ambyas dara ekā ekā gecohā keras.

Āulam saītnū oṇṭā bēlas ā ḍabrēnum sendrā tartī kirrālagyas. Ās jōk͟hārin ānyas. 'Isan ērā. Hukan onta'ā'. Ār oṇṭā mann nū argyar kī attrā-ittrā ērā helrar. Ortos bācas: 'Abai gā ṭuiṭuira'ā mojk͟hā cu'ī'.[2] Ā addā gusan āṛsyar kī ānā helrar: 'Nā ra'adar?

---

[1] Or. Dict. *bekkhnā.*

[2] *Cu'ī*, from *ce'gna.* See above l. 1 *pulli.*

Cicc ci'ai'. K̲h̲anē ād hebṛā hebṛā ci'ī. Ār nirk̲h̲nar tuppā tuppā, dara ānnar : 'K̲h̲ekkhā nū, k̲h̲ekkhā nū ci'ai'. K̲h̲anē ād ciocā. Ār kerar dara bēlāsin ānyar : 'Ort ālī asan ra'ī : ād bīṛintī koṛhem sughaṛ itthri'ī'. Bēlas tānim keras, mundhtar lekh'ā cioc nēcas. Ād āsgc hō hebṛā hebṛā ci'ī, ās hō tēbdas dara k̲h̲ekkhānum nē'edas. Abīrī adin dhardas dara hō'odas...Ād endr nanō ? Tanghai kiorin khaṇḍā khaṇḍa, ḍahrē nū ṭīḍḍā ṭiḍḍā kerā.

Ormā bhāir ā aḍḍā nū barcar k̲h̲anē, endr ērnar, ārgahi tangṛī malkī. Ār bācar : 'Gucā, beddā kālot'. Sannis jokk gecchā īkyaskī ērdas adigahi ledrā ledrā ḍahrē nū khatrkī ra'ī.. Lakh'ā lakh'ā petkas keras. Annem annem bēlasgahi mahal īṛsyas.

Bakhṛē ulā kōrcas k̲h̲anē, asan cạṭā bisāhī paccō cukumuku ukkī ra'ī. Ād eka'ārem saṭh'anā khisār'ā helrā dara āsin mākgahi muṭṭhan nū badlācā. Ā k̲h̲attā kukkos gohom-k̲h̲all nū bongas ; pahē, īryar-kī, ā paddantā ālar gaṇḍas dara ballū dera taṛrī dara barchā dara urmī piṭnā-hathyārin dharcar kī khed'ā helrar. Ābīrī ā kukoi eṛpā mañyā argyā dara mēk̲h̲ālagyā : 'Bongā dadā ! bongā dadā' ! Ās āndas : 'Kīyyā gā k̲h̲eḍḍ mulk̲h̲yā, dara mañyā marg ṭhekcā : eksan[1] bongon' ? Ālar āsin balnum piṭā k̲h̲acoyar...

Ahṛan khaṭcar ; bēlasge hō iṛtāge occar. Khaṭ'us-iṛtus ā ahṛan iṛyā helras k̲h̲anē, ād ānā-dara cīk̲h̲ā helrā : 'Hō'ō babū, durō[2] : ālargahi ahṛan malā mōk̲h̲on'. Bēlas meñjas dara bācas : 'Nīn endr ba'adī' ? K̲h̲anē ād tingyā 'Engdadas (bā[illegible]ā) māk-mañjas-kī barcas ; āsin piṭyar : āsgahi k̲h̲ēs ahṛā talī'. Idin menā tapṛem, bēlas urmī ahṛā dara k̲h̲ēs rahcā, adin nēcas dara k̲h̲uppyas, kī kierī jhapcas...Ābīrim ā kukkos kirr ujjyas ; dara ās tangṛī ganē ra'ā helras.

—Five children were orphans. Of the cares which attend agriculture the boys knew nothing. They subsisted on the produce of their chase and, whatever happened, they did not trouble about it. They had a little sister : she used to stay at home. One day the

[1] Here *eksan* ? does not mean *where* ? (for this, *eksāvrā* should be used). The meaning is : *how possibly* ?

[2] Meaningless words to appease a child or lull him to sleep. The girl talks to herself in a mournful mood, to attract the king's attention.

youngest boy came back with a most beautiful flower in his hair. His elder brothers had told him : 'Don't put on that flower ; if the girl sees it, she will want to come with us'. But he did not throw it. No sooner did the girl see that flower than she started questions : 'Where's the tree which bears this flower' ? Her brother said : 'Where crows never go, where men cannot reach'. She replied : 'I too must go there'.

When they got up next day, her desire to go with them made her weep, but the elder brothers did not mind her. They hastened off, in advance of the youngest boy. The latter was delayed by his efforts to dissuade her (*lit.* to cause her to go back), and finally allowed her to accompany him. On her way she grew so tired that she was unable to carry her very rings and armlets ; he then carried her. The sun set down when they were (still) in the depths of the forest. As the elder boys were not to be found, he dug up some wild roots, and he and she had a meal. On the next day, he left her by herself to start in search of the others, and he went far away.

Just on that day a king returning from a hunt passed by that road. He said to his servant : Have a look about here. Give me my hookah'. They climbed up a tree and began to look all round One of them said : 'Down there, some smoke is curling up'. They went to the place and said : 'Who's here ? Give us fire'. She, from a distance, threw them some live embers (*lit.* fire). They extinguished them with their spittle and said : 'In our hands, in our hands' ! She complied. On their return they told the king : 'A woman is there, who looks more beautiful than a queen'. The king himself went to her and, like his servants (*lit.* like the preceding ones), asked for fire. She threw embers to him too ; he too put them out, and asked to be given some in his hand. That moment he seized her and took her along... What could she do ? She went, tearing (meanwhile) her garment to small pieces and dropping them on the road.

When all the brothers arrived at the spot, what do they see, but that their little sister has disappeared. They said : 'Come along ; let us search for her'. The youngest had not walked far, when he notices that rags (having belonged) to her are on the ground. He picked them up, recognizing them more and more clearly. And thus he arrived at to the king's residence.

As he entered the yard, there was an old witch squatting (in a corner). She somehow got suddenly angry (with him) and turned him into a deer. The pcor boy fled into a wheat-field ; but, having caught sight of him, the villagers went for him with hatchets, pole-axes, long knives, spears and other weapons. That moment the girl ascended on the house-top and was shouting : 'Run away, brother ! run away, brother'. He said : 'Below, my feet are caught (in the mud) ; upwards, my antlers are caught (in branches) : how can I flee' ? The (hunters), all unconscious (of his identity), did kill him...

They divided the meat and brought some to the king for his curry. When the cook wanted to roast it, the girl began to sob, saying : 'Sleep, o boy, do sleep ; I will not eat human flesh.' The king heard her and asked : 'What doest thou say' ? She told him : 'My brother, turned into a deer, had come this way ; they have killed him, this is his flesh and blood'. The king no sooner heard this than he asked for all that was left of the blood and flesh, he put it all in a heap and covered it with a cloth...instantly the boy returned to life. He henceforth remained with his little sister.

32.—*Raṇḍī Paccō dara Sārū Kuãras. The Widow and Prince Sāru.*

Ort raṇḍī paccō rahcā, ād bēlasgahi eṛpā nū pellō rahcā. Dālīgahi muṛguṭṭhin[1] ara adarguṭṭhin hō'ar hō'ar mōkhā-ōuālagyā ; biṛiguṭṭhiarge, pup malkō bīrī, ād ārge tokkhā tokkhā ondor ondor ci'ālagyā. Undul ennē manjā, bēlasge sakhin mōcālagyā khanē, ā mukkan bāoar : 'Īd malā bi'ō ; ambai mōcai'. I accō ānyā : 'Innā engāge cunī khudī ambō ci'ē[2] : idin ci'ē'. Ā sakhin eṛpā occā, annuhō̃ pāce ullā gūṭī malā mūcyā dara malā amkhī iṛtyā...Khōkhānū ād lajjen khōkhyā kī bāoā : 'Engdābagāro, āulā uēo'an dara occ'an, ā sakhin-

---

1. *Muṛ*, properly the 'reproductive germ' of pulse grains.

2. A woman, talking with persons of her sex or (as here) to herself, uses special forms of verbs. The first two paragraphs of this story offer several instances of this. Gramm. pp. 68 to 72.

kukk, tīkhil goṭṭam malkātī, malā mukkhin ra'en'. Biṛīguṭṭhiar adigo ōnd āṛkō tīkhil bakhrā ciccar.

Ād ā sakhingahi kukkan mōcāge basgā helrā khanē, oṇṭā cāl mendrā: 'Ān paccō, mendī kā? engan tani tani basgai'. Ād ānyā: 'Nē ba'anai?, bācā, dara ultī bongkī bongkī urkhā. Khōkhā kirryā darā, basgī khanē, annem minī: khanē basgyādim. Palkā helrā khanē, ā sakhin ānā helrā: 'Ān paccō, mendī kā? majhīnum majhīnum palak'. Majhīnum palkyā-dara endran īrī? oṇṭā kukkō-khadd! Ād jiyā jiyā bācā: 'En isin betro'on hōle, ālar ānor īd eksan khadd biddyā (ba'or) kī alkhor'. Ennē ā khaddan eṛpā ultī malā otthrā. Ād āsgahi nāmē Saru Kuār pinjyā.

Ās pardā helras khanē, ekā ekā sōbhdas. Jōkh mañjas, ābīrī ās undul 'ekāsē rājī ra'ī'? bācas-kī eṛpantī chachem urkhas[1]. Ḍahrē nū ukkyas kī bāgra'ā helras: āsgahi cuṭṭī dighā dighā rahcā.

Laṇḍī luhāṛī[2] mañjā khanē, bēlasgahi tangdā em'āge kālālagyā, ābīrī ād Sārūsin īryā dara mōghārā[3] kerā. Hāṛī ēkāge malā biddyā. Ād khōkhā tarā kirryā, tambasgahi eṛpā kōrcā kī cūtyā, dara naṛī kach'ā helrā, dara maṇḍī amkhī ambyā ḍhilcā. Bēlas ōnāge ukkyas khanē, beddā helras: 'Kukoi ekhō[4] ra'ī'? Bīṛī ānyā: 'Endrge[5] ād ōnā malā biddī'. Anti adin khōb meñjar. Munjā nū ād bācā: 'Sārū kukkōsin eng gane beñjor hōle, maṇḍī ōnon' bācā. Bīṛī bēlas ā raṇḍī paccon ēṛ'arkī adin ānyar: 'Ningdāsin ci'ai'. Ād ciccā, dara irbārim rāe lekh'ā benjrar.

Undul bēlas dara bēl-kukkor ormar, dara Sārus hō, oṇṭā gecohā ṭoṛang nū sendrā kerar. Neokhrā khanē, ūr ammōnkā sār'ā helrar. Pahē ekā gusan amm ōnāge kānar, asānim amm sath-saṭh'anā khāyī. Oṇṭā gaḍḍī pōkhārī nū kerar: īd hō battī kai. Khanē bēlas yād nañjas ī ṭoṛang nū ḍherim nād ra'ī. Ās ānā helras: 'Cī, pōkhārī, amm, ēn mankhā dāṛē ci'on[6]'. Nannā ortos ānyas 'ēn khēr ci'on':

---

[1] In this idiom *rājī* has the sense of 'world'.

[2] *Laṇḍī luhāṛī*, breakfast time, about 9-30 a.m.

[3] This verb has two forms *mōghārnā* and *mōghrnā*; both have the same meaning.

[4] *Ekhō*?, and not *eksan*? because the speaker assumes that his daughter is somewhere near by, though not actually seen by him.

[5] Pregnant use of interrogatives. The sense is: '*I do not know* why she does not want to eat'. See Gramm. p. 51, 23.

[6] *Dāṛē ci'inā*, to offer in sacrifice, to immolate; *lit.* to give as victim.

nannas : 'ēn meṛhō ci'on'. Khōkhānū Sārus, ghōṛō argkā-bārī, ār gusan āṛsyas. Ghōṛōgahi khaḍḍ rittā mulkhā belrā, anti mūkā, anti keṛmā, anti kūl, anti eōkh : ennē mannum mannum ghōṛō dara Sārus hō mulkhyar khanē, amm urkhā...Khanē gā ōrmar khōb eicā helrar kī eṛpā bongar. Ā kukoi menā helrā : 'Okhō bang, Sārus? Okhō dadā, Sārus'? Tingyar ; khanē ād beldāge urkhā dara ā mulukhkā pōkhārī gusan āṛsyā : 'Ekhō, enghai Sārū, ra'adai'. Ās bācas : 'Ohrē, oṇṭa nād engan pokhārī ultī urkhā malā ci'ī'. Ā kukoi lūr-akh'ū a'ālagyā. Ād āulantim Sārusge hō, dara ā nādge hō, dau dauim ōnnā-mōkhnan ullā ullā ondra'ā helrā. Nād bēs lekh'ā copkārkī rahcā khanē, ād undul dighā-aoc-ra ū jiñjon ondrā kī 'Ondai, nād' bācā. Nādgahi melkhā nū oṇṭā aoc hiṭingyā : āganem Sārus cāṛē urkhas Irbar eṛpā kirryar kī kōṛem ra'ā helrar.

—There was a widow who had some employment in the royal household. She used to have the waste of pulse grains and pounded rice to live upon, and, when the queens wanted flowers, she went to pluck some, which she brought to them. One day, as she was about to cut a pumpkin open for the king, the queens said to her : 'This one won't cook (well), do not open it'. The old woman said : 'To-day give me neither broken pulse grains nor broken rice : give me this'. She took that pumpkin to her house, but for five days did not cut it up to make curry with it...At length, laying shame aside, she said (to the queens) : 'Daughters, the pumpkin which I asked for and obtained the other day, I have not eaten yet for lack of unbroken rice grains'. The queens gave her one measure of rice as a gratification.

When she set about peeling that pumpkin previous to opening it, a voice was heard : 'Look here, old woman, peel me just a little.' The woman said : 'Who is talking ?' and she ran out of her house. She came back and, on resuming her work, hears the same voice : this time she did peel the pumpkin. As she (next) wanted to split it, the pumpkin said : 'Look here, old woman, split me just in the middle'. So she did, and what does she find but a baby-boy ! She said to herself : 'Were I carry him about in a cloth at my back, people would wonder whence I have got a child and laugh. So she did not take that baby out of her house. She named him 'Prince Sāru'.

In growing up he became very beautiful. One day, when he was a lad already, he said: '(I must see) how the world is made', and he secretly went out of the house. He sat down by the roadside, and combed his hair, which was very long.

About nine o'clock in the morning, as the king's daughter was going out for her bath, she saw Sāru and felt fascinated. She did not want to go further. She returned to her father's house and lost all appetite for curry and rice. When the king sat down to meal, he asked: 'Where is the girl'? The queen replied: 'She does not want to eat, (I do not know) why'. They pressed her with questions. At last she said: 'If you marry me to young Sāru, I will eat'. The king and queen called the widow and said: 'Give us thy son'. She did so, and the pair was duly married.

One day the king, with all his sons and also Sāru, went to a distant forest for a hunt. As the sun was still very high, they became thirsty. But wherever they go for a drink, the water suddenly dries up .. They went to a deep pond, this also sinks down .. The king then remembered that, in that forest, there were many demons. He said: 'O pond, give us water, I shall offer thee a buffalo'. Another said: 'I shall offer a fowl'; another still: 'a sheep'. Sāru on horseback came up (only) after this. Immediately his horse's feet sank (into some quicksand), then its knees, haunches, belly and chest: and, when degree by degree Sāru and the animal disappeared, water welled up. The whole party took fright and ran for home. The girl began to ask: 'Father, where is Sāru? Brother, where is Sāru'? They told her. She went out in search of him and reached the pond into which the man had sunk (*lit.* the pond of the sinking): 'My Sāru, where art thou'? He said: 'Alas! a demon keeps me from coming out of this pond'. The girl was clever. Henceforth she brought, day after day, excellent food and drink for Sāru, and for the demon as well. When the latter had lost all distrust, she once brought fish with long bones. 'Eat, demon', she said. One bone stuck in the demon's throat, and Sāru at once got out. He and she went home and they had a happy life together.

33.—*Lūr-uyyurgahi Katthā. The Horoscope.*

Oṇṭā urbasgahi ort roṭ'ō tangdas rahcas. Is kundras khanē, lūr-uyyar barcar. Tambas meñjas ī khaddasgahi ekāse ekāse uliā ka'ō. Ār bācar: 'Is gā jokk ullāge iyyam barcas: ekā uliā īsgahi beñjā manō, āulā lakṛā hō'ō.' Ī katthan meñjar-kī tangyō tambas dara sendrā kālā malā ciccar, dara ṭoṛang-aḍḍā nū otkham iklā hō̃ mal ambyar.

Ā kukkos pardyas khanē, ār āsgahi beñjāge kharā baggē ōnnā mōkhnāguṭṭhin, kiorī sañjgiguṭṭhin khindyar, dara naumahlan[1] hō̃ kamtācar. Kukkos barāt occas dara ekā kōṛhē [2]ōhmā ganē keras. Beñjā mañjā khanē, irbar rokkā bidā mañjar dara erpā kīrrā helrar.

Pahiē nū, jahāj ulam, ās lācas: 'Innāgem, ānyar lūr-akh'ur, engan lakṛā dhar'ō. Pahē kōṛem -urmī mañjā kerā, dara daulē kālagdat'. Ād meñjā: 'Nin lakṛātī kharā elcdai hūtā'? Ās lācas: 'Ekāse muṭṭhan trū ād ra'ī, adin ērā hō̃ argan'[3]. Anti kanyā meñjā: 'Ēroi'? Khanē ād, bālkā khasskā asmāgahi engrkā uikā rahcā,[4] adin dharcā kī lakṛāgahi muṭṭhan kamcā...Īd āganem ujnā mañjā dara āsin dhar'arkī ṭoṛang tarā occā. Munddhtā ānkā lekh'ā mañjā.

—A rich man had an only son. Casters of nativities came at his birth. The father asked them how this boy would fare in life. They said: 'This child has come into the world for a short stay only: on the day of his wedding, he shall be caught by a tiger'. Knowing this, his parents did not allow him to go hunting, and never left him by himself in a jungly spot. When he had grown up they made, for his marriage, large purchases of eatables and drink, of clothes and other things, and ordered a huge wedding-litter for

[1] *Naumahāl, lit.* a nine-storey litter, a huge wedding litter in which as many as fifty persons can find place.

[2] *Ekā koṛhē,* ohmā, lit. any amount of splendour.

[3] *Argan,* see Or. Gramm. p. 91 n. 36, and Dict. |*arg(nā).*

[4] *Lit.* what had been put by, as remainder, of a cake sprinkled over with turmeric.

him. The young man led out the bridal party and had a very brilliant progress. After the ceremony he and his bride left immediately for home.

On their way back he, within the litter, remarked: 'It is to-day, according to horoscopists, that a tiger must catch me. But everything has come off very well and we are going back quietly'. She inquired: 'Probably thou art much in fear of tigers'? He said: 'So far, I do not even know what a tiger is like'. His bride asked: 'Wilt thou see'? And, taking in her hand what was left of a saffron cake, she kneaded it into the figure of a tiger. It immediately became endowed with life and, catching him, carried him off to the woods. The prophecy came true.

34.—*Sirupādes dara Ekkā.* *The Jackal and the Tortoise.*

Oṇṭā bambhnas rahcas, ās ullā ullā tembā tembā tanghai kūlan uṛdālagyas. Undul āsge ḍahrē nū oṇṭā ekkā-khadd khakkhrā, ās adin pettas kī bācas: 'Innā gā bēs tembon-kī ahṛā mōkhon'. Kānum kānum oṇṭā khāṛ gusan āṛsyas khanē, ā ekkā ānyā: 'Anā bambhnā hoi, ī khāṛ gusan engan uyyar ci'ā: khāṛ nū baṛhī nīndō hōle, ēn argo'oñ'kī kaṭṭo'on ci'on'.' Ā bambhnas bujhras: 'Bēsim ba'ī; ēn gā ullā ullā tembāge bardan'. Adin asānim uyyas ciccas.

Pardyā khane, undul baṛhī nīnd'ā khanē, bambhnas ekkan eḍḍas. Ād barcā dara āsin argā[1] kī hō'ā helrā. Majhā majhīnum āṛsyā kī āsin ānyā: 'Anā bambhnā hoi, āulā gā engan mōkhā beddālakkai; Innā endr? innā mulkhto'on ci'on'. Ābīrim salt nū oṇṭā sirupādes[2] ā khāṛ tarā bar'ālāgyas. Bambhnas ānyas: 'Ṭhaukam, mulkhto'oi gā mulkhto'oi; pahē tani ū Sirupādesin menai endr ba'das: anti ek'am nanoi'. Ekkā gecchantī mīkhyā: 'Endr, sirupādē, ī bambhnāsin mulkhto'on? āulā engan mōkhā beddālagyas'. Sirupādes bambhnāsin bacchāba'āge tihā nañjas. Ās meñjas-kī bēgar meñjkā mañjas[3] dara ekkán ānyas: 'Oṇṭā khebdā mal minī; tani kūṭī tarā barai. Endr ba'adi'? Antī ekkā ṭani kūṭī tarā barcā kī onghon

---

[1] *Arga'ānā* is a synonym to *argta'ānā*, to cause one to mount. The Perfect tense of *arga'āna* has two forms, one regular *argāchan*, and one irregular (see l. 9) *arghan*.

[2] *Sirupādes*, though properly a nickname of the personified jackal ('Pandit Siru') is occasionally used, without change in accidence, as a common name.

[3] Having heard, he made as a (man) who hasn't heard.

meñjā: 'Endr bambhnāsin mulkhtō'on? undul engan mōkhā beddālagyas'. Sirupādes bācas: 'Tani kūṭī tarā bar'ar kī ānai; hōle katthā mendro'ō'. Ennem ṭhaknum ṭhaknum Sirupādes ekkan kūṭī gūṭī eḍḍas. Kūṭīnum āṛsyā khanē, bambhnāsin Sirupādes ānyas: 'Ḍeg'ā bambhnā hoi! endran ērdai'? Bambhnas ḍegcas cicas dara bongas.

Aulantim ekkā Sirupādesin dhirāba'ā helrā. Ād ānyā: 'Āmm ōnā bar'oi hōle, ēn ningan dhar'cn'. Ā cigālō amm onā kerā khanē, ekkā adigahi kheḍḍnim dharcā dara bācā: 'Dharckan; eksan bongoi'? Sirupādes bācas: 'Dhar'ā gā pulkī: pōṛoi pādan[3] gā dharckī'! khanē ekkā cāṛē cāṛē kheḍḍan ambyā dara heddetā pōṛoi pādan dharcā. Sirupādes baechras.

Antile ekkā bācā: 'Ērke! nīn ḍhekārı sekra'ā bar'oi, ābīrī ningan dhar'on'. Undul Sirupādes attrā ḍhekārī sekhra'ā keras; ās jiyā jiyā āndas: 'Hō, ād dinkī ī aḍḍā 'okkā okkā' ba'ī: pahē innā gā endr hō mal ba'ī.' Khanē tān ekkāgahi cāltī mēkhā helras: 'Okkā! okkā'! I cāl menarkī adige ānābiṛdā urkhā: 'Okkā! okkā'! Sirupādes angal alkhyas kī bācas: 'Ha'ī; asānim ra'adī'. Astik bongas.

Antile ekkā endr nangū nañjā? Tangdābagārin ānyā: 'Kalā babū: Sirupādesin ānke: 'gucā, ingyō kecoā; māṛāge gucā'. Ekkāgahi khaddguṭṭhī adigahi ānkā lekh'ā, Sirupādes gusan kerā dara ānyā: 'Gucā; ingyō gā kecoā kerā'. Tangdābagārin sikhābackī rahcā: 'Nīm, māṛā ho'ōbīrī, kukk tarā dharta'ākē; hōlē en āsin khakkhon'. Sirupādes bācas, pahē kukk tarā malā dharcas: ekkāgahi tangdābagarīnim attrā dhartācas. Ḍahrē nū Sirupādes ānyas: 'Mār rē, kecokā gā khann aṇḍri'ī! id minkhī eklā rahcā'! Khanē gā Sirupādes khisār'ā helras. Uiyāge bācas, kōhā pakhnau cōdas dara ekkāgahi kukk nū kacrācas. Ād āsin ek'am örtī dhar'ā pollā.

—There was a brahmin who kept body and soul together by continual begging. One day he found a young tortoise on the road;

---

[1] Passive voice of *mennā*.

[2] See story 31, l. 41.

[3] *Pōṛoi mann* or *poṛhō mann*, a tree which grows along streams and gullies, its roots plunging into water. The roots bear a small guava-like fruit.

he picked it up and said: 'Good begging to-day; I shall have meat'. As he came near a river, the tortoise said: 'Eh brahmin, put me down in this stream: whenever there will be a flood here, I shall take thee on my back and carry thee to the other bank'. The brahmin thought: 'She is right, for my begging brings me here every day'. He did put her down there.

When she had attained her full size, one day as the river was in a flood, the brahmin called for the tortoise. She came, made him mount and started. When she was in middle stream, she told him: 'I say brahmin, that other day thou wantedst to eat me; what of that to-day? to-day I shall drown thee'. Just then a jackal was coming (down) to the river side. The brahmin replied: 'All right, drown me, do drown me. However, just ask yonder jackal for his advice: after that, thou wilt do whatever (thou likest)'. The tortoise shouted from afar: 'Sirupande, should I drown this brahmin? the other day he wanted to eat me'. The jackal had a mind to save the brahmin. He made a pretence of not having heard and said: 'I am deaf of one ear; come a little this side; what doest thou say'? So the tortoise took some steps towards the river side and asked once more: 'Shall I drown this brahmin? once he wanted to eat me'. Sirupande replied: 'Speak when thou art a little nearer: then I shall be able to catch what thou sayest'. By tricking her in this way, Sirupande got (*lit.* called) the tortoise quite close to the streamside. When she reached it, he said to the brahmin: 'Jump down, thou brahmin! What art thou looking at'? The brahmin jumped down and ran away.

From that day the tortoise was engaged in laying traps for (*lit.* in threatening) the jackal. She said: 'When thou comest to drink, I shall catch thee'. And as the jackal went there (one day) for a drink, she, sure enough caught him by the foot; she said: 'I have got thee; try to run off'. The jackal answered: 'Thou hasn't got me; it's a poroi-root that thou hast caught'. The tortoise immediately let the foot go and seized a poroi-root near by. Sirupande went scot free.

Next, the tortoise said: 'Take care! When thou comest to warm thee in the morning sun, I shall have thee'. One morning Sirupande went that side to warm himself. He thought: 'Halloo, here every day she shouts *okkā okkā*; to-day she is silent'. There mimicking the tortoise voice he himself shouted: *okkā! okkā!* The reply escaped her: '*Okkā! okkā*'! Sirupande laughed heartily and said: 'Yes, thou art there', and he decamped.

What was the tortoise's next trick? She said to her children: 'Sons, go and tell the jackal to come, that mother is dead, that he should bury her'. The tortoise's children went as they were told and said: 'Come, mother is dead'. She had recommended to her children: 'When the moment comes for removing the body, make him take hold of me on the head side; thus I shall have him.' Sirupande came, but he did not catch hold of the head side; he put there (*lit.* had her seized on that side by) her children. On the way Sirupande, exclaimed: 'By Jove, the dead opens her eyes! she was only closing her lids'! Then the jackal got angry in real earnest. He had (the stretcher) laid down, lifted up a big stone and flung it at the head of the tortoise. Never had she succeeded in getting the better of him.

35.—*Irb Bhuccaṛ khaddar.* *The Two Little Scamps.*

Kā̃nā dara Kujā nāmē irb bhāir rahcar; ār ort gōllas gusan jō̃kh ra'ālagyar. Kā̃nāsin ēṛā khāpta'ālagyar dara Kujāsin khadd bēstāta' ālagyar.[1] Undul eṛpantā ālar nalakh tarā urkhuar ābīrī, Kujāsin ānyar: Babus erkhos hōle, pakhṛā'ake dara jhaṭṭā nū arta'āke. Kānāsin ānyar: 'Nīn ēṛan, māsi-khall[2] nū ghāsē ra'ī, ayyam menta'ā hō'oke'.

Īs māsī-khall nū ēṛan menta'ā occas. Māsīguṭṭhi cankārkī rahcā Kā̃nas cabdas mōkhdas. Khatrkā māsin ēṛā hō̃ pesī dara kaṭarkuṭurra'ā mūkhī. Khanē Kā̃nas khisār'ā belras. 'Ē̃ṛā enghai cabnan bhesri'ī mil'ī'? bācas'. Ās abṛā urmī ēṛan piṭyas ciccas.—Ā madhem gollasgahi eṛpā tarā endr mañjā? Lelles Kujas mañyā irkhyas. Ās

(1) Double causal of *bēcnā*, to dance, to play. The first causal (irreg.) is *bēsta'ānā*, to cause one to play, to amuse one. The root of the latter is *bēstā*: hence the 2nd causal *bēstāta'ānā*, to order one to amuse (e.g. a child).

(2) *Masi*, a roundish black bean, in Hindi 'urid' (*Phaseolus Mungo*).

babūsin pakhṛācas dara thelthelambācas kī jhaṭṭā nū artācas ciccas.

Ērā-khāpus eṛpā barcas khanē, Kujas meñjas : 'Ekhō, Kānā, ēṛā hō' ? Kānas urmī katthan tingyas; dara khōkhānū meñjas : 'Anā kō, ekhō khaddas' [2] Kujas hō urmin tingyas. Anti Kānas bācas : 'Ana Kujai, ningan kicrīnim pakhṛa'āge bācar. Khanē khaddāsin pakhṛāckai ! Ningan eṛpantā ālar lau'or' ! Kujas hō ānyas : 'Anā kō, ningan ēṛā menta'ā taiyar, khanē piṭkai : ningan hō lau'orim : gucā ho, istā bongot'. —'Bongot hōle, endran ōnot hō' ?—Gucā kō, piṭkai abṛā ēṛān mōkhot'. Oṇṭā ēṛan ṭoṛang tarā occar. Mokkhar khanē, adigahi poṭṭan hō'arkī hāṛī kerar.

Mākhā mañjā khanē oṛtā mann nū argyar. Ennē mañjā ā aḍḍānum ort bēlas dara āsgahi jōkhar ḍērā nanā barcar. Bēlasgahi khaṭi ṭhaukam ājgo ([2]) attkā rahcā' ekā ajgō Kānas Kujas argkar rahcar. Ormar khandrar khanē, Kānas ā ēṛā-pottan bēlasgahi Kūlnum alghem alghem ettācas dara ciccas. Ukhā rahcā, jōkhar madher nē nē saītnū oōcar kī bēlasgahi poṭṭā urkhkā bujhrar. Khanē ōrmar gobār nanā helrar. dara urmin ambā bongar. Bēlas ejjras kī ās nantaram bongas keras. Khanē ā khaddar manntī ittyar. Kānas dharcas dhulkin, dara Kujas dharcas phirī taṛri, dara kerar. Ā ṭoṛangnum ōnd aḍḍā eō dumbā dara bhaōrō khakkhrā : abṛan Kānas tanghai dhulkī nū sajjas dara muṇḍhcas.

Ārge khōkhānū ā bēlas gane laucnakhrnā mañjā. Āsgahi ḍhēr bagge telengar ra'ālagyar ! Īr, Kānas dara Kujas, irb rot'ō. Kānas dhulkin khōb assdas, dara Kujas phirī taṛrī trū uchlār uchlār nāldas. Ekābīrī khōb bandukgahi gulī ār mañyā hebṛar'ālagyā' ([3]), ābīri Kānas tanghai dhulkin umpyas : khanē antham ḍhēr baggē dumbā bhaōrō urkhā dara telengārin parmā ntgā helrā. Telengar mīkhyar : 'Erā, Kānai Kujai, eman bacchāba'ā. Manāba'ā, manāba'ā ! Em nimāge ī rājin ci'om'. Kānas abṛan manābācas. Irbarge kainōgoṭang paddā khakkhrā, dara ār abṛā paddā trū ujjā okkā helrar.

([1]) *Thelthelamba'anā* to render quite soft by hammering, kneading, etc.

([2]) *Ajgō* (opp. *ijgō*, *hujgō*) in that direction, on that side. See Dict. *ujgo*, *ajgō*.

([3]) *Lit.* were throwing themselves (reflex. of *hebṛnā*, to throw).

—Two brothers, Kāna and Kuja, were employed in a landowner's house. Kāna was put to tend the goats and Kuja to amuse the child. One day, the people of the household going out to their work told Kuja: 'Should the baby soil thee, thou shalt just give a knock against the ground, and hang it up to dry on the wooden fence'. They told Kāna : 'There is grass in the urid plantation : take the goats there to graze'.

The latter took the goats into the urid plantation. The bean-stalks were shedding their seeds : some of these Kāna munches with a noise. The goats in turn pick up the fallen seeds and make them crackle under their teeth. Kāna felt offended : 'These goats (he said) are mimicking the noise of my teeth ! they are making sport of me' ! He simply killed all of them. Meanwhile what was happening in the zemindar's house ? The baby-boy sullied Kuja, and Kuja knocked him against ground till he became soft like linen ; then he hung him up on the wooden fence.

When the goatherd came home, Kuja enquired : 'where are the goats, Kāna' ? Kāna related the whole story, and then asked : 'I say, boy, where is the child'? Kuja in his turn told his story. Kāna said : 'Eh Kuja, it is your garment that they had told you to knock on the ground, and you have knocked the child ! The house people will give you a licking'. Kuja replied : 'Boy, they had sent you to tend the goats, and you have killed them : sure, they'll thrash you as well. Come, fellow, let us clear out of this place'. 'If we run away, what shall we live upon' ? 'On the goats you have killed. Come boy'. They carried one of the goats to the forest. When they had had a meal, they walked off with the guts of the animal.

At night they climbed upon a tree. It so happened that a king and his servants came and made halt at that very spot. The king's bedding was spread precisely under the tree on which were Kuja and Kāna. When all fell asleep, Kāna gently let the guts slip down upon the king's stomach. In the dark, a few of the servants, who for some cause had got up, thought that the king had been disembowelled. They all raised an alarm and fled, leaving everything behind. The king on awakening ran elsewhere (i.e. did not take the same direction as his servants).

Then the two boys slipped down the tree. Kāna seized a drum, Kuja took hold of a shield and sword, and they went their way. At a certain spot in the same forest, they encountered a large number of wasps and big hornets: Kāna put them in his drum, which he closed. In the sequel they had to fight against that king. Many were 'his soldiers; (on Kāna and Kuja's side), just the two of them. Kāna beats the drum vigorously and Kuja executes a dance, flourishing his sword and shield. When the bullets of many guns were being hurled at them, Kāna pierced his drum: a cloud of (*lit.* exceedingly many) wasps and hornets got out and began to sting the soldiers. The men shouted: 'Stop, Kāna, Kuja, save us! Call them back, call them back! We shall give you this kingdom'. Kāna called back the wasps. He and his brother were given a number of villages, and on (the revenue of) the same they led an easy life.

86.—*Sattō Bhāiguthyar. The Seven Brothers.*

Sattē bhāir rahcar. Sattōjhan nū chaujhan beñjkar rahcar, dara sannis ḍinḍam rahcas. Ās ikla'am khall kā n ankhā tarā mal kālālagyas; ās erpā nū cūtkam ra'ālagyas dara an'rman'ā puthī nū bāc'ālagyas. Asgahi bhāir īyar-kī khisār'ālagyar, pahē endr hō nanā pollālagyar.

Undul ār tām tām nū bācar: 'Gucā, isin ujjnā-barī kūbī saj'ot dara u ārot ci'ot.'[1] Ār annem nanjar, rahē ās onṭā usangin tanghai kicrī nū nuḍḍkas rahcas, adi trū umpyas kī urkhas, dara tangdadābagar munddhim erpā nū ārsyas. 'Mār rē (bācar), isin mārkat; ekastī barcas'? Ār ās gane pollar.

Anti undul bācar: 'Gucā, ī lūr akh'ū-in ṭorang hō'ot dara lakṛatī dharto'ot'. Asin akai ṭorang nū otkhā-īnim ambyar dara tām ōnd cokkh manjar[2]. Onṭā lakṛā āsin dhar'āge barcā khanē, ās ānyas: 'Onṭā lakṛā endergē barckī? Kalai, nākh mūnd barkē: hōle engan mōkhā ongor'. Dhērekan lakṛā asānim jummrā khanē, kukkos malkas: ās onṭā kōbā mann nū angkas ra'as.

(1) The sense is: 'let us throw and bury him in a well' From what follows the well must have been a dry one, or rather it was a burying pit.

(2) Apart out of the way.

Nanna ullā, tangdābagar onghon ṭoṛang kerar bā̃s ondra'āge dara kūm kam'āge. Sannis ār gane keras dara onghon otkhas ambras keras: ār gā cāṛē cāṛē khaṇḍyar dara eṛpā kirryar. Sannis oṇṭā bā̃skhoppā gusan kāldas dara ba'adas: 'Hīrā bajhaba'ā ongoi'? Bā̃s bācā: 'Ēn gā pollon; nannā bā̃s gusan kalke dara menke'. Ennem menā menā jokk gahṛi kuddyas: munjā nū oṇṭā bā̃s gacchrādim. Adin tāryas kī eṛpā ondras dara kūm kamcas. Pahē̃ kōhar āsin tam gane eksa'ānim ic'ā malā ci'inar; tām bēsım khall nū icnar; sannis ōnd aḍḍā, eksan khūṛītā amm ittī, asan icdas. Dhēr ullā gūṭī ār iñjō khettā[1] ondrar-kī eṛpā barnar; āsgahi nū oṇṭā hō̃ malā bajhri'ī. Pahē̃ undul adi nū oṇṭā hīrā bajjhrā kerā.

Iñjō bī-ā bīsā, kōhar ḍhibā khōṇḍar, dara ōrmar mēlā kerar ghōṛō khēndā. Ḍahrē nū oṇṭā sattē pursāgahi[2] ḍā̃ng ijtācar dara salhā nañjar: 'I ḍāngan ḍeg'ā lekh'ā ghoṛōguṭṭhin khēndot'. Mēlā nū āṛsyar. Ār gā mecchā mecchā ghoṛon khindyar; pahē̃ sannis urmī ghoṛō gusan kuddas dara mendas: 'Endr, ghoṛō, sattē pursāgahi ḍāngan ḍeg'ā ongoi'? Munjā nū oṇṭā ṭiṭū-ghoṛō gacchrā, dara bācā: 'Ēn ḍeg'on'. Ās adīnim khindyas. Ā ḍā̃ng gusan āṛsā tapṛem, adin ṭiṭū ghoṛō ḍeg'ā khaccyā. Nannar tang'ā tang'ā ghoṛon bongta'ā bongta'ā helrar, pahē̃ nēkhai hō̃[3] pollā ḍeg'ā. Khōkhānū ā kōhā kōhā ghoṛō khaṛdyā dara khattrā dara abṛāgahi kheḍḍ essrā. Āulanti kōhar tangṛisin iklā hō̃ malā sādhācar oiccar.

—There were seven brothers. Six of them were married men, the youngest was (still) a bachelor. He never drove ploughing teams nor worked in the fields; he was staying in bed at home and reading all kind of books. His brothers seeing this were angry, but could do nothing (to mend matters).

One day, the elders said among themselves: 'Come, let us bury him alive in a pit'. They did so; but he, with a plough-coulter which he had concealed under his clothes, worked his way through (the earth), got out (of the pit) and was at home even before his

(1) *Khettnā*, to shake off or out by imparting jerks, to knock out or off by beating with a piece of cloth, with the feet, etc.

(2) *Pursā* is properly the height of a man from his feet up to the top of his raised-up arm and hand.

(3) The horse of none of them.

brothers. 'Good heavens! (they said) we had buried him; whence does he come from'? They were no match against him.

Another day, they said: 'Come, let us take this clever man to the woods and have him caught by a tiger'. They abandoned him in a deep forest and went away. When a tiger turned up to catch him, he said: 'Why hast thou come alone? Go and come three or four of you, then you will be able to devour me'. (But) when a goodly number of tigers had collected, the boy was no longer (within reach): he had climbed up a high tree.

Another day, his brothers went once more to the woods to fetch bamboos and make fishing-baskets. The youngest accompanied them and was again abandoned by them: they cut hastily (what wood they wanted) and returned home. The little man goes to a bamboo cluster and asks: 'Bamboo, wilt thou be able to catch a diamond (for me)'? The bamboo answered: 'Not I; go and enquire from other bamboos'. Thus he went about for a while, repeating his question. At length one bamboo made the undertaking. This one he cut down and carried home, and (out of it) he made his fishing-basket... His elders however do not allow him to set it down anywhere near their own fishing-baskets (*lit.* anywhere with themselves). The latter they laid in a select field; the younger brother lays his own at a spot where the waters of the village lane collect (*lit.* descend). Many a day, on coming home, they knock a quantity of fish out of their baskets, while not a single one has been caught in his own. One day however a diamond was caught therein.

By the sale of their fishes the elder brothers had made money, and they all went to the fair to purchase horses. On the road they set up a perch seven times the height of a man, and agreed to buy animals able to clear that perch. They arrive at the fair. The elder brothers purchase very tall horses. The youngest however walks to every one of the animals (brought to the place for sale): 'Horse, wilt thou be able to jump over a perch seven times the height of a man?' At length a tattoo (was found who) undertook the feat. 'I shall do it', he said. The boy purchased the tattoo. As soon as the party reached the perch, the small poney jumped clear over it. The other brothers put their mounts at a gallop many a time, but no horse was able to clear the perch. Finally those tall horses got tired, fell and broke their limbs. From that day the elders ceased to tease their cadet.

37.—*Bharīyas dara Lakṛā. The Water-Carrier and the Tiger.*

Oṇṭā lakṛā oṇṭā kūbī gusan amm ōnāge kerā khanē, ād ek'am ōrtī adi nū khattrā dara ulam ra'ī. Ā kūbī nū orot bharīyas[1], amm nind'āge keras. Lakṛā, āsin īryā-dara, nē'ā belrā: 'Anā bharīyai, engan otthra'ā ci'ā'.

Ās meñjas: 'Ekāse otthro'on'? Lakṛā bācā: Ēnā, ninghai geṭhyan etta'ā: hōle ēn ayyā kōr'on, nīn natgoi'. Bharīyas tanghai geṭhyan ettāeas ciccar, dara lakṛā mañjā rukkhā. Anti endr mañjā? Lakṛā ā bharīyāsin mōkhāge nigirdigir nani! Ās bācas: 'En otthorkan dara nīn engan mōkhā biddī'? Irbar oṇṭā aḍḍon pañc badcar[2]. Āḍḍo lakṛan ānyā: 'Mōkhai ci'ai; ālar gā eman sogarkhanē dik nannar, mēd nū ladnar, khesṛti natagta'ānar'. Anti ṭaṭkhā-mannan pañc badcar. Ṭaṭkhā-mann hō bācā: 'Mōkhai ci'ai, lakṛā; ālar engan sādha ānar; khañje'on hōle, oṇṭā khañjpan gā mōkhnar, oṇṭan lebda'ānar ci'inar. Khōkhānū Sirupāden badcar. Sirupādes ānyas: 'Nīm kōṛē-kōṛē tang'ā tang'ā[3] katthan. tengā; hōle ba'on'. Tingyar ciccar.' Sirupādes lakṛan muñjā nū bācā: 'Nīn ekāse kurckī, adin emāgē ēd'ā'. Khanē lakṛā ā geṭhyā nū onghon kōreā, ēd'āge. Sirupādes āganem bhiṛtāeas; khōkhānū bharīyas lakṛan lau'ā helras dara piṭyas ciccas.

—A tiger, which had gone to drink at a well, somehow fell into it and could not come out (*lit.* remained inside). A bhisti went to the same well to fill up his goat-skin. The tiger began to entreat him: 'O bhisti, take me out of this'. The man asked: 'How shall I take thee out'? The tiger said: 'Look here, you let down your goat-skin, I get

---

(1) *Bharīyas* means a carrier, a porter. In this story (no doubt adapted from Hindi) it refers to a water-carrier. Likewise *geṭhyā* or *gēṭī*, a sack for the conveyance of goods by sumpter bullocks or packhorses does here duty for the bhisti's goat-skin.

(2) *Panc badnā*, to choose or accept as arbiter, to refer the case to.

(3) *Tang'ā tang'ā* may like its Hindi synonym *apnā*, refer to the 1st, 2nd or 3rd person.

inside and you pull upward'. The bhisti did so and the tiger came out. What happened next was that the tiger showed its teeth to the man, previous to devouring him. 'I have taken thee out', says the latter, 'and thou wantest to eat me up'? They took an ox as arbiter between them. The ox said to the tiger 'Devour him. Men constantly annoy me, put burdens on my back and by means of a halter pull me along'. They next referred the case to a mango-tree. The mango-tree also said: 'Tiger, do eat him. Men are foes to me; if I bear fruits, they eat part of them, and throw the rest about'. Finally the jackal is chosen as judge. Sirupande said: 'Let each of you expose the case with all details. I shall then decide'. They did so. In the end, Sirupande said to the tiger: Show to the court how thou couldst get into this goat-skin'. The tiger went into the goat-skin once more, just to show. Sirupande had the goat-skin tightened up immediately, and the bhisti beat the tiger to death.

38 —*Bāṇḍā Cigālō.* *The Tailless Jackal.*

Orot pacgis nitkī Khosrā ānakkhē niā kālālagyas, dara paccō nitkī maṇḍī hō'or ci'ālagyā. Undul oṇṭā Sirupādes paccon khakkhyas dara meñjas: 'Endr kādī, paccō'?— 'Anā babū, pacgisge maṇḍī hō'odan ci'idan'. Sirupādes bācas: Ē paccō, paccō-ālī taldī dara khāṛ nū bagge amm ra'ī; ekāse kaoi? Ēn karta'ādan ci'idan'. Kūṭi gusan āṛsyar khanē: 'An paccō, maṇḍin ēn kum'en[1]; nīn enghai kholan dhar'ai'. Kaṭṭnum kaṭṭnum Sirupādes maṇḍin adhā ōndas ciccas. Nannā nannā ullā hō ennem nañjā; dara paccō ullā ulla tang ālasge khīṛbī maṇḍin ho'ālagyā. Pacgis undul meñjas: 'Ān paccō, endrge nitkī koo'ā nandī-kī[2] maṇḍī ondrdī'? Paccō ānyā: 'Ē pacgī, oṇṭā cigālō ḍabrē nū ullā ullā khakkhrī'ī: ādim ṭhak'ī dara ūnī'. Khanē pacgis ānyas: 'Ē pacco, nin ī khallnum innā ra'ai: nēlā īnim ningāge maṇḍin hō'on'. Ānkā lekh'ā nañjar. Pacgis eṛpā nū chachem kirryas, dara paccō khall tarā rahcā Luhāṛī beṛā nū

(1) *Kum'nā* (pron. kummnā), to carry on the head.

(2) *Koo'ā*, as a noun, means a chip, a bit or piece cut or broken away from; *aṛigahī koo'ā*, a potsherd. As adjective, it means notched, chipped, scooped out. In the last meaning, however, the proper word is *khīṛhī* (l.9) or *khiṇḍhī*.

pacgis kukan bāgrai dara kicrin kūryas[1], dara oṇṭā khollā-kanton oakcas kī maṇḍin ku'nmyas-dara kā'ālagyas. Khāṛ gusan Sirupādesin khakkhyas. 'Endr kādī, pacgiō'?— 'E babū, pacgisge maṇḍī hō'odan ci'idan'. Sirupādes bācas: 'Khaṛ nū amm baggē ra'ī, ekāse kaṭṭoi? ēn kum'on maṇḍin, nīn kholan dhar'ai'. Cigālō munddh lekh'ā maṇḍin ōnā helrā khanē, pacgis kanton otthras dara kholānim mūcyas ciccas. Sirupādes ajgut manarkī kirr īryas dara lakhcas pacgīsim taldas, paccō malāl ...

Khanē Sirupādes pacgīsin dhirāba'ā helras: 'Ra'ā, pacgī, ēn ninghai ugtā-kaṛbā nū corgon[2]. Pacgis pannāgahi khuṭī kamtācas dara ugta-kaṛbā nū ṭhōkcas ciccas. Sirupādes chachem barcas kī asan corgā helras khanē, liṇḍīnim hotrācas.

Sirupādes onghon ānyas: 'Ra'ā, pacgī! Ṭhakackai: ninghai khēran ēn khaṛ'on', Dhirābācka lekh'ā, as undul ḍhēr cigālon sangī occas dara pacgisgahi khēr khaṛ'āge kerās. Pahē pacgis khēran munddh gucchābāckas rahcas dara tān tātran dhar'arkī kuslīnum ukkas ra'as. Nannā nannā cigālō kōrcā khanē, pacgis abṛan tani tani ṭhōṭhcas. Abṛa ba'ā helrā: 'Anā harō, oṇṭa kōha gayā ra'ī; ād gā ṭhōṭh'ī dara ambī.[3] Urminti khōkhānū ā baṇḍā Cigālō hō kōrcā: khanē gā adin pacgis jōrtī ṭhōṭhcas ciccas. Ād bongā dara mīkhyā: 'Nīns khēr ba'adar, pacgis taldas kā, harō'!

Sirupādes khisāras: 'Ra'ā, pacgī (bācas): ninghai kohṇḍan khaṛ'on'. Khanē pacgis tanghai urmī kohṇḍan mesgā mañyātī cokkhas, dara tanghai mēd nū cind khasseras: ennem-ās asānim aṭkhā majhī nū nūkhurkas ra'as. Sirupādes onghon sangī occas dara khaṛ'āge barcas. Ekdā ekdā mesgā nū argī: abṛan pacgis tukkas[4] ci'idas; khanē cigālōguṭṭhī ba'ā helrā: 'Anā harō, pacgisgahi kohṇḍā gā kussī dara ambī'! Khōkhānū bāṇḍā hō argyā. adin pacgis kōṛhem tukkyas ciccas. Anti bongā dara mīkhyā: 'Pacgisgahi kohṇḍā

(1) *Kūrnā*, to put on and tie a *sāri* round one's waist, gown-like fashion

(2) *Corgnā*, prop. to move forward with one seat rubbing against the ground or in grass (as dogs do), hence to sully.

(3) *Ambnā* here simply denotes *extreme action* in the first verb. 'The cock pecks *with a vengeance*'. See Or. Dict. *ambnā*, I, 8, last example.

(4) *Lit.* 'pushes'. The push in question is given with the head, as shown by *kussi*.

kussī ba'adar, paoglīsim taldas kā, harō'.—Anti, paegis hō ek'am ōrti Sirupāndesin piṭā pōllas, dara Sirupāndes hō āsgahin endra[1] hō khaṛ'ā pōllas.

Muñjā nū salhā nañjar pacco-pacgī[2] : 'Ekāsē abṛā urmī cigālon ṭhak'ot dara piṭā khaccot ? endr ōr otthro'ot ? Undul pacco cālī nū ukkyā dara cīkhā helrā : ' Enghai paegis keocas karas ! ekāse nanon ' ? Cigālōguṭṭhi ānyā : ' Ān pacoō, bhōjā nanai E nan eṛ'oi kā malā ' ? Pacoō bācā : ' Endrge malā eṛ'on , natti' ? Pacoō endr nanjā ? Ḍhēr baggē goēṭhā khōṇḍā dara pakhnā. Paeglsin naḍḍā kī cigālōguṭṭhin urmin bhōjē ōnāge eḍḍā. Abṛā jummrā khanē, paccō ā goēṭhā kudhā nanjā, ā pakhnā muñyā ; khōkhānū dagcā ciccā. Pakhnā otthor otthor amm nū sajj'ī : ābīrī choēgorgoṛ ba'ī. Abṛā cigālō onṭan onṭan ni'ī : Engā cī, ajjī ; engā cī, ajjī ! — ' Ra'ā, natti ; bi'ā ci'or hōle, ōrmarge manō ; khutton.'. Khōkhānū bācā : ' Barā, nattībagārō ; akkū biccā. ' Barcā khanē, paccō bācā : ' E nattibagārō anuem ra'or, hōle gā nīm biccānakhro'or kā. arbānakhro'or ; aōnge barā ; ōrmārin paghātī khuṭ'on '. Dara ād nannā cigālon gā paghātī khuṭcā, pahē ā bāṇḍā Sirupāndēsin sikṛītī khuṭcā. Abṛā urmī pātī pātī ukkyā khanē paccō mēkhā helrā : ' Pannā kotgā ! cāṛē barke, pacgī hō hō ' ! Abṛā cigālō minī : ' Endr bi'alī, paccō ' ? ' E nattī ēkh gā mīkhkan '. Muaddhtāge[3] ekaan paegis kaprkas rahcas, asanti onṭā kōhā mugran otthras kī barcas ... Abṛā urmī cigālon tarkuṭintī lau'ā helras. Bāṇḍā guṇan āṛayas khanē, adin koṛhom lau'ā helras ekattī sīkṛī cssā. Idin iryā kī nannā cigālā hō, paghan natgā natgā, khaccyā khaccyā, dara urmī ekātarā ekātarā bongā.

—An old man crossed the Koel every day to go and plough his fields ; his wife every day carried him his rice. . One day a jackal met the old crony and asked : ' Where are you going, old dame ' ? ' Child, I am taking rice to the old man'. Sirupande said to her : ' Mother, thou art aged and the river carries much water ; I am going to help

(¹) Two pronouns in apposition. *Lit.* ' He could not steal anything of his whatsoever '.

(²) Adverbial sense : 'between husband and wife'. Mukkā-mēt is often used with the same force.

(³) Beforehand, in advance.

you across'. When they reached the (near) bank: 'Mother, I shall take the rice upon my head: you just hold my tail'. During their walking across, Sirupande ate half of the rice. He repeated this on the following days, and each time the old woman brought a scooped out rice portion to her husband. One day the latter asked: 'Wife, why doest thou bring me regularly rice, part of which thou hast scooped out'? The woman said: 'Husband, every day on my way here, I meet a certain jackal: it is he who plays the cheat and eats off that rice'. The old man replied: 'Wife, to-day you stay in this field, and I myself shall bring the rice to-morrow'. It was done accordingly. The old man went home on stealth and his wife remained in the field. About nine o'clock in the morning, the old man combed his chignon, put on a sārī, sharpened a razor, and was off with the pot of rice on his head. Near the river he came up with Sirupande: 'Where do you go, old dame'?—Child, I am taking rice to the old man'. Says Sirupande: 'There is much water in the river; how shall you cross? I will carry your rice, take hold of my tail'. When the jackal fell to the rice as usual, the old man took out his razor and cut the (glutton's) tail clean off. Sirupande in great surprise turned round and knew (it was) the old man, not the old dame... Sirupande then came out with threats: 'Wait a bit, old man; shan't I cover the handle of thy plough with filth'! The old man ordered some iron nails to be made and drove them into his plough-handle. When the jackal came to rub itself there, it (only) got its seat scratched.

Once more Sirupande said: 'Wait a bit, old man! Thou hast cheated me, I shall have (*lit.* steal) thy fowls'. One day he, true to his threat, took with himself a pack of (other) jackals and went to rob the old man of his fowls. But the latter, after removing the fowls, was sitting in the very poultry house, armed with a scythe. As the minor (*lit.* the other) jackals made an entrance, he just gave them a touch of his weapon. They shouted: 'O brothers, a huge cock is there, which pecks very hard'. The tailless jackal came in (also), as bringer up; the old man made a good gash into him. It ran off shouting: 'You fellows, what you call a cock, why it's the old man'! Sirupande was angry: 'Wait a bit, old man (he said): I shall have thy pumpkins'. The old man plucked all his gourds off his roof, covered his body with ashes, and hid himself there amid the leaves. Once more Sirupande took associates and came for his robbery. Some of the (minor) jackals got upon the roof; the old man gave them a shove (with his head), and jackals to say: 'O brothers, the old man's gourds are butting frightfully'! After them the Tailless one, in turn, went up: to him the old man gave a master thrust. It ran away shouting: 'You fellows, what you call the old man's gourds, why it's the old man himself'. So, neither could the old man kill Sirupande, nor could Sirupande rob the old man of anything.

In the end the old pair held a council: 'How shall we allure all those jackals and make an end of them? What means'? One day the old crony seated herself before her door and cried: 'My old man is dead; What shall I do'? The jackals said to her: 'Old dame, prepare a funeral repast; you will invite us, won't you'? The woman said: 'Why shouldn't I invite you, children'? (Then) what did she do? She collected a good quantity of dry cowdung and pebbles. After hiding away her husband, she invited all the jackals. When they had gathered, she made that cowdung into a heap over the pebbles, and set fire to it. Each time she takes a stone out, she drops it into water: (the stone) hisses violently. Every jackal asks for one: 'Give to me, granny! Give to me, granny'!—'Wait, children; if you allow the cooking its time, there will be (cakes) for all! I will make the shares'. Finally she said: 'Come near, children: now the cooking is over'. As they approached she said: 'Children, if you remain as you are, you will rob one another or have a fight; so come, I am tying down all of you with ropes'. And she bound them all, the minor jackals with ropes, and the tailless Sirupande with a chain. As they were thus seated in a row, she shouted. 'The iron bludgeon! come quick, old man, ho! ho'! The jackals asked: 'What do you say, old dame'?—'Children, I was calling for his manes'. Out of his place of concealment came the old man with a wooden mallet in his hand...He began to lay about all those jackals from one end of the row onwards. When he reached the Tailless one, he gave him such a thrashing that the chain snapped...At the sight, the other jackals too, by dint of tugging at their ropes, broke them, and they all decamped, each in a different direction.

39.—*Ōrt chikuṭ ālas.* *A Cautious Fellow.*

Ḍahrē ekoi hole, sange sange ekke ; ekṣa'ānim okkoi Lōle, kaprke kī okke ; nannā guyā[1] kāloi hōle, cihuṭṭī ra'ake '.

Ī ankan parkh'āge oṇṭā ālas urkhas. Kānum kānum ōnd aḍḍā amm ōnāge ijjas. Ḍobhā nū oṇṭā kakṛon īryas dara ānyas : ' Ankā ra'ī : ' ḍahrē ekōbīri, sange sange ekke ' ; pahē enghai sange gā nē hō malkar '. Ennē ba'anum ās ā kakṛōnim pettas kī tanghai kukkhe'enā nū ghusyācas. Jokk bāṛī keras kī ontā mann gusan cūtvas dara khandras keras. Abirī oṇṭā ajgaṛ nerr a'ānim rahcā, āsin nunkhāge bar'ā helrā : ād ekannē ekannē heddē bar'ālagyā, annem annem bayyam kōbā angla'ālagyā. Kukk nū ghusyācā rahcā, kakṛō adin īryā dara, nerr ekannē ekannē heddē bar'ālagyā, annem annem kakṛō pāgantī urkhā dara tanghai bakkan anglta'ā[2] helrā Nerr ' āsin parmon ' bācā āganem, kakṛō a ligahi phēnim parmyā : nerr ajgut uphṛār'ā uphṛār'ā, asānim kecā kerā. Khōkhānū ālas ejjras dara, kakṛōgahi nalkhan bujhras-ki, haikaṭ mañjas. Mundhbhāre kālā helras, dara bācas : ' Ī katthan parkhākan ra'adin : ' ḍahrē ekoi Lōle, sangē sangē ekke '.

Kānum kānum ōnd aḍḍā īṛsyas, asan ḍhērekan ṭhakuar ukkar rahcar : ār ḍahrē-īkū ālarin phasta'ālagyar. Ār āsin hō okr'āgē eḍḍar. Ār endr nanjkar rahcar ? Oṇṭā kūbin patgālī trū aḍḍar-dara, ā mañyā piṭrī attyar-kī, tām kūṭī kūṭī nū ukkar rahcar. Nīk'im bar'or hōle, ārin majhī nū okta'ālagyar : khattar kūbī nū mulkhar kālālagyar,[4] dara ṭhakuar ārgahi laṭṭi-phatī cō ra ī, adin hō'ālagyar. Ār ā ḍahrē-īkūsin eḍḍar dara bācar : ' Majhī nū okkā' khanē, ās ōnd kūṭī nū pitrin dharcas dara cōcas, kīyyā ērāge Ormā ṭhakuar kūbī nū

---

[1]. *Gusan*, at, near. *Guyā*, at the house of, Fr. chez.

[2]. The crab's claws are conceived by the narrator as a sort of tongs distinct from the animal : hence the use of the causal verb : ' the crab caused its claws to open '.

[3]. *Ukkhnā* means ' to sit down ' ; *ekrnā*, ' to sit for a rest '. *Ṭhakuā* means *Thug*.

[4]. *Mulkhālagyar* would simply mean : ' they sank '. The gerund with *kānē* is descriptive of the action : ' down they went '.

khattrar kerar. As orgā helras : 'Mānī mānī katthad : 'eksa'ānim okkoi hōle, kaprkē kī okkē'.

Ās astiklē hāṛī keras kī oṇtā paddā āṛsyas ; khanē biṛī puttyā. Ās ā paddānum ḍēṭā nanjas dara ort kumbhras gayā kaṭṭū tauā nē'āge keras. Endran ērdas ? Kumbhras guyā, oīkhoar olokhnar-dara, āsin bācar : 'Innā gā em guyā kattū tauā malā ; innā emhai kukkogahi jiyā kālō' ! 'Ekāsēnū' ? meñjas khanē, ār tingyar : 'Bēlasgahi tangdā ra'ī, ād rakas[1] ra'ī. Adīgahi beñjā pālī pālī ī ṭolantā ḍhēr kukkor gane mañja : ād arin ōrmarin beñjāgahi mākhānum pityā ciccā. Innā engdasgahi[2] jiyā kālō : aṅṅge ēn oīkhdam olokhnam'. Anti ḍahiē-īkus bācas : 'Ēn gā ḍiṇḍam ra'adan. Engāge ci'ā : ēn, ningdasgahi uijī nū bēl-kukoi gane beñjro'on'. Ā kumbhras khus mañjas, ongdasgahi jiyā bacchrō'ō : āge eōndā cāṛ laggyā, ciccas ; āsin ontācas, mōkhtācas, sapṛācas. Ūkhyā khanē barāt urkhā. Beñjā manjadim Adhā-idhi mākhānum, ā bel-kukoigahi muīti ēṛ'otā nerr urkhālagyā[3] : idin as ērdas dara, kuk'ī otthrā khanē, kainīitī khaṇḍyas eiccas. Nerr uphṛārā dara urkhā kerā. A kukoi niman manjā dara āsin pitā pollā Pairim ālar khōṇḍrar uītkīgahi mañjkā lekh'ā, mārin otthra'āge. Ār ōrmar ajgut manālagyai inna endīge malā tisgī ; khōkhānū endr ērnar ? ibārim urkhnar ! Anti dahiē-ikus idin īryas : 'Nannar guyā kaoi hōle, cihuttī ra'ake', dara tanāalin onlras kī eṛpā kirryas.

—'If you travel, travel in company, if you sit down, look where you sit ; if you go to strangers, be on your guard'.

In order to test this proverb a man set out on a journey. At one spot he halted for a drink of water He caught sight of a crab in a puddle and thought : The proverb says : 'if you travel, travel in company' : now, I have no one with me With these words he picked up the crab and thrust it into his headgear. Some distance further he lay down under a tree and got asleep. Meanwhile a huge snake which was living there advanced to swallow him up : the nearer it came, the wider did it dilate its jaws. The crab in the turban noticed that snake ; and, as the latter was approaching more and

---

[1]. Corresponding to the Hindi 'Rakshas' or 'Rākas'.

[2]. Engdas and l. 37 ningdas mean 'our, your son'.

[3]. The use of the Imperfect tense suggests that the 'coming out' was still in process.

more, the crab was moving out further and further, opening its claws wider. When the snake was on the very point of stinging (the sleeper), the crab pinched its hood. The snake writhed in agonies and died on the spot. Subsequently, on awakening, the man realized the crab's doing and admired it. He resumed his journey, saying : (One part of) the proverb is tested : 'if you travel, travel in company'.

He came later on to a place where a number of thugs were sitting (in a circle) : they used to lay snares for travellers. They invited him to squat with them for a rest. What had they devised (*lit.* done)? After covering a well with leaves (sown together), they had spread a mat on top, they themselves squatting all round the brim. If any (likely victims) presented themselves, they made them sit in the centre : down into the well went the poor wretches, and the thugs carried off whatever baggage might be his. When they invited (our) traveller and said : 'Sit down in the centre', he seized and lifted up one end of the mat to look underneath. All those thugs fell into the well. The man thought : 'True is the saying : 'wherever you sit down, look at what you sit upon'.

He proceeded further and came to a village, when the sun went down. He stopped there and went to a potter's to ask for pots and pans. What does he see? At the potter's house, they told him, amid tears and laments : 'Oh to-day we have no pots (for sale); to-day our son must die'. 'How is that'? he asked. They then said to him : 'The king has a daughter who is a ghoul. A number of young men of this hamlet have, one after the other, been married to her, she has killed them all on the very night after the marriage. To-day our son shall die : this is why we weep and bewail'. The traveller said : 'I am a bachelor. Allow me : I will marry the king's daughter in lieu and place of your son'. The potter felt glad that his son's life should be saved. He gave (the traveller) whatever he needed, food, drink and fine clothes. The wedding party started after dark, and the marriage did take place. At midnight two snakes began to emerge from the princess's nostrils : he notices the fact and, when (the snakes) let out their heads, he cut these off with scissors.

The snakes writhed and fell out. This purified the princess and she did not (*lit.* could not) kill him. Early in the morning people assembled as they had done ever before (in front of the palace), to take out the corpse. They were marvelling why on that morning she did not open her door; in due time, what do they see? both of them are coming out! The traveller had experienced (how wise the proverb is): 'If you go to strangers, be on your guard', and he went home with his wife.

40.—*Āl-piṭū Lakṛā. The Man-Eater.*

Ort ālī ṭoṛang kerā khaṛrā[1] ondra'ā. Khaṛrā hō̃ bēsim baggē khakkhrā kera: ād baggem mūjyā. Tētrā pollā khanē, oṇṭā lakṛā asānim rahcā, adin ā ālī ānyā: 'Ē babū, barā, tēttrā' Lakṛā bācā: 'Endran ci'oi-dara[2], paccō?' Ā ālī bācā: 'Anā babū, endran ci'on? Idigā, otthā-ēkh ra'ī: kukoi manō, hōle gā beñjon ci'on, dara kukkō manos hōle, sangī jōṛto'on'. Anti lakṛā tēttā ciccā. Jokk ullā kerā khanē, lakṛā oṇṭā ḍhicuā-oṛan[3] menāge taiyā endr lellē mañjā; ālī tingyā: 'Kukoidim mañjā' Baggē candō kirkī rahcā khanē, lakṛā ā ḍhicuan onghon ērā taiyā kukoi eō̃ kōhā pardyā. Ḍhicuā tingyā: 'Akkū tani tani ammguṭṭhin undri'ī'. Dara onghon ērāge taiyā, khanē gā ḍhicuā tengr ciccā: 'Akkū kanyārī mañjā'. Anti lakṛā barcā, dara adin beñjrā dara ondra'ā helrā.

Ondrnum ondrnum, ōnd aḍḍā mañyā̃ ḍippā dara kiyyā gaḍḍī rahcā,[4] asan lakṛā ā kukoin bācā. 'Lagē, nīn isan kaḍrkā[5] nanai: ēn attrā lahrī urkhā kādan'. Pahē ād mūhī mū̃jhra'ā lakkī rahcā, ābīrim lakṛā mañyā̃ tartī bongkī barcā, dara asānim adin piṭyā kī mokkhā.

Jokk ullā khōkhā, lakṛā tanghai sasrār nū kerā dara tangsāsan kūlī urkhkā[6] oṇṭā katthan tengā helrā: 'Ān ayō, ningdāge gā, kālā khanemtī, khann-nuñjnā mañjā. Urmī nalakh ukkyā kerā

[1]. Bamboo shoots plucked for greens. They are eaten either cut into bits and roasted (*bangā*), or as a pulverulent condiment (*haṇḍhuā*). See Dictionary.

[2]. Grammar, p. 286, 6.

[3]. A king crow.

[4]. *Lit.* at a place which upward was high and downward (was) deep.

[5]. Sāl-tree twig used as a tooth-brush. *Kaḍrkā n.*, to rinse one's mouth.

[6]. Trumped up story. Compare the idiom '*to suck out of one's thumb*'.

Jokk ullā khatrī sannī engsāṛin[1] susār nanāge taiyai'. Ā ālī lakṛāgahi ānkā lekh'ā sannī tingsāṛin taiyā ciccā. Ḍahrē nū ḍhicuā-ōṛā ḍaṇḍī pāṛī: 'Bongai koi, bongai koi'! Ā kukoi meñjā: 'Hudā, bhaṭū! hū ōṛā endr ba'ī'? Ād bācā: 'Endr ba'ī, maī; gucai[2]. Ennem kainō dhaō ā ōṛā pāṛnum barca.. Eksan tanghai ālin mokkhā, ā aḍḍā nū āṭsyar khanē, ā kukoin hō kaḍrkā nanāge bācā, daran tān mañyā tarā kerā Ād mūhī mūjhra' ālagyā, ābīrin lakṛā mañyā taṛtī rittam ittyā dara adin hō mokkhā ciccā.

Idigahi[3] onghon lakṛā sasrār nū kirryā dara bācā: 'Ē ayō, majhlī hō bērām khattrā; uoñge kōhā mayyan taiyai, ārgahi susār nanō'. Tangsās pattācā dara taiyā ticcā. Ḍahrē nū ā ḍhicuāgahi ḍaṇḍī mindri'ī: 'Bongai, koi, bongai, koi'!—'Hudā, bhaṭū! endr ba'ī hū ōṛā bhaṭū'?—'Endr ba'ō maī; gucai'. Hāṛī kerar; dara ā aḍḍānum, eksan irbārim ijjhī ṛahcā, asan adin hō kaḍrkā nanāge ānyā; dara, mūhī mūjhro'ō bīrī, barcā ki adin mokkhā ciccā.

Khōkhanū onghon lakṛā sasrār kirryā dara tangsāsan bācā: 'Kōhad hō, kūl nuñjnātī, uphṛār' ī kuddī: kōhā dadāsin taiyai. Malā ra'os; ēros kī bar'os'. Lakṛāgahi ānkā lekh'ā, ā ālī kōhāsin hō taiyā ciccā. Ās khisārnum ḍahrē kālālagyas. Saītnū ā ḍhicuāgahi ḍaṇḍī-pāṛnan ās hō meñjas dara urmī katthan bujhras. Soṭṭan ceḍḍas: dara, lakṛā ānyā: 'lagē dadā, nīn isan kaḍrkā nanā, ēn bahrī urkhā kādan.' ābīrī, ās chachem darangā heddē nū kaṛrkas rahcas. Ād bungkī ittyā khanē, adigahi kukknim passas dara ciccas. Asānim khōkhānū mūjhras khanē, tangṛībagargahi punan īryas..Ibṛan kōllam mañjas-kī pettas dara eṛpā ondras, dara tangyon urmī katthan tingyas ciccas.

—A woman went to a forest to fetch bamboo saplings. She found a large quantity of them and made a good crop Being unable to raise (the basket) to her head she said to a tiger who was near: 'Come child, help me to get this up'. The tiger asked:

---

1. 'The youngest of my sisters-in-law.' She, being older than the wife, is referred to, on l. 20, as *majhlī*, your second daughter.

2. On this construction see story 26, l. 28.

3. For *idigahi khokhā*.

'Woman, what do you propose to give me'? Says the woman: 'Child, what can I give? You see that I am in the family way: if it is a girl, I shall make her your wife, and if it is a boy I shall make him your chum'. The tiger assisted her in lifting up the basket.

A few days later, the tiger sent a kingcrow to enquire what sort of child it was; the woman said: 'It is a girl'. Many a month passed, and once more the tiger sent the kingcrow to see how big the girl had become (*lit.* grown up). The swallow reported: 'She now can fetch a little water and do such things'. Once more he sent the kingcrow and the bird's message was: 'She is (now) of marriageable age'. So the tiger came, married her and departed with her.

On their journey, at a spot where high banks overhang (a stream), the tiger said to the girl: 'Come, cleanse (here) thy teeth; I am going to the privy that side'. But, as she was busy washing her face he, from a height, pounced upon her; he killed her on the spot and devoured her.

Some time later, the tiger went to his mother-in-law's house, and told her a trumped up story: 'Mother, your daughter, from the very day she left, got sore eyes. Every work is at a standstill For a few days allow my little sister-in-law to come and take care of her'. As the tiger requested, the woman did send his little sister in-law. On their way the kingcrow began to sing a song: 'Flee away, girl! flee away, girl'. The girl asked: 'Up there, brother-in-law, what does that bird say'? He said: 'How can I know, girl? Come on'. The bird repeated its song again and again...On reaching the spot where he had eaten up his wife, the tiger said to her also to cleanse her teeth, and he himself went up. As she washed her face [1], the tiger suddenly came down and devoured her.

After this the tiger returned once more to his wife's house and said: 'Mother, your second daughter also has been taken ill; do

---

[1]. This detail is invariably repeated at each fresh murder. The moment chosen is when the victim is looking away into the stream

send the big girl, that she may take care of them'. His mother-in-law believed him and did as requested. On the way the kingcrow's song was heard: 'Flee away, girl! flee away, girl'—'Up there, brother-in-law! what does that bird say, brother-in-law'?—'What can it say, girl? Come on'. They went on; at the spot where her two (sisters) had stopped, he told her likewise to cleanse her teeth, and when she was washing her face, he came and devoured her.

After this the tiger went once more and said to his mother-in-law: 'Your eldest daughter also is writhing with colics, send my big brother-in-law. He won't stay; he will just see and come back'. Accordingly the mother sent her elder son. The latter set out in anger. It happened that he also heard the kingcrow singing, and he understood the whole (tragedy). He threw a club on his shoulders; and when the tiger said 'Come, brother, cleanse here thy teeth, I am going to the privy', he hid himself at the foot of the embankment. When the tiger came down at a run, he smashed his head up clean. When he next washed himself, he saw beads of his sisters' (necklaces). In deep sorrow he picked them up, brought them home and related to his mother all that had happened.

41.—*Danō-Daīt.* *The Dragon.*

Oṛt urbas urbnī rahcar; ārgahi eṛpā ṭoṛang heddē rahcā; ārgahi irb k͟haddar rahcar, oṇṭā kukkos dara sannī kukoi. Undul irbārim ultī bongkar urkhnar dara cīk͟hnar. Ghōṛō meñjā: 'Endrgē cīk͟hdar'? Tingyar ciccar: 'Emhai eṛpā ulā oṇṭā danō-daīt ([1]) embāsin dara ingyōn mōk͟hālaggī, dara eman hō k͟hōk͟hānū mōk͟hā biddī.' Ghōṛō bācā: 'Engan kollā dara irbārim eng mañyā argā' bācā. Ārin occā dara bongā kerā. Danō-daīt ārgahi tangyō tambāsin mokkhā cappyā, dara abṛā k͟haddārin khed'ā helrā.

Khednum khednum āṛsā helrā k͟hanē, oṇṭā bāsargahi [2] jhūṛ nū ennē ba'anum ghusyārar: 'Bāsar-k͟hoppā taldī, hōle gā eman bacchāba'oi'. Ā bāsar-k͟hoppā ḍhēr jhūṛ rahcā: ulā kōr'āge Danō-daīt aḍḍā beddā kuddyā, muñjā nū bāsnim caṛrā helrā: ābīrī ghōṛō urkhā dara ā

[1]. *Danō-daīt* (from H. dānar), a demon half man and half animal, with a crested head, enormous claws, and eyes and mouth which spout fire.

[2]. *Bāsā*, hollow stem bamboo-tree; *bās*, full stem bamboo-tree. A third kind of bamboos, the strongest and heaviest, is called *bāsin*; whether full or hollow, it does not float.

khaddārin hāṛī bongtāoā. Bongnum bongnum oṇṭā khāṛ gusan āṛsyar ghōṛō ārin kaṛtāoā ; pahē Danō-daṛtge lau-laṛang argāge maññjā Ād argālagyā khanē, laṛang khaccrā kerā. Danō-daṛt ārin āṛsā pōliā. Ā khāṛ āpakkhē ghōṛō dhakārkātī khattrā dara keccā kerā. Ār adigahi khebdan dara kheḍḍan occar. Kheḍḍan gā ēṛeth dara khebdan phirī kamcar, dara ā toṛangnum ra'ā helrar : mākguṭṭhin luc mōkhālagyar.

Undul ā rājintā bēlas sendrā lēcā keras ; ṭoṛang nū ās gusan oicc ghaṭṭrā kerā, dara ās tanghai ālarin cicc beddā tayyas. Ār mann nū argyar kī ērā helrar. Ond aḍḍā ciccgahi mojkhā-cō'onan īryar dara asan nē'ā kerar Ayyā abṛā bhayā-bahingahi eṛpā rahcā. Kukoi cicc ci'āge ultī urkhā khanē, ār mogbārar kerar. Tambai urbāsin barcar-kī tingyar : 'Ninghai tatkhā hō adigahi kheḍḍ lekh'ā malā jumro'ō[1]'. Bēlas ā kukoigahi tangdadāsin eḍḍas kī ās gustī tangṛin nēcas, pahē ās malā ciccas.

Aunlantim bēlas āsin pitāge tihā nanā helras. Āsin bācas : 'Enghai rājī nū ujjdai : kalā, engāge māk pitā ondra'ā'. Ā kukkos tanghai ghōṛō-kheḍḍ ēṛetthan occas dara māk piṭā keras. Ekābīrī oṇṭā māk mañyā ēṛeth calābā'ālagyas, ābīri oṇṭā hartu[2] cicyār'ā helrā : māk bongā kerā. Anti kukkos ā hartun eṛethtī tukāckas kuddas. Hartu bācā : 'Endr lau'ā beddai ? nīn ba'oi, ā lekh'am nanon ! engan ambā lau'ā'. Kukkos bācas : 'Engan bēlas māk lau'ā tayyas khanē, nīn cicyārkī dara bongtāckī'? Khanē hartu : 'Gucā (bācā), ēnim bēlas gusan kādan. Enghai khēser nū paghā lagāba'ā dara bēlas gusan ho'ā'. Kukkos adin ghisya'ānūtim occas. Āṛsar-kī bācas : 'Idin engan māk lau'ā malā cicoā' !

Pahē bēlas irbarīnim ambyas[3] dara ā kukkōsin bācas : 'Kalā, dara lakṛan lau'ar ondra'ā'. Kukkos hartun ānyas : 'Akkū endr nanon'? Hartu bācā. 'Engāge nau mangahi oṇṭā mugrā kam'ā dara gucā : lakṛan lau'ot'. Kukkos sarnan keras dara mugraṇ kamcas. Ār nannā ṭoṛang kerar. Ṭhaukam ārin Danō-daṛt khakkhyā.

---

[1]. *Lit* 'Even thy tongue will not be compared (bear comparison) with her feet.'

[2]. In Hindi *kalumān*, baboon, the black-faced long-tailed monkey.

[3]. *Lit.* let them go, dismissed them.

Ād ā kukkōsin dharcā khanē, hartu ā otthā mugrātī ōnd mugrā lancā. Khanē Danō-dalt : 'Ambā lau'ā ; ba'or indri'im ba'or, ēn nanon ci'on'. Hartu bācā : 'Oṇṭā lakṛan emāge piṭai'. Ā lakṛan bēlas gusan on'rar. Anti bēlas ek'am ōrtī ā kukkōsin ṭhak'ā pollas dara āsgahi tangṛin hō hō'ā pollas.

Khōkhānū bēlas ās gane laṛ'āge ṭhannca, dara āsin ānyas : 'Lagē, enghai dara ninghai majhī nū laṛai manānek'ā' ! Kukkos ā hartun mañjas : 'Ekāsē nanāge manō ? ēn gā otokh ālan ra'adan'. Hartu bācā : 'Ēn ningā,e telengārin khōṇḍ'ā kādan' bācā, dara ā Danō-dalt gusan kerā dara ānyā : 'Eō ninghai sanger ra'anar, ārin khōṇḍ'ai '. Ād ḍhērekan danō-daltguṭṭhin khōṇḍā dara ondrā dara oṇṭa heddetā ṭungṛi nū ijtācā. Hartu abṛan bācā : 'Ekātarā hō ambke kalā enghai bēgar ānkāṭī'. Tān oṇṭā khoppā kōrcā, khēṛ ērāge Kukkos ghōṛō-khebdā phirin dharcas. Majhī nū ijjkas ra'as . Aoñdā bagge cār calābācar : pahē oṇṭā hō āsin malā laggyā. Khanē telengar tām tām kacnakhra'ā helrar : 'Ībaggē cār munjr'ālaggī, āsin oṇṭā hō malā laggyā : ī katthan hū hartun menā harō '. Āganem hartu abṛā urmī danō-daltguṭṭhin cḍḍā : 'Innā eō baggē mōkhā ongdar, ā baggē piṭā mōkhā '. Anti urmī danō-daltguṭṭhi bungkī barcā, dara eō ālarin dharcā, carrā carrā mokkhā ciccā. Bēlas hō munjras keras. Āsgahi uiji nū ā kukkos bēl cajjras,keras dara ā rāji nū rāji nanā helras

– There were a rich man and his wife. They lived close to a forest and had two children, a boy and a girl. These two one day ran out of the house weeping. The horse asked them. 'What are you crying for ' ? They said : 'There, in our house, a dragon is devouring our parents, and he wants to eat us afterwards'. The horse said : 'Untie me and mount, both of you, on my back'. He gallopped off with them. The dragon made haste to finish off the parents and started in pursuit of the children.

As it was no longer far behind, they threw themselves inside a cluster of bamboo-trees, saying : 'If you are (true) bamboos, you will save us' The bamboo-cluster was a very thick one, the dragon went all round to find an entrance and finally began uprooting the very trees : then the horse came out and, with (renewed) gallop, took the children further. They arrived at a river the horse crossed it, but the dragon had to pass over a creeper bridge. As it was ascending (this bridge), the creeper snapped. The dragon could not overtake them. On the other side of the river the horse fell for want of breath and died. They took off its ears and legs: out of the latter they made a bow, and with the former a shield; and henceforth they lived in the forest, living on the deer which they killed.

One day the king of the land went a-hunting. In the woods he ran short of fire and sent his men to fetch some. They climbed on a tree and looked round. They saw smoke rising up, and went there to ask for fire: this was the brother and sister's house. As the girl came out to give them (what they wanted), they were struck with admiration. On their return they said to their master: 'Your tongue itself is less tender and delicate than are her feet'. The king summoned the girl's brother and asked him for his sister. But the boy refused to give her away.

Henceforward the king sought to encompass the boy's death. He told him:- 'Thou art living in my dominions: go, kill a deer and bring it to me'. The boy, with his horse-legged bow, went out for a deer. As he was on the point of discharging an arrow, a monkey gave a shrill shout and the deer escaped. The boy then steps about, aiming at the monkey. The latter said: 'What do you want to strike me for? I shall be at your service for whatever you want. Do not strike me'. Says the boy: 'When the king sends me to kill a deer for him, thou shoutest and makest it run away'? Then the monkey: 'Come (he said), I am going myself to the king. Pass a halter round my neck and take me to him'. The boy dragged the monkey along. On arriving he said: 'This is the fellow that prevented me from killing a deer'.

But the king did not mind them, and said to the boy: 'Go kill a tiger and bring it here'. The boy said to the monkey: 'Now what to do'? The monkey said: 'Make for me a mace of the weight of nine maunds and come along: we shall kill a tiger'. The boy repaired to a sāl-tree wood and fashioned a mace. They then went to another forest. As chance would have it, the dragon met with them. It had got hold of the boy, when the monkey gave it one knock of that heavy mace. The dragon said: 'Don't strike; whatever service you (both) want from me, I shall render it'. Says the monkey: 'Go then and kill a tiger for us'. They carried that tiger to the king. So the latter could neither entrap the boy nor have his sister.

Subsequently the king made up his mind to wage war against him and said 'Come, there must be war between us'. The boy enquired from the monkey: 'What shall I do? for I am single-handed'. The monkey said: 'I am going to levy soldiers for you'. He went to that dragon and said: 'All the compeers thou hast, collect them into one body'. This dragon assembled a good number of other dragons which she brought over, and posted on a neighbouring rocky plateau. The monkey said to them: 'Do not move until I tell you'; and he, the while, entered a thicket to watch the fun. The boy seized his horse-ear shield. He stands up in the centre...The enemy let a cloud (*lit.* any number) of arrows fly at him: not one struck him. The men then began to remark to one another: 'So many arrows (gone: our supply is) coming to an end; and not one but has missed him. Eh fellows! ask yonder monkey what this means'. Instantly the monkey called in all those dragons: 'To-day kill and devour to your heart's content'! The dragons, one and all, came at a run, caught men after men, ripped open and devoured everyone they caught. The king himself lost his life. The boy was elected king in his place and took up the government of the land.

II. Religious Myths.

42.—*Cicc-Cēp.*

The well meaning Dharmes wants to dispose by fire of the carcase of a huge man-eating monster, which he has just killed with his own hand. But in the world-wide conflagration mankind perishes. Its only survivors are two infants, whom the god nurses, rescues from savagery and instructs in good morals. The two become in time the renovators of mankind.

Hullo bīrī kohā nād rahcā; ād ālargahī kānā-barnā ḍahrē nū angikī ra'ālagyā. Ād kohā ṭungṛī lekh'ā meccha rahcā. Adin ballālagyar aoṅge, ālar adigahi baī nū kōr'ālagyar : eoṅdā ālar ā ḍahrē nū kālālagyar, eōndar malā kirrālagyar. Khanē Dharmes ānyas : 'I ḍahrē nū ḍhēr ālarin nitkī nitkī kānā ērdan, anti oṇṭā hō kirrnā malā ērdan'. Antile Dharmes ārin beddāge ittiyas. Khanē endr ērdas ? Kohā mudai asan ra'ī : eōndar attrā kānar, ār ormar ā nādgah kūlnum kōr'ar

Khanē Dharmes ālargahi muṭṭhā nū maṅjas, darā oṇṭā kohā aḍḍō nū nau nau mangahi ēṛ balman laccas kī keras. Ād āṛsā helrā khanē, 'arē, banḍā aḍḍo' bācas. Antile Dharmes ā nādgahi kūl ulā keras kī, oṇṭā balman kīyyā jobcas darā oṇtan maṅyā jobcas : a nād keccā kerāi

Kittā helrā khanē, adigahi gamkārnā merkhā gūṭī āṛsiyā, darā Dharmes ānyas : 'Idin cicc trū malā basson hole, ḍhēr ullā gūṭi gamkōr'ō' bācas, kī ciccan taiyas. Pahē, ciccan tainantī mundh, halmānan ānyas : 'Anā, bhagnā, ēn nād bassāge cicc-cēp taiyon, ād ōlō. Nīn ērā : cicc sagre aḍrā lagā helr'ō hōle, ḍamuan ṭhokke, hole ēn ciccan tēb'on. Antile Dharmes cicc-cēp taiyas, darā ā nād ulliyā kerā. Pahē cicc urmī khēkhel nū aḍrā laggā helrā. Halmānas, oṇṭā telā-mann nū khob telā paṅjkī rahcā, abṛin mokhā lōbhras keras ; ḍamuan ṭhok'āge modhras keras : cicc aḍrā lagnum urmī khēkhel bīḍrā kerā. Halmānasgahi mechā endrā jholrā kerā Khanē ās, tanghai mechan telā-mann nū niṛgr'ā khanē, telā-mann mōkhārō manjā, darā innā gūṭi ennem lakkā bārī ra'ī. Anti saōse rājī, darā saōse rājintā ālar, darā urmī sanjgīguṭṭhi ulliyā.

Abīrim Sirāsitā nālgahi oṇṭe kakṛō-lātā nū bhayā babin irb sannī khaddar kōrcar, kī ciccantī bacchrar. Khōkhānū Dharmes, Caṅrā, Bhaṅrā, Tilkā, Lodhā allan occas-kī, Sirāsitā nāl nū kuddā keras : endrā hō malā khakhrā, urmī ulkā rakhcā. Ekā aḍḍā nū bhayā babin rahcar, attrā allāguṭṭbi bāṛnum bārnum aṛsā helrā khanē, abṛā khaddar kakṛō-lātā nū kōr'āge bongcar. Dharmes, īryas kī, mīkhyas 'Ambā elcā, umbā elcā' bācas. Anti ās ārgahi khekkhā nū dhan-bihnin ciccas darā ānyas : 'Khetī nanke' bācas.

Abīrintim ullā ullā Dharmes ār gusan kālā-bar'ālagyas. Khōkhānū abṛā khaddar jokk jokk pardyar khanē, Dharmes, oṇṭā ḍhingran ār gusan occas-kī, ā kukkōsin ānyas : 'Idī, babū, ort ī ḍhingrantī īpakkhē cūtke, ort āpakkhē cūtke; nīm ḍhingrantī āpakkhē ambke kāla' bācas-kī, Dharmes keras Khanē abṛā khaddar, Dharmesgahi ānkā lekh'ā, ḍhingrāgahi āpakkhē ort, īpakkhē ort, cutā helrar Khōkhānū, ār khōb kōbā manjar khanē, undul ā kukkos ā ḍhingran kaṭṭiyas. Khanē ā kukoi ēkh mañjā. Darā ārgahi khaddārim sañse khēkhel nū bindyar. Ārgahi bārenū oṇṭā ḍaṇḍī pāṛnar :

' Bhayā bahin urkhar, koi :
Sirāsitā nālenū ra'anar.
Kakṛō-lātā eṛpā, koi :
Sirāsitā nālenū ra'anar '.

43.—*Karmas darā Dharmas.*

How did the Karam feast, formerly one of the tamest in the Oraon calendar, acquire a tribal character, and its present grade of solemnity and sacredness? It was all due to the heavenly chastisement which overtook a profane jester and happily brought him to his senses.

Karmas dara Dharmas name irb bhāir rahcar. Dharmas khall-ukhṛ nanālagyas, backan Karmas malañg lad'ālagyas

Undul Bhādō candōgahi hullō nū, Karmas malañg lad'ā keras. Ā candōgahi ekādasī ullā nū, Dharmas, tanghai eṛpambārir sange, karam tāryar kī ondrar, dara, tāli nū gaḍḍar-kī, kiṛā-ammōnkā nembāti, adigahi nēgcār nannar, adigahi mundhbhāre pāṛnar bēcnar.

Abirim khaṛdkā kīṛāsārkā Karmas kirr āṛyas, darā cālī nu dahuṛā gaṛrkā īryas-darā meñjas: 'Id endrā talī'? Ār gā 'karam-gōsāīn talī' ba'anar. Ās kadrāras darā bācas: 'Ort Karman ēn: nannā ekā karam isan ra'ō'? Khanē caḍḍas kī hibṛiyas ciccas. Annūtim Karmasgahi kapṛē bagṛārā. Dharmasgahi nalakh pardkī kālā helrā, pahē āsgahi tangdadas kīṛā manā helras, darā āsge ōnāge hō mal khakkr'ā helrā.

Undul Dharmasgahi ro'ā idnā rahcā. Khanē Karmas tanghai paccon ānyas: 'Ān paccō, gucai: innā gā namhai guṭhiyasgahīdim[1] ra'ī. Ēn biṛā ohiṭ'on, nīn id'oi Hole gā paohait ci'or '. Irbārim kerar, darā ās biṛā ohiṭdas, ād id'ī —Puttbirī Dharmas ormārin pacaiṭ ōnāge eḍḍas, pahē īrin malā eḍḍas. 'Eṛ'ā bar'or' ba'anar-kī, pāb ērnar; pahē nē hō eṛ'āge malā barcar. Khanē Karmas

[1] To-day, it is (the turn) of our kinsman. Grammar, p. 277c.

kadrāras, darā tanghai pacoon ānyas : 'Ān paccō, gucai : nīn ekā ekā ujgō iddkī, abran abṛan caṛ'ot ci'ot. Ormarge ciccar : naman endrnā malā eḍḍar'? Paccō kerā, darā tamhai iddkāujgontā caṛ'ā caṛ'ā hebṛā helrā. Adigahī ennē nannum, Dharmasgahi ālar, barcar-kī īryar-kī adin ānyar : 'Nīn ekā urtī taldī'? Ād ānyā : 'Ēn Karmasgahi ālin'. Ār bācar : 'Nīm endrnā iddkā ro'an caṛdar'? Ār bācar : Ēm irbāmim taō iddkam; eman pacaiṭ ōnāge eṛ'ā hō malā eḍḍar'. Dharmasgahi jōkhar ānyar : 'Nimhai kapṛē bagṛārā. Nīm karam-gosāīn ohmā malā nañjkar. Nanor hole, nimhai kapṛē paltār'ō'.

Khanē Karmas kobrār'ā helras, darā geochā geochā rājī nū Gangā tarā keras, karam-go-sāīn beddāge.

Kānum kānum, kīṛāsārkas mañjas. Oṇṭā dumbārī-mann nū khanjkan[1] īryas kī, heddē keras : 'oṇṭan mōkhon' bācas. Ouṭan caṛryas darā, ērdas gā ayyā pocgō ra'ī ! Malā mokkhas, hibṛiyas ciccas.

Anti ērdas ort mahras dūdhī bīnā bīnā jūtan opdas. Ās gusan keras darā ānyas : 'Ē bhāi, eṇgā tanikunā dūdhī ci'ā : kharā ammōn-kā sārkan ra'adan'. Mahras ciccas gā ; pahē Karmas bai gusan occas khanē, ērdas gā ād khēsō mañja darā kerā. Adin hō malā ōndas : annem hibṛiyas ciccas.

Gangā heddē āṛso bīrī, endr ērdas? Gangā nīndkī ra'ī, dara āpaklē oṇṭā karam-mann ra'ī. Ās mēkhā helras : 'Ē karam-gosāīn, barai eṇg gusan. Niṇgan hibṛkan āulantim, eṇghai kapṛē bagṛārā : aoṅge ningan beddā barekan. Innantim ennē malā nanon'. Karam-mann ānyā : 'Ēn gā niṇg gusan malā kaon ; hō'odai hōle[4], ninim bar'arkī, eṇgan conhātī cōd'arkī hō'ā'. Anti ās, amm nū helras[5] darā, khanē mulkhdas, khanē urkhdas : annē annem ajgut gahanḍī nū āṛsyas kī ōdas darā ondras. Karmasgahi dasā palṭārā, dara ās urb manā helras.

Āulantim ormar, cān cān, Bhādōgahi punaitī ulmūnd mundhim[6], karam-gosāīngahi ōhmā pūjā nannar.

---

[1] She began to uproot (the seedlings) in-the-direction-of her planting.

[2] See Grammar, p. 279, n. 3.

[3] Or Dict. under *opnā*.

[4] Grammar, p. 279, at bottom.

[5] Grammar, p. 279. n. 4.

[6] Exactly three days before the new moon of Bhado. See Grammar, p. 177, 6.

44.—*Lodhar dara Assurar.*

Dharmes, inconvenienced by some large iron smelting works underneath, sends word to stop them, but is not obeyed. He then, under the garb of a child, comes down and lures the iron-smeltors to their doom. For being displeased at this, their wives are changed into trees

The story looks like an adaptation of several biblical reminiscences: Noah's dove, tower of Babel, tale of Lot's wife. — It is also remarkable that, in this legend, the Lodhars, lit. *Lot's people, are associated in work with the Assurs, just as in Psalm 82, 7. A common designation for Dharmes is Bēlas: which reminds of Baal, the Assyrian god.*

Bārā bhāi Lodhā dara tērā bhāir Assūrar ōnd ullā nū kuṭṭhin dhuk'ālagyar khanē, mojkhā merkhā nū argyā. Adin Dharmes sah'ā pōllas, dara, ḍhicuan manā nanā taiyas khanē, ār adigahi ānkan malā pattācar. 'Ī sār ḍhicuā manā nanā barcā' ānyar, dara adigahi khōlan sāṛsītī dharcar : ābīrim ḍhicuāgahi khōlā khambhā lekh'ā mañjā, dara innā gūṭī annem ra'ī. — Ā khōkhānū bak'lan taiyas : khanē adigahi khēsran sāṛ-ītī dharcar kī natgyar : khanē bak'lāgahi khēser dighā mañjā, darā innā gūṭī digham ra'ī. — Munjā nū kerkeṭan taiyas : ād barcā darā manā helrā. Adigahi katthan hō malā meñjar, backan adigahi narṭin sāṛsītī pedkhar : āulantim, kerkeṭāgahi narṭi gusan, mokhārō mañjā, dara innā gūṭī mokhārod ra'ī. — Antile Dharmes manā nanā hārcas, dara, khasrā-khusrū kukkos lekh'ā mañjas-kī, tānim barcas, darā ārgahi kuṭṭhī-dhuknā gusan keras. Khanē gā endr ērdas ? Bārā bhāī Lodhar darā tērā bhāi Assūrar, mukkar bārī, kuṭṭhin dhuk'āge lakkar ra'anar.

Khanē khasrā-khusrū kukkos ārin ānyas : 'Nīm ekāse kuṭṭhin dhukdar darā pannā cāṛe malā bi'ī ? Ēngan kuṭṭhī ulā kōr'ā ci'ā' bācas-kī, kōrcas. Kōrnantī mundh ānkas rahcas : 'Cico khōb handkār'ō hole, punā aṛī nū khēnā amman ondrke darā ecchke.' Bācas rahcas khanē, ciccan darā kuilan kuṭṭhī nū sajjar, kī khōb dhuk'ā helrar ; ara, cico khōb handkār'ā helrā khanē, punā aṛī nū khēnā amman ondrar, kī ecch'ā helrar, kī dhuk'ā lagyar. Annē annem, urmī kuilā ōlā ōlā cind mañjā khanē, kuṭṭhin calkhar. Khanē Dharmes, khasrā-khusrū mañjas-kī kuṭṭhī nū kōrchas rahcas ās[1], sonārūpā trū khōb jhabrāras-kī urkhas. Ārin ānā helras: 'Ērā gā nīm ekāse pōldar dhuk'ā! Ērā, ēn akkun, bēs bēs singār-hīrāguṭṭhin biddkan-kī jhabrārkan-darā, urkhkan[2]. Akkun, nīm bō̃ khakkhdar hole[3], lagē, kuṭṭhī nū ormar kōr'ā: nimbai mukkar dhuk'or', bācas. Khanē abṛā bārā bhāi Lodhā, darā tērā bhāi Asūrar bō̃, ormārim kuṭṭhī nū kōrear. Khanē ārgahi mukkar, kuṭṭhi nū kuilan darā ciccan nindar-kī, dhuk'ā helrar. Cicc handkār'ā helrā khanē, ār ōlā helrar, darā ulā kāir-kōer[4] manālagyar, dara uphṛār'ā kacṛār'ā lagyar. Khanē Dharmes mukkārin āndas: 'Khōb dhuk'ā akkun; ār arbānakhr'ā lagnar, bagge bagge hō'āge'. Khanē ā mukkar khōb dhuknar: eō̃dā ār uphṛārnar, aō̃lā adkō capuan dhuknar. Khōkhānū, urmī kuilā ullyā kī cind mañjā khanē, kuṭṭhin calkhnar.. Darā ērnar gā, ōrmar ullyar kī cind mañjar.

Khanē ārgahi mukkar, Dharmesin dharcar-kī, malam kālā ci'inar, darā ānnar: 'Nīn emhai mētārin ṭhahackai, darā eman ārin kuṭṭhī nū dhuktāckai: eman ningāge pōsnā manō. Ningan em malam ambom'. Antile Dharmes hārcas, darā abṛā mukkārin ānyas: 'Akkū nīm, ṭoṛang nū kālarkī, kaisaigō-khoppā manā: hole nimāge ōnāge khakkhr'ō' bācas-kī ṭēṛas. Khanē abṛā mukkārim ṭoṛang nū kirkī-da'ā kaisaigō-khoppā manjar.

Aōñgem, akkū gūṭī, ālar, ṭoṛang kānar hole, kaisaigō-khoppā nū aṛjhārnar: ād ārgahi kheḍḍan khō̃sī[5], kī khēson urkhti'ī. Dharmes annūhoñ, bar cicckas ra'adas aoñgem, ālar, karam ullā, kaisaigo-khoppan darā telā-khoppan sangem gaṛnar; dara, gaṛ'ō bīrī, arkhin bhel munō, jharan adi maiyā tunduar. Abṛan kabsī-khall nū, kā ro'ā-khall nū bō̃ gaṛnar ci'inar.

---

[1] *Ās, ād*, etc., at the *end* of a clause, means *who*. See Grammar, p. 293, 2d and 3d examples.

[2] For the tense, see Grammar, p. 223, n. 6.

[3] Grammar p. 315, n. 4.

[4] Onomat. for confuse wrangling.

[5] *Khō̃snā*, to scratch.

III. Tribal Traditions.

45.—*Ruidastā Kuṛukh Bēlas.* (*Or. Gramm. p.* 311).

The Oraon traditions have it that, in remote times, the tribe was established in and round the Ruidas stronghold—a fortress 28 miles in circuit, now ruined, in the Shahābad district. The name is usually spelled Rohtas.

The present story relates how one Oraon king, as a heavenly reward for his boundless generosity to the poor, was restored to the throne, and built the fortress of Ruidās, which he named after the young prince, his son and heir.

The Hindu Puranas have a similar legend about one Haris Chandra and his queen Saivya, voluntary slaves in Benāres. But this Hindu variant is marred by the incredible and revolting rapacity of the Brahmin hermit Viswāmitra. Whichever be the original sketch, we find this objectionable person replaced, in the Oraon account, by a deity who simply wants to test the king's virtue and recompense it.

Ort bēlas arā bīṛī rahcar; ārge oṇṭā eklā tangdas rahcas. Ā bēlas bhagat rahcas: darā nēt-nēg uiyū, dara andhrā langṛā ṭhuṭhāguṭṭhiarge ci'ū khaṭṭū rahcas. Ek'am ōrtar tembā bar'ālagyar hōle, ārin nīdī-khekkhā malā kirrā ci'ālagyas Nīk'im oṇṭā ḍhibā nē'ālagyar hōle, ḍhibā-ēṛ ci'ālagyas; nīk'im ōnd ānā nē'ālagyar hōle, ārge nākh ānā ci'ālagyas; nīk'im pañce auṛkā khess nē'ālagyar, ārge dassē auṛkā ci'ālagyas. Nēkhain hō baccā-puccā malā nanālagyas, muīn ērā erā raibāṛī hō malā nanālagyas, baccā-barci kacnakr'ā hō malā ci'ālagyas. Ās em'ardara, ullā ulla pairī bīrī ci'ā khaṭṭālagyas.

Undul ennē mañjā Dharmes, timbū ālargahi[1] muṭṭhan dharcas-kī, bēlasgahi gaṛhē gusan keras, dara, bali gusan ijjas-kī, tembā helras. Khanē bēlas uṛung menjas-dara, urkhas dara bācas: 'Endran beddai, ēn niṅgāge ci'on'? Ās bācas: 'Anā belāyō, ēn tengāge sakcārdan:

[1] See Or. Gramm. p. 180, n. 28.

endr akh'oi, ci'ā ongoi kā polloi'. Ās bācas : Ēn pollon ci'ā-dara[1], nē ci'ā ongō ? Enghai gā urmī ra'ī ; ḍhēr timbū ālarge ciockan hole, anti ningā ci'ā pollon ? Nē'ā ; akkūnim ci'on'. Khanē timbus ennē biggē ḍhibā nē..as ā bēlas ci'ā hō pollā helras. Khanē gā bēlas endr nanjas ? tanghai gaṛhen, aḍḍō-mekkhō mankhā-bhaisā bāthighōṛōgutthin urmin bīsyas: annūhō ci'āge malā manī. Khanē munjā nū tanghai ālin khaddāsin tillī-eṛpā[2] nū bīsyas, dara tān oṇṭā dōmas guyā bīsras[3]...Dara timbusge ḍhibā ciccas.

Ābīri, nik'im khē'alagyar hōle, dōmārim bassālagyar : abṛā ullā[4] nū, ī nēgdim rahcā

Bisrkāgahi dhēr ulla khōkhanū,[5] undul ennē mañjā bēlasge tangdas bēṛām mañjas dara keccas kera.. mākhā mākhadim keccas. Mākham hō tilliyargahi jōkhar dōmar gusan bassāge, cēṛ'arkī hō ā helrar ; bīṛī hō khōkha cīkhnūtī kālālagyā. Adhāidhī mākhā ḍōmragahi ṭeṛpa āṛ-yar dara mēkhā helrar. Khanē urb ḍōmas cōcas, dara bīṛī gu-an dhiba nēras . khanē, adigahi bakhrā nū, tanghai urbar ciccar. Khanē urb dōmas ā bēl-jōkhasinim[6] bassāge cōdas. Ās, ciccan dharcas-kī, ār gane masṛā kālā helras.

Ḍabrē nū, adigahi cīkhnan meñjas-kī āsge soggē laggyā, dara adin menā menā helras. Enrēgē ās adin lakh'ā ṭōllālagyas : bisrkā ullantī ērā hō mal nakrkar rahcar, ara, tillyar lekh'am, adigahi kicri hō marakhkam ra'ālagyā. Ād hō āsin lakh'ā pōllā : ās gā hebṛkā[7] ālar lekh'ā etthr'āiagyas. Khanē ād hō, cīkhā cīkhā, bēlas anr timbusgahi dara tanghai urmī ktthan ōrentī tingyā Ās, meñjas-kī, tān hō cīkhā helras, dara olokhnum olokhnum bācas · 'Ēnim ra'adan'. Khanē irbārim khōb kalpār'ā helrar

[1] See Or. Gramm. p. 286, n. 6

[2] *Tilliyar*, Hindoos of the *tēli* caste.

[3] *Bisras*, he sold himself.

[4] The sense is : In those remote days, the bodies of *Oraons* were burnt *at ghats* (what) is no longer the case nowadays.

[5] *Bisrkā* is a past participle used as a noun. See Grammar, p. 244, nn. 40, 60. — The child had been sold together with his mother to the *tēli* people

[6] The royal slave in person.

[7] Castaway, from *hebṛnā*.

Abīrim Dharmes, ongh'on timbū ālargah'[1] muṭṭhan dharcas-kī, ittiyas, dara ārin bācas : ' Nīm engan khōb lōlā nanjkar kī manackar[2] songe, ēn hō nimāge dau ci'idan ' bācas. Khanē kecckā khaddāsin ujjtācas, darā ārin ānyas : ' Kalā, ī Ruidāsin lō'arkī Nimbaidim rāji manō'. Antile ayang-bang-guṭṭhiyar khaddāsin occar-kī kerar. Dara, tangdasgahi nāmetī, Ruidas nāme onṭā punā garhen kamcar, ekdā innā gūṭī ra'ī. Antile ḍher ullā rājī nanjar dara kōṛem kecar.

46.—*Kūṛukhargahi Ruidasti bongnā.*

Fort Rohtas, was destroyed by Aurangzeb. A full description with accompanying plan of what remains of that fortress may be seen in Montgomery Martin's History and Antiquities of Eastern India, 1838. *This author says page* 432 : ' *Hari Chandra* [*was*] *a king of the family of the sun in the most remote periods of the Hindu legend...I have learned nothing of the persons who held Rohtasgarh* from the time of Hari Chandra until the 12th century *of the Christian era* '. *So, if one may doubt the genuineness of the Oraon legend, he can certainly not say that it is clumsily timed or located.*

Hullo bīrī Kūṛukhar Ajabgaṛh[3] nū rahcar. Ayyantī bongarkī Hardiban barcar : eō ullā gūṭī ayyā rahcar. Asantī hō bongarkī Pipripāṭ barcar. Khōkhānū Ruidas nū ra'ā helrar, darā isan kōṛē kōṛem ōnālagyar.

Isānim, ārge Kurur[4] gane laggānakhrnā mañjā khanē, khōb laṛcar, dara Kurūrin ikla'am hō harāba'ā malā ciccar. Kurur gā, endr hō ōr nanā pollar khane, onṭā mabrā-mukkan galsī lagābācar.

Kuṛukhargahi majhi nū ennē nēgcār rahoā. Onṭā candō darā onṭā ullā nū khaddī man'ālagyar : ābīrī, urmī eṛpā nū, ḍher ḍher jharā lad'ālagyar darā arkhin hō kam'ālagyar : khōb onā mōkhālagyar, darā ungkhā ungkhā ormar kecokā lekh' am manar kālālagyar.

---

[1] See Gramm, p. 180, n. 28.

[2] From *man'na*, 4.

[3] Perhaps the petty state of Ajabpūrī, near Ahmednagar. *Hardiban* may be a mispronunciation of Hardwār, and *Pipripāt* of Pipraintī, a place just north of the Rājmahāl hills.

[4] The Mohammedans

Ā mahrā mukkā-ḍhcr cānti ullā ullā, dū lhī bisāṛe, Ruidas nū hālālagyā : aōge ād aiyyantā urmi nēgcāran īrkī darā akkhī rahcā Ād Kurūrin ānyā : ' Nīm ārin aubārī ullānū harāba'ā pollor '. Khane ār meñjar-kī ānyar : ' Anti, ekā ullā nū harāba'ā oṇgom ? ' Ād bācā . ' Iklā khaddī mano aulā kaor hōle, ārin harāba'ā oṇgor.'

Ād mānī mānim tiṇgkā rahcā. Kuṛukhar, khaddī manarkī, jharā darā arkhin ōṇḍar kī khōb uṇkhyar : khane, Kurūr tamhai gohoṇḍan ondrar-kī baroar, darā Ruida-gaṛh nū kōrcar. Ērnar gā ormar uṇkhyar, darā keccka lekh'am mañjkar ra'anar ; anti ārin lau'ā piṭā helrar. Pahē Kuṛukhnī mukkar abīrim, kaṛeā cōo cōc, tuṛsin darā manan dharcar kī laṛ'ā helrar, darā Kurūrin harāba'ā malā ciccar. Kurur, kadrārar-kī, mahra-mukkan anyar ' Nīn eman thakackī ! ' bācar. Ād ānyā : ' Thū thū[1] ! Nīm mukkar gane lar'ā pōldar ? ' Khane ār ba'anar . ' Nīn ānkī rahackī, khaddī ullā ormar jharā arkhī ōnnar kī keccka lekh'ā ra'anar, bācckī. Okhō uṇgkhyar ? ormar gā, īrdīdim[2], laṛnar. ' Ād ānā kirtācā : ' Nīm gane laṛnar, ār mukkārim talnar : ār gane nīm laṛ'ā pōldar ?' Ar bācar : ' Kaṛean cōckar rā anar ? ' Khane ād ānyā : ' Ha'ī gā. Mukkārim kaṛea cōcār : tuṛsī darā manan dhar'ā dhar'ā laṛnārim. Nīm eṇghai katthan malā patta'ādar hōle, ērā kalke, kaḍrkā nanō bīrī ekāṛē mūhin muñjhrnar : oñtā khekkhā trū muñjhrnar hōle, mētar talnar ; ēṛ khekkhātim muñjhmar hōle gā mukkar talnar. ' Anti Kurur joh'ā helrar : khane gā ērnar, mukkārim kaṛeā cōckar ra'anar, darā ēr khekkhā trū mūhin muñjhrnar. Iin akkhar-kī, kirryar kī Ruida-gaṛh nū oṇgh'on kōrcar, darā ormārin laúā piṭā helrar.

Ort gā Kuṛukhas nijṛiyas darā boṇgā helras : Kurur, āsin hō piṭāge gecchā geecham khedcar. Boṇgnum boṇgnum, ās Chota Nagpur guṭī āṛsyas. I rājī nū ābīrī Mūṇḍā bhāīr ra'ālagyar. Ōṇṭē paddā nū ek ' am ek'am Muṇḍar ḍaṇgrā paskar rahcar, darā abṛan mōkhāge khonḍrkar rahcar. Buṇgkāsim[3] ā ḍaṇgrā-mucūrin ānā helras : ' Eṇgan bacchāba'ā, bhāirō, eṇgan bacchāba'ā, bhāirō.' Khane ār ānyar : ' Ninghai janain hebṛā, darā emhain

[1] Thu Thu ! pshaw, pshaw !

[2] Irdīdim, Indicative present of ērna.

[3] Bungkāsim, the fugitive.

mōkhā; hole gā ningan baccbāba'om. makhle, ningan malā baccbāba'om. (Ābīri, Kuṛukhar majhī nū, ormā mētar janai ṭang'ālagyar). Khane ās, elenā trū, tanghai janain hibṛiyas, kī ḍangrā-ahṛan hō mokkhas ciccas[1]. Kurur āsin khednūti ondr'ālagyar[2]. Āṛsyar ki ānā helrar: 'Ijgonū ortos bnngkāsim bar'ālagyas; ās ittrā barcas; āsin nīm eksan nuḍḍkar?' Ār bācar: 'Ittrā gā nē hō malā barcar. Ērā se, isan embai ālārim ra'ānar; Kuṛukhargā janai ṭangnar: ērā se nekh'aidim ra'ī hole.' Khane ā Kurur ērā kuddnar: nekh'ai hō janai mala rahcā. Khane ār kerar; darā ā Kuṛukhas (Choṭā) Nagpūrnum ra'ā helras, darā asgabi khaddārim asan akkū gūṭī baṛharkar ra'anar.

IV. Domestic events and tribal festivals.

47.—Kuṛukh Beñjā.

The first proposal.—Pūsē bhēl Māghē candō nū Kuṛukhar beñjrnar Benjanti mundh, benjru'ū kukkosgahi tambas, pāb-īd'usgahi[3] leke, ek'am paddantā ek'am ortosgahi tangdan ānta'ādas. Ās kādas arā kukoigahi tangyō kā tambāsin mendas: 'Ek'am tartī ī ninghai kukoige āṛsor hōle, bīsor kā malā?' Antile kukoigahi tangyō tambas ānnar. 'Ek'am tartī āṛsor hōle gā bīsom.' Khane pāb-īd'us ēṛ-tartā katthāguṭṭhin attra-ittrā hōodas oodrdas: anti, ēṛ-tartim katthā ukki hōle, pāhīge kānar barnar.

The exchange of visits.—Kukkos tartile kālō bīrī, ālar sagun īrnum kānar: attī ār akh'ā beddnar, īrgahi beñjā ṭhaukam manō kā malā. Kānum kānum, eksa'ānim chucchū kā coṭṭō keockā khakkhor kā ēror hole, ba'anar. 'Ibṛargahi beñjā dau mal manō: beñjr'or hōlē, kukkos kā kukoi nīd'im cāṛē gā khe'or kālor'. Ī caḍḍē ibṛar arr brnakhrnar... Mundā, kālo bīrī, murkhur ḍhicuan mennar hōle, ba'anar: 'Id gā authan dau sagun mañjā. Attī ār oṛgnar: 'Ī punā khai khōkhānū oṇṭā narmiyā, dhirijā, cōnhā arā nalakh-nanū ālī manō.' Pābēnū, eksa'ānim māṛā-bassnan ērnar hole, ba'anar: 'Ibṛā punā biñjru'ūrge kharā dau tali'; ār ghokhnar ibṛā kukkō-kukoirgahi punā kundrnam

[1] See Or. Gramm. p. 149*c*.

[2] Were still pursuing him. See grammar pp. 146*b* and 242.

[3] *Lit.* through a scout, i.e. a friend sent out to reconnoitre how the wind blows. *Pāb īd'us* is derived from *pāb* and *īdnā*.

manālaggī, darā īr-irbārim paconā gūṭī juṛi-pāti ra'ā oṛgor. Eṛpā āṛskantī, endran endran bar'ōbīrī pābe nū meñjar kā īryar, abṛāguṭṭhī teṅgar arā mennar.[1]

Ceremonial of the visit.—Punā pāhiyargahi barekō bīrī[2], amm-aṛī khoṭr'ō, kā billī tēbr'ō, hōle hō 'sagun lēs mal mañjā' a'anar-kī kacnakınar. Mundā ennē malā manō, hōle gā daulem ōnā mokhāge oi'inar.—Urmintī mundh, ek'am ālī pāhiyārin kheḍḍ nūṛī, anti kheḍḍ-nūṛū ālīge pāhiyar oṇṭā ḍhibā ci'inar. Khōkhānū kukkō-kukoi tartar ōṇḍ aḍḍānum okknar. Pāhiyarge arkhī ondrnar kā jharā tundnar. Antile ormārim, mukkar mētar, ōnnar mōkhnar, darā kukkō-kukoirgahi bare nū mennar arā teṅgnar. Gōtar ēṛ-tartādim oṇṭam manō hōle, beñjā malā cicenakrnar. Ār oṛgnar: 'Ibṛār gā oṇṭā eṛpantā talnar, īr ōnd kūliyar manjar: īr-irbārimgahi beñjā ekāse manō'? Mundā nannā gotrantar ganẹ, beñjā cicenakrnar. Kukkos arā kukoigahi kundrkā cānguṭṭhin mennar teṅgnar.—Ēṛ-tartārim pattārnar hōle, pattārkāgahi cinhā ēd'āge ēṛ-tartā kheppar cō'onar, arā 'samdhī, samdhī' bā'anum, baṛin dharnar, antile eōkhan emarnakhrnar darā phīn okknar. Ōndkā okkā khōkhānū, tang'ā tang'ā eṛpā kirrnar kānar.

Ennem, beñjā argī mannā gūṭī, ēṛ-tartim pāhī kānar barnar, beñjāgahi ullan cājnar. Pāhī-eḍḍkā kukoi tartile hō, ālar kukkōsin ērāge kānar. Ār hō sagunguṭṭhi ērnum kānar: pābē nū urmidīm kōṛe-kōṛem mañjā hōle, kukkosgahi eṛpā gūṭi āṛsnar khane, kukkos tartar ārin kheḍḍ nōṛnar arā pāhī khōjnar.

Settlement of the money payable to the girl's father.—Kukoigahi eṛpā nū kālō bīrī, dālī-ḍhibāgahi katthā otthornar. Ābīrim ēṛ-tartārim an'ā-man'ā alkhnāgahi katthan kacnakhrnar.

Kukoi tartā kheppar mennar; anti kukkos tartā kheppar ānā-kirta'ānar:

Kukoi tartar: 'Nīm ekā ōrtar taldar? ēm niman baldam. Ekā tartī barekar? Endran beddar?'

[1] They relate all this, or else *their hosts* question them as to such happenings. *Mannā teṅgnā*, to talk a thing over.

[2] On the arrival.

[3] Engaged, betrothed.

Kukkos tartar: 'Ēm kharā geochamtī barckam. Gollasgahi cirkbī ondrkam be'edam, puttbirī iyyā āṛskan. Ī paddā nū, ha'ī ī eṛpānum, emhai oṇṭā osar bachiyā kōrcā: ēm bēs bēs akhdam Ād eõdā eõdā ullantī ibsirkī ra'ī; innī ēm adin iyyā khakkhon[1].'

Kukoi tartar: 'Anti ninghai osar ekāse ra'ī? Khē-ō, kā mokhārō, kā paṇḍrū? Endr adigahi marg hõ ra'ī? nīm adin akh'ā ongor?'

Kukkos tartar: 'Ha'ī, mānim, ēm alin akhlam. ād enghaidim talī.'

Kukoi tartar: 'Akkun, endr ā osargahi mullī ci'ā ongor? Ēm adin biddkam, pōskam be'edam: adigahi kharā baggē ḍhibā manō. Ēm anti bisoi-ēṛ doye (kā bisoi-ēṛ, kā ōnd bisoi doye)[2] rupiā ba'adam' ba'anar.

Ennem kacnakhrnum alkhnum, ḍhiban etta'ānar[3], arā dāli-ḍhibā pānce rupiā manī. Phīn doye-nākhannan hõ oṇṭā rupia kamnar: idi lekkhā nū pānce rupiyāgahi dāliḍhibā rupiā nākh soye annantā manī[4]. Īdim Kuṛukh beñjāgahi dalī-ḍhibā talī.

The fixing of the marriage-day.—Cirdīgahi ullā har' ālaggī khane, kukkosgahi tambas kukkosgahi tambas guyā pāb-īd'ustī menā taidas. Ās mendas: 'Beñjā iklā manō?' Khane kukoi-tambas tengdas: 'Engdā hanuī ullā kundrā: anti āulā adigahi beñjā mal ban'ō'. Khokhānū kacnakhrnum ullānim okta'ānar[5].

The wedding pageant.—Ibṛā urmī khōkhā, barāt kalāge saprāṛnar. Beñjā kālō bīrī, jokk jharā-amm khēkhel tundnar pācbālarge. Antile, khusmārnāgahi cinhāge, kāṛsā cōlnar, darā kānantī mundh, urung cālī nū assnar, pāṛnar, nālnar. (Kāṛsā nū[6] oṇṭā khajjgahi bhaṇḍā talī; adin khessgahi bāltī tessnar[7], pīp mējbnar) Anti ort mēt arā ālī, adin kummū-darā, nalti'ī. Antile barāt kālī. Beñjru'ū kukkos oṇṭā khaṇḍan hō'odas arākādas: ī khaṇḍā mēt arā saññgyā mannāgahi oṇṭā cinhā talī. Beñjā-ālar kukoigahi paddā gusan

---

[1] We shall take it back.

[2] Rs. 50 (or 40 or 30).

[3] They beat down.

[4] At the rate of 14 as. per rupee, Rs. 5 becomes Rs. 4-6-0.

[5] They fix the very day.

[6] An earthen pot is (i. e. does duty) *for* a wedding urn.

[7] Figure of speech, *lit.* they plait the wedding urn with rice-ears.

barnar hōlē, kukoi tartar hō nalnutim urkhnar: antī ēṛ-tartārim ōnd aḍḍānum k͟hōnḍrnar, arā asan uṛung paikī ḍēgnar. Ābīrim, kukoi tartile, mukkar loṭā nū amm ondrnar, arā ṭatk͟hā-ḍahurātī beñjru'ū kukkōsin arā pāhiyārin chiṭka'ānar[1]; antile ār eṛpā kōrnar.

The marriage rite.—Beñjru'ū kukkos, tanghai khanḍan dhar'ar, chachem ijjkas ra'adas : k͟hane kukoi-tambas, kā tangdadas, bar'ar kukkōsin pākdas, antile manṛbā ulā hō'odas, asan āngahi k͟heḍḍan nōṛnar, k͟hōkhānū kukoin darā ormā pāhiyārin hō eṛpā nū eṛnar ci'inar.

Kukkō kukoi irbārim ijnar; kukkos kukoigahi k͟hōk͟hā tarā ijdas arā tanghai ēṛ k͟heḍḍgahi anglitī kukoigahi guṛk͟hin emardas: kukkosgahi enrē nannā ā kukoin tanghai ālī kamnāgahi cinhā talī. Kukoi āsin tanghai guṛk͟hin emara'ā ci'ī: īd tabē nū mannāgahi onṭā cinhā talī.—Ennē mañjkā k͟hōk͟hā, ār irbārim onṭā piṭrīnum okknar: ā piṭrī kiyā mañyā ālār kaṭikunā dubbā-jargan ondrnar: ittī punā beñjru'ūrge ujjnā baggē ullā mannan ēḍnar[2], kā īr irbārim kōṛē-kōṛem arā khusmārnum tambai ullan khēp'or. K͟hane irbarīnim mukkāmēt manāge gacchrta'ānar[3]. Beñjr'ō bīrī kicrīti ārin ochor nannar. Kukkos, tanghai ḍebbā k͟hekkhāgahi nāk͟htā anglītī, kukoigahi kapṛē nū i-ung arā sindrī tuddas; anti kukoi hō, tanghai ḍebbā k͟hekkhāgahi nāk͟htā anglītī, kukkosgahi kapṛē nū isung arā sindrī tuddī: īd gā tām tām nū beñjrnāgahi onṭā chinhā talī. Beñjā-aḍḍā gusan onṭā ugtan bhēl onṭā pagsin kukkosge, kukoige paṭcācan kā lūṛhin uinar: ugtā arā pagsī mētasgahī cirkhī (anti nalakh)) gahi, paṭcācā arā lūṛhī mukkāgahi kumnā[4] (nalakh) cinhāge ra'ī—Antile ōrt paccō ālī (adigahi mētas keccas hōle) beñjāgahi nēgcar nanī; adigahi mētas gandas, ujjnum ra'adas hōle Ā paccō beñjāgahi katthan ennē tingāba'ī: (Kukkōsin :) Ērā hannī, īd hannī ninghai mukkā mañjā. Nalakh nanō bīrī, kā aṛk͟hā tokkhō bīrī, manntī khattr'ō arā k͟heḍḍ k͟hekkhā esr'ō, kā kāṛī kā sonḍē manō, kā ek'am sastītī adigahi mūhī muṭṭhan bigṛāṛ'ō hōle,

---

1. Generally with turmeric water.

2. *Lit.* they symbolize the prospect of many days of life.

3. *Lit.* they make them engage to become man and wife.

4. *Cirkhī* and *kumnā* (ant. infinitive with noun-value) stand as emblems of the various occupations proper to each sex.

annūbō idin ambke ambā. Endr'ānim īd niṅgāge bīt'ō, adinim ōnke mōkhkr, arā tarkai rā'ake. Antī nannā ek'am urtī[1] tarā ambkem ērā.'

(Kukoin :) 'Ān hanniyo, ērāī. hannis ninghai mētas taldas. As, nalakh nanāge kā sendrā bēcāge, ṭopang kā partā kālos, darā āsgahi kheḍḍ kā khekkhā esr'ō, kā kāṛā manos hōle, nīn āsin ambke ambā. Endr'ānim ās ondr'os, adinim bītā'āke arā ci'ike. Anti nannā ek'am ortos tarā ambke era.'

Banquet and bride's departure for her new home.—Beñjā mañjkā khōkhā nū, ormā ālar ōnnar mōkhnar. Adhā-idhī mākhā bīrī, kukoin tainar[2]; ābīrī eṛpantar nīd'im adin pāknar, arā paddantī jokk geochā otthornar ci'inar. Antile kukkos tartar adin pāknar, arā kukkosgahi paddā tarā hō'onar : Khane, kālo bīrī, kukoi ennē ennē bāe bāe cīkhālaggī : 'An ayō! Anā babā hoi! anā dadā bagārō! nīm engan chipā-amm lekh'ā eṛpantī otthorkar, khall-sārē lekh'am hibṛkar[3].'—Aulā ālī gane irb nubb kukoiguṭṭiyar kānar; anti, jokk ullā, adigahi hebṛnā ullanti adi gane ra'anar. Āntile khōkhānū ād utkhīdim[4] kālī bar'ī.

48. *Kuṛukhargahi khuṇḍī.*

I. *The ordinary case* (immediate cremation).

1. *The ceremony.*—Kuṛukhar nīd'im khē'enar hōle, aulam bassnar. Urmintī mundh, māṛan emta'ānar arā isung khassnar, kapṛē nū sindrī tundnar, anti bai nū maṇḍī arā ḍhibā tindna Antile māṛan kicrī bācnar, darā eṛpantī otthornar. Khane eṛpan ēṛnar, arā eṛpā nū cindan bīṇḍnar; khōkhānū balin muccnar. Māṛan sāṛā nū ceṛ'arkī masṛan gusan hō'onar. Ār jokk jokk khess cākhnūtim kānār : ī khessan, uruṅg mundhim, ormā paccō mukkar keockā ālas (kā ālī) gahi cālī nū ondrkar ra'anar, darā tām ās (kā adi) gahi eṛpantī bō jokk khess otthorkar ra'anar.

Masṛā gusan āṛandr ; asan kaṅktī oṇṭā tāṛā kamnar, darā kaṅk malyā māṛan uinar ; antile eṛpantā urbas pār-mūnḍ keockasgahi bain cicctī dāgdas ; khōkhānū goṭṭā mēlan ōldnar.

---

[1] *Urtī*, femin. of *ortos*.

[2] *Tainar*, the bride's relations 'send her away', i.e. see her off. *Ótthornar ci'inar*,' accompany her when she leaves.

[3] *Hebṛnā*, a verb very different from *hēbṛnā*.

[4] See Or. Dict. *otokh*.

2. *Observances on way back and at home.*—Masṛā gusan ḍiṇḍā-kukkō, kā kukoi-khaddar, kā pellō-āligutṛhiyar mal kānar. Nannā mukkar, mēd ōldkā khōkhānū, kheḍḍ khekkhā nōṛornar darā eṛpā kirrnar. Balin tisignar arā ērnar: eṛpā ulā, cind nū endr endr cambī mañjā, kā malā[1]..Cind nū murgī, nerr, bhirkhāgahi kheḍḍ-cambin ēror hole, ba'anar: 'Isin (kā idin) nād mōkkhā[2]; mundā, cind nū mērgahi cinhā ērnar khane oṛgnar isin (kā idin) Dharmē occā.'

Mētar khōkhānū eṛpā barnar. Asan ār, keeckā ālas (kā ālī gahi nāmētī, oṇṭā kisan piṭnar, arā adligahi jokk ahṛan pannpīk[3] gane mōcnar, arā eṛpā-balī gusan mārnar.—Ābiri paddantā ormā mukkar paobāl-tīkhil ondrnar. Mētar mūndgoṭeng oṭkhā aṭkhāti oṇṭā dhukṛī ōjnar: aiyyā oṇṭā kā mund' oṭe iñjō, arā kaṭikunā baṅgur arā mani sajnar; anti jokk goṭmāsin pūkhnar, arā abṛan mundgoṭang maṇḍī gane pataglī nū khaṭṭnar arā kētr nu uinar ci'inar.

3. *Going to pick up the bones.*—Khōcol pesā kalō bīrī, abṛan māsṛa gusan hō'onar, darā kukk tarā uinar; ḍahrē nū ā paobāl-tīkhlan cākhrum kānar. Keeckasgahi urmī pōrentā, oṇṭā oṇṭā, khōcol pesar, punā sanjgī nū uinar: antile eṛnāgahi khōkhā tartā cankhī gusan mārnar.

Khōclan kūnḍī nū argī huṛāba'anā gūṭī, abṛāgahi mārkā-aḍḍā gusan ullā ullā ōnd khetā maṇḍī āṛsta'ānar.

II. Case of differed cremation.—Olā kā mātātī khē'enar hole, ārin mārnar ci'inar. Antile, cirdīgahi, ārgahi māṛan bisō bīrī, kukkan kheḍḍ cappōtarā nannar arā bissnar. Ulka khōkhā nū[4], kukk, kheḍḍ, khekkhā, anti raggantā oṇṭā oṇṭā khōcol pesnar.

III. Final disposal of the bones.—Cīrdī āṛsyā khane, khōclan kuñḍī nū huṛāba'anar. Kuñḍī khāṛ nū kā nāl nū kamckā ra'ī. N tambai addī paddā nū malkar, ār tambai ālargahi khōclan ad paddantā kunḍī nū āṛsta'ānar. Pahē inelā tambai ra'anā paddānur addiyar gusti aḍḍā khēdā khēdā, abgam ālar tamāge kuṇḍī kamnar[5].

[1] They observe whether any markings have (during their absence) been made on the ashes.

[2] *Asan nād mokkhā*, he was killed by a *bhūt*, or by witchcraft; *Dharmē occā*, he died a natural death.

[3] With (a knife made of) cast iron.

[4] *Ulkā*, a contraction of *oldkā*. See Dict. *ōlnā*.

[5] Hence, the only essential [illegible]

Khōclan kuṇḍī nū hō'onagahi nēg Kuṛukhar ennē nannar. Cirdīnum kā Pūse candō, tambai kecckā ālargahi beñjāgahi nēg nannar ; darā, ā beñjantī mundh, ārge nembā mannuā caṛ ra'ī : keockargahi khōclan argī huṛāba'anā gūṭī, eṛpantā ālar rīn nū hērkar bē'enar aõge.

Nembā mañjkantī, māṛkā sañjgin otthornar. Adin pāp mējhnar ; anti, asmā kuṛ'arkī arā attī pūn kam'ardarā, adin atta'ānar. Antile, khōclan kūṇḍī nū etta'āge, assnum, pāṛnum, sanjgin nalta'ānūtim kānar. Mundh, kūṇḍin umdā ēgnar, balkā-amin eohnar, astā cācā nū sindrī ṭūḍnar arā aḍḍan nembā nannar, anti khōclan huṛāba'anar ci'inar.

Ibṛā urmī nēg gā, keockā ālārin pacbālar gusan āṛsta'āge Kuṛukhar nannar. Ī nēg nanō bīrī hō, kharā bagge ōnnā arā mōkhnā manī.

49.—*Pacbā ālar.*

This tale may be aptly placed here, as illustrating the popular belief in ghosts in a most lively manner. The piece is particularly full of idioms.

Ort ālas undul bemār mañjas kī keccas keras : khane āsin masṛā occar darā bassyar ciocar. Antile puttbīrī maṇḍī occar, darā, sōṛā patagliguṭṭhīnū[1] khaṭṭā khaṭṭā, uiyar ciccar. Ennē bācar-kī masṛan ambyar : 'Hudī, pacbā ālarō, nimāge ci'ar kāldam ; mōkhke ōnke darā ra'ake.'

Ittī ort ālas ānā helras : ' Pacbā ālar ōnnar mōkhnar ' ba'anar : idin ēn ērā bar'on', bācas. Khōkhānū otkhas[2] masṛā kirryas, darā masṛā-gustā oṇṭā mann nū argyas-kī chachem joh'ā helras. Adhā-idhī mākhā mañjā khane, endr ērdas ? pacbā ālar urkhar-darā tām tām nū kaonakhrnaṛ, darā khaṭrnakr'ā[3] mōkhā ōnā helrnar.

Khanē oṇṭā pacbā ālas bācas : ' Ānā harō, ortosge gā modhrkar[4].' Ār meñjar : ' Nekā ? ' Khane ās bācas : Adā, ā mann maitasgē[5]. Ormar

---

[1] into a big leaf-cup *and* upon leaf-plates.

[2] See Dict. *otkh*.

[3] The word ' khaṭrnakr'ā ' implies that the weird guests do not help themselves, but are given each his portion by one of their number.

[4] Understand ' ci'ā ' before ' modhrkar '.

[5] To the one on the top of that tree.

mann tarā ūrā helrar ... Khane gā mann-maitas ittyas cappyas, darā boṇgā helras, darā tanghai eṛpantārin bācas : 'Mānim, harō, pacbā ālar ujjnar, darā khaṭrnakr'ā ōnā mōkhālagyar : adin īrkan ra'adan.'

Ī ketthan menō bīrī, kecokāsgahi[1] bhāis ānyas : 'Bhōjē gā bākim ra'ī : āsgahi[2] nāmētī ōnto'on ci'on.' Aulantī keeckā tanghbhāis mākhā nū tambai[2] eṛpā bar'ā helras ... Ekābīrī ormar cūtnar, ābīrī ālar lekh'am ēknūtī bardas ; darā tambai allā hō malā bhūkī; pabē ekāsem 'ujjnā[3] rabcas ābīrī, ās gane lebhṛeṛerkī kuddkī kuddālagyā, annē akkū hō nanālaggī. Ennem mākhā mākham bardas khane, eṛpantar joh'ā helrar : ār sachem ērnar āsim talyar ... Eṛpā nū bhokṛontī kōrālagyas, darā mundhantā lekh'ā āl manar kālālagyas...Antile, okkā ka cūtā kā ijkas[4] ra'ālagyas hole, āsin dhar'ā beddālagyar : khane ās cāṛem lātantī[5] kōrālagyas, darā chayā manar bongālagyas ... Ennem, ekāgūṭī malā bhōjē naññjar, ā gūtī bar'ālagyas. Munjā nū bhōjē āsgahi nāmētī maññjā kerā : āulantim ās barnan ambyas ciccas.

Āoñge ālar ba'anar, ekāgūṭī bhōjē malā nanom, āgūtī keeckar āsē nannar. Ige bhōjē nannar, darā, 'pacbā ālar ujjnar' ba'arkī, urmī tihā nū asmā kiccnar[6], darā khēkhel nū arkhī kā boṛ'ē tundnar, anti mōkhnar darā ōnnar.

50.—*Khaddī parab.*

Phāgū kerkā khōkhānū Kuṛukhar khaddī man'nar. bīrī urmintī kōṛhē jhakhrā-mannan[7], idātō cālā-paccon, ohmā nannar : anti adige dāṛē argnar.

---

[1] Viz., the dead man referred to in the opening lines of this story. 'The meal (I was to give in his honour) is, as a matter of fact, (still) due.

[2] *Tambai*, their, viz., his own and his still living brother's.

[3] 'Just as when he was alive'...The Oraon infinitive frequently takes adjectival value. (Gramm. p. 238). On 'kuddki', see Gramm, p. 150, n 231.

[4] The final '*s*' of 'ijjkas' is to be mentally supplied also at the end of the other two past participles 'okkā' and 'cūtā'.

[5] 'He would pass through the chinks *of the door*.'

[6] 'They thread cakes' in bunches for the dead.

[7] That tree is regarded as the embodiment of a deity, the 'lady of the grove.' Of the various spirits honoured on the Khaddī day, she receives the largest share of veneration (urmintī kōṛhe)

Priestly fast and first begging tour.—Iklā khaddī maññage ōr manī, aulam naigas arā iṛbus darā ārgabi mukkar pairī bīrintim ubsnar. Naigas arā iṛbus irbārim paddā nū erpā eṛpanti jokk jokk ābdā-tikhil ūjnar: mukkar idin ār gusan ondrnar khane, naiças hō ā mukkarge jokk kirta'ādas[1]: ennē mannāti, naigas urmī eṛpantā khurjī-paññjā nū dau ci'idas[2]. Mukkar naigas gustile iññjrkā tīkhlan eṛpā ondrnar, arā taṇghai eṛpā ula cākhnar: ār oṛgnar, enne nanā khane, eṛpantā khurj-ī-paññjā baggē mano.

Pujā preparations.—Kukk cappōbīrī, naigas arā iṛbus arā kainō ālar, nāggahi ālon cāla-paccōgahi nembā aḍḍā gusan hō'onar: idāto khēr, ābdā-tikhil, ābdā-mēr, punā aṛī, kaṭṭū, tauā, ḍabnā, anti isuṇg, sindrī, punā kantō, kalcur, arā naōr-pūp. Oṇṭā kēter nū, ād[3]'cān biṛdantim naigasge ciockā ra'ī, ās jokk ābdā-tikhil arā naōr-pūp uidas; jharā arā arkhī arā jokk ābdā-tīkhil guṇḍā, ibṛā urmī ālōguṭṭhin naigas sapṛa'ādas. Iṛbus hō, idhī mākhā[4], ōnd cirkhī amm punā aṛī nū nindcas, arā jhakhrā gusan āṛtācas. Mākhā nū aṛintā amm battī hole, ālar ānnar: 'Idnā cēp jukkī manō;' mundā ā amm mal battī hōle, ba'anar: 'Idnā baggē cēp poññō.'

The khaddi pūjā.—Antile, pairī bīrī, naigas nēg nannāge ōr nandas. Urmintī mundh, ās jhakhrā-mannā mūlī nū ābdā tikhil guṇḍan bīṇḍdas; antile ābdā-tīkhlan aḍḍā mūnd[5] jokk jokk khaṭṭdas arā uidas. Idin khēr pisī mūkhī hōle, ālar kacnakhrnar: 'Jhakhrā pattārā.'—Ī khōkhānū, naigas jhakhrāmann mūlin isung arā sindrī tūḍdas, darā pār-mūnd ābdā mērau mann nū pojjdas, idātō[6] cāla-paccon punā kicrī kurta'ādas: adin beñjrdar[7]. Khōkhānū tān isung arā sindrī taṇghai kapṛē ēṛ-barī cōkh arā khebdāguṭṭhī nū ṭūḍrdas.—Anti khēran asan eṛbdas-arā[8], naigas gohrārdas-kī ba'adas: 'Anai jhakhrā-paccō, nīn kōṛē-kōṛem idnā cēp-amm taike: paddā,

[1] The pahan takes their rice, and returns a little of it to them.

[2] *Lit.* bring a blessing on all their domestic interests.

[3] Ās, ād take occasionally the meaning *who, which*. This is one instance.

[4] I.e. in the course of the hours from midnight till morning.

[5] 'On three spots.' He drops rice, in three distinct little heaps, near the foot of the tree.

[6] Idāto, 'which emblematically signifies that'

[7] 'he marries her to himself.' Ṭūḍrdas, he anoints his own body.

[8] *Lit.* 'Then, (while) sacrificing a fowl, the priest shouting says.'

eṛpā-pallī, khall-ukhṛī anti urmī khurjī-pañjā nū dau ci'ike.' Anti nannā urmī nādguṭṭhīge onṭā onṭā khēr asānim eṛbdas.

Treat given to the male population.—Ikkun iṛbus ā punā aṛinta ammtī suṛī manḍi bita' ādas. Manḍī argī bi'inā gūṭi, naigas, jokk kheppar gane, paddantā khūrī khūrī kuddas: assnum pāṛnum, kēter ara naōr pūpgutṭhin ockas-kī kuddas, darā mukkarge onṭā onṭā pūp khuṭṭdas; khōkhānū ā cālā gusan kirrdas. Phīn kāldas, darā metārin suṛī manḍī ōnāge eṛāge paddā kōrdas. Ennem ās arā kheppar pār-mūnd paddā kānar barnar; kālo bar'ō birī, ennē dandī pāṛnar:

Sarinda gosāī sārem	Sarinda gosāī sārem
Hare khaddi nanot	Innā khaddī kerā,
Hare phaggu nanot:	Nelā phaggu kerā:
Hiyō hī, daldal, hiyō hī!	Hiyō hī, daldal, hiyō hī!

Suṛī manḍī bickā khōkhānū, nubb kā pañcē ceplōguṭṭhyar mūnd ōnnar: ābīrī naigas urmī nādguṭṭhīge khērgahi umbalkhon arā suṛī manḍin argdas. Antile ormā kheppar ōnnar mōkhnar.

Treat to women and children.—Biṛī puttī khane, ortos naigāsin pākdas, darā āsgahi eṛpa ondrdas. Cālī nū āsgahi kheḍḍan naignī nūṛī: anti ās eṛpā kōrdas. Āulam naignī hō, paddantā ormā mukkar arā khaddarge, tanghai eṛpā nū, manḍī biti'ī, darā ormārin ōnti'ī mōkhti'ī, darā khusmarti'ī Āulam hō, naigas ṭanghai eṛpā nū naōr-pūp kherrdas[1].

The 2nd day's begging tour.—Nelantā ullā pairī birī ās arā iṛbus, ormā addiyargahi eṛpantī ōr nanar gaurorgahi eṛpā gūṭī, naōr-pūp kherrnūtim kānar: ābīrim mukkar, irbargahi kheḍḍan nōṛnar-kī, ārge ōnd auṛkā ābdā tikhil arā onṭā ḍhibā ci'inar: khane naigas pastī nū iñjrdas, pahē ās mukkarge jokk tikhil kirta'ādas darā pūp ci'idas: abṛan ār tamhai kēter nū iñjrnar. Khane iṛbus mesgā maīyā amm tunddas: idin hō mukkar tamhai kēter nū iñjrnar arā eṛpā mankhnar. Ennē nannātī abṛar ōṛgnar, ēm naigas tartile dau khakkhdam.

[1]. That is, he drives the stalk of the flower into the roof thatch.

Meaning of these celebrations.—Ennē ennē nēgcār nannātī Kuṛu-khar oṛgnar : 'Akkū gā urmī nādguṭṭhī tangā tangā aḍḍā nū ukkyā.[1] Dara khēkhel beñjrā.' Ār khal-ukhṛī nanāgo ōr nannar arā ba'anar : uyā khōsā, bihnī cākh'ā : akku endr elonā hō malā maṇō. Onā mōkhā, kōṛē kōṛem ullan khēp'ā.'

Naigas, ibṛā urmi nēgcār nañj khacdas khanē, tanghai kētran[2], onṭā khēr eṛbdas-arā, tanghai eṛpā ulā okta'ādas : ā keter, cān malā biṛdā gūṭī, āsgahi erpānum ra'ī.

51. *Karam parab.*

Kuṛukhar majhīnñ, Karam onṭā kohā parab ra'ī. Īd bhādō candōgahi ekādasī ullā nū manī.

Remote preparations.—Ā parab mundhintim, nahṛā nanarkī samā nannar. Ondrkā-khaīgutthyārin mundhim naihār nū āṛsto'or ci'or. Karam āṛsnantī aṭhē ullā mundh, eṛpā nū 'jawā khoppnar'. jokk jokk jawā calkurnum cākhnar, darā ullā[3] nitkī bālkā-amm chiohra' ānar, adin parab nū mējhrāge.

Reason of the regale on Karam-eve. Karam gaṛnantī mundh-mākhan 'senjot' ba'anar. Ānlam bīṛī puttyā khane, khuṛtī nū dālī, iñjō darā an'ā-man'ā aṛkhā kamnar, darā ābīrī pakā urnifigha'ā ōnnar : pairintī gā ubsnā[4] manō, Īge. Pahē kukkō-kukoikhaddar, darā jōkhar pellor hō, nē ubsā beddnar, ārim ubsnar.

First day (morning). Pairī bijj-ghaṛintim ubsur bēcage urkhnar, darā ekā ḍiṇḍā khaddar mal ubsnar, ār karam tarā[5] kānar. Pahē beddarkī āganem malā tārnar. Asānum khāpnar, 'conhai karman nē hō ambnar khaṛnarnek'ā' ba'arkī.

---

[1] Have settled down to their own dwellings, have ceased to prowl about. *Beñjrā* conveys the same idea : the earth is at peace and has fallen to business, has ended its wild life.

[2] *Kētran* refers here to the pahān's sacred winnowing-basket.

[3] Ullā nitkī, assiduously.

[4] Those alone do not fast who volunteer to go to forest early next day, for selecting the karam-bough and bringing it over. It is understood that these are not to return earlier than 2 p.m. or so.

[5] Tarā, *lit.* towards, for ; i.e. in order to fetch.

Paddā nū ra'ū ubsur, biṛī dū-pahar mannā gūṭī, akhṛā nū khōb rijh nanor, darā, tamhai urmī attnā-pundrnan attor-darā, hēcor. Khēl, soēko jhājh jhalī-singār nañjar-kī, bajā assnar Ārgahi madhent' gā nē nē pūrnar, idātō, cuṭṭī kollrkā-bārī, attrā ittrā bongrnakhr'ar kuddnar darā baramba'ā helrnar.—Karamgahi āṛsō biṛī heddē manālaggī khane, bēonantī udhrār'or darā taṅg'ā taṅg'ā eṛpā kaor: pahē maṇḍī mal ōnor: bēgar kaḍrkā nanam, nīdī jharā-amman eklā ōnor.—Karam ondr'ā kānā berā mañja hōlē[1], ār assnā-bajā darā singārguṭṭhi (ghughrī, cāor) hō'orkī urkhor. Pellar hō isuṅg sindrī hō'or-kī ār gane kaor. Ibṛā ormā jōkhar pellar sert'ō, emnā-khajrnā aḍḍā nū em'or, khajr'or, kī bēonā aḍḍā nū phīn kaor. Eō gahṛī[2] mal ubsur, karmam ondr'or-kī, malā bar'or, āgūṭī bēonum ra'or. Karam āṛsālaggī hōle, ōrmar ṭoṅkā nū kālor kī khōṇḍr'or. Punā ubsūrim, ābīri, karam nū sindrī ohiṭ'or, an'āmen'ā bēonan bēcor, darā bagge nēgcar ṭoṅkānum nanor.

(*evening*). Biṛī puttbiṛī, ormar, karman majhyāckar[3], tīnā ḍebbā assnum pāṛnum bar'or, darā akhṛa nū gaṛ'or, kī uruṅg bēcor. Khane ortosin khāpāge asan uyyor, darā, usgo oṇṭa jharā ci'arkī, tām taṅgs'ā taṅg'ā eṛpā kālor.

Khōkhānū, phīn akhṛā nū khōṇḍarkī, assnum paṛnum pāṛnum, ukhā-bārī mēkhā helrnar. Kukoikhaddar punā baugī nū (ekdan ' karam-dōṛo ' ba'anar) oṇṭā billin kisgō-aṭkhātī kullarkī ayyā ondrnar, darā karman ōnd bēṛhā kirrnar kī tamhai aḍḍā nū okknar.

Khane ormārim khōṇḍnaṛ; oṇṭā mancī darā kullā ondrnar. Nīk'ım cān cān khīrī teṅgdas[4], ās mancī nū okkos, darā, kullātī ēkh manos hōle, khīrī teṅgā helr'os. Khīrī munjrkantī, ubsū kukoikhaddar ā khīrī-tinguage ālkhṛā, isuṅg, māsī oi'inar. Darā ormar taṅg'ā taṅg'ā eṛpā kānar; antile asmā, bōṛ'e, arkhī, jharāguṭṭhī onar mōkharkī, oṅghon cāṛē beoā bar'or; makhlē uruṅg khandrnar. Ormar hijta'ā gūṭī nalor bēcor.

---

[1] Ondr'ā kānā, to go and meet.

[2] Gahṛī (=gahnḍī), a word to be distinguished from ghaṛī.

[3] An instance of the past participle of a transitive verb being used with a reflex meaning, ' having surrounded'

[4] *Lit.* Whoever is every year appointed to tell stories, i.e., the man who has been appointed for *that* year.

Second day (*morning*). Nannā ullan 'parnā' ba'anar. Annē jōkhar pellor mūjhrōr'or, darā ormar, sannir kā kōhar, elkhrnā gūṭi bēcor. Pahē mal ubsur aḍḍō-mankhā tarā kaor.

(*evening*). Puttbirī mañjā khane, ōrmārim karman caṛ'ā kālor. Adin mundh naigasgahi, panbharasgahi, mahtosgahi eṛpā kutt'oror; ha'ī, annē annem sadse paddantā khūṭ khūṭ nū āssnum pāṛnum kutta'ānar. Urmi gusan pūroā khane, assnum pāṛnum karman bohāba'āge kānar. Urmī aṭkhan mundh cokhnar, darā kaḍrkāguṭṭhī nannar*: khōkhānū karman, endrā endrā ṭangckā bārī, amm nū hebṛnar ci'inar. Kheḍḍ khekkhan nōṛorkī, asan alkhṛāguṭṭhī mōkhor; darā, kukoikhaddārgahi palkhañjā ra'ō, adin khadd kam'or. Antile taṅg'ā taṅg'ā eṛpa kaor, kī jharu asmā, manḍī-amkhī ōnor mōkhor.

52. *Kuṛukhargahī jatrā kānā.*

Origin and popularity—Kuṛukhargahi majhi nū jatrā kānā khōb manī. Nīk'im, Kuṛukhārim kā Khaṭṭārim madher, khōb urbar mañjardara, tambai ohmā cōd'ā baddnar, ār jatrā okta'āge tambai khurjīn hō uṭhāba'anar; ār, paddā paddantā ālarin eṛ'arkī, ārge tīkhil, dālī, arkhī, lōṛ'ē, mankhā onā mōkhāge ci'inar. Innelā ennē jatrāguṭṭhī Kuṛukhargahi majhī nū ḍher ra'ī; darā abṛā nū hō ekdā-ekdā gā khōb naujaddī ra'ī, idāto Muṛmādarā Guṭuantā jatrā: ibṛā ullā darā mākhā hō laggī.

Proceedings.—Neḍḍā ullā nū, jatrā-ṭoṅkā tarā, nād-pūjā nannar, ekattī lauouakhrnā amban manānek'ā, darā ormar bēs-bēsim eṛpā kirrnarnek'ā; ī khatrī nādge dāṛe ci'inar. Khōkhānū jatran okta'anar: mākhantim dosar ullāgahi adhā biṛī gūṭī khōb bēonar. Antile, uḍhrārnarkī, manḍī onā kānar: khane aṛtī bīrī, mukkar mētar, khaddārin hō'onarkī, jatrāge aur oṅghon kirr urkhnar.

Jōkhar, tam ganē bairākhī ṭōpor, khēl, ḍamuā, jhājh, soēkō, ḍhōl, ḍhāk, penḍrē, tiryō, murli hō'onarkī kānar: ibṛā gā urmī surrā saprau talī; ormar ibṛan hō'ā ongnar. Nēkhai ra'ī ār kāṛā-bairākhī. rampācalpā, kaṅkgahi lakṛā, aḍḍō, injō, godō, mākmarg, teṅgrākullā, ṭemḍāg, darā endran endran argnar. Ibṛā urmī saprau jōkhar hō'onarkī, jatrā-ṭoṅkā argnar, dara asan āṛsnarkī, oṅghon hohkārī

*They make tooth-sticks (from its slenderer branches).

nanaūṭī jatrā ṭonkan kindrārnar. Antile, taṉg'ātaṉg'ā buhī mārnar[1], darā paddantā bairākhlguṭṭhin majhī nū uinar: khanē jōkhar, oṇṭā oṇṭā pellon dharnarkī, ḍaṇḍī pāṛ'ā pāṛ'ā bēonar.

Unpleasant incidents.—Pahē ek'am birī nik'īm, urb ālar majhī nū, bṛā mētā likhickā saprau ambardarā, ekdan ekdan punā kampar. Ennē ennen jatrā-ṭoṉkā nū arg'or hōle, khob launā manī ... Bēonā-ṭonkānum sendrā ṭonkantā khīsan khettnar[2]; darā jiyā-kānan[3] hō balnar, annem launakhrnar.

End of festivities—Biṛī puttbirī, ormar uḍhrārnarkī, nē gā pāhī kānar, nē gā eṛpā kirrnar, kā ā paddantā akbṛā nū hō adhā mākhā gūṭī bēonar. Āulā khōb bōṛ'ē arkhī ōnnar, darā, pāhī ērāge, ālar khēr kiss pīṭnar. Oṇḍkā-mokkantī, pāhiyar eṛpā kirrnar, makhlē ullēṛ gūṭī hō pāhī ōnnar.

V. Riddles.

Pandrah bhāir rahcar, ār gusan oṇṭā asmā[4] rahcā. Idin candāhē sannī bhāir ōnd[5] mokkhar darā kohasge phīn saēsem ciccar. Endrā talī ?—Candō.

2. Ek'am āli oṇṭā khaddānim pacci. Endr talī ?—Kerā-mann.

3. Orot kukkosge, kundras khane, cār-ṭhur kheḍḍ rahcā ; jōkh mañjas khane, ēṛ kheḍḍ mañjā ; paogī mañjas khane, mūnd kheḍḍ mañjā. Nē taldas ?—Āl-khadd.

4. Ulā kukk, darā bahrī panjrā ; adi maīyā ēṛā-poṭṭā Endr talī ?—Carkhā[6].

5. Kiyyā ṭhaṭhrā, maīyā hō ṭhaṭhrā : majhī nu nalī mokhārō paṭhrū. Endr ?—Kicrī-essnā ḍuṉgī[7].

---

[1] *Lit.* they bury a pen ; i.e., they fence off an enclosure with a row of posts.

[2] 'pay off old scores due since the last hunt', or more probably 'display wraths worthy of a hunting ground'.

[3] See Dict. under *jiyā*.

[4] *Asmā*, a round flat cake.

[5] *Ond mokkhar*, ate it all.

[6] In the spinning wheel, the thread rests on an assemblage of slender pegs, the reel inside

[7] See Dict. under eaning

6. Konkṛō-bonkṛō dassō bhāir, ārge kukk malā, darā kūl nū baī ra'ī. Endr ?—Kakṛō.

7. Khoṭṭkā khāsī merkhā tarā mēn īrī[1]. Endr talī ?—Khess nāṛā.

8. Nannā paddā nū cicc laggyā, nannā paddā nū mōjkhā ca'ī, nannā paddā nū gohār nannar. Endr ba'adai ?—Hukā.

9. Ort ālas, tanghai āloguṭṭhī nū cicc lagābacas-darā, alkhdas : 'Akkū engāge ḍhibā khakkhr'ō'. Īs nētanghai ?—Kumbhras.

10. Ālarin īrī-kī, balin muccī ? Nē talī ?—Ghunghī.

11. Ujjō bīrī onṭā nāme, piṭkantī kainōgoṭang nāme. Endr talī ?—Bās.

12 Ulā ahṛā, bahrī poṭṭā. Endr talī ?—Mōṛā.

13. Ulā khamī, bahrī kāṭh-korwā. Ekālekh'ā mesgā—Gūngu.

14. Onṭa pūp ullā-bīrī dulkhī, makhā-bīrī bīndri'ī. Talī ?—Piṭrī[2].

15. Cēp poṅṅō hole, onṭā pūp bithrār'ī ; cēp idro'ō khane, dumpho'ō[3]. Endr talī ?—Etta'ānā kullā.

16. Onṭā mann nū bāgrkadim-bāgrkā. Endr ?—Kornjō-aṭkhā.

17. Ort kukkos pairī bīrim mulkhdas, kukk-cappō bīrī urkhdas. Īs endr ?—Lsangī.

18. Ort kukkosin pāknar khane, cǐkhdas ; kīdnar khane, chachem ra'adas. Endr talī ?—Ḍhāk.

19. Ort kukoi, irrī[4] nippī-kī, collā nū ukkī ṛāī. Īd nē talī ?—Bāgrka.

20. Ort kukkos kohā sōgyā, khōb jōr-uyyū, ālarin hō paṭka'ādas. Īs ne taldas ?—Boṛ'ē.

21. Ort cicī kukkos konkō soṭṭan ceḍḍkas[5] kuddālagdas. Ek'am ōrtās ?—Allā.

[1] Notice the alliteration between *khāsi* and *khess*,

[2] After the night's rest, mats are rolled up and tilted against a wall : in this position, they often topple over.

[3] From *domphnā*.

[4] From *errnā*.

[5] From *ceṛnā*.

22. Ort bēl-khaddas endran bō malā sahdas. Nē taldas ?-Khann.

23. Urmī pūpantī ekdā subhi'ī[1] ?—Kicrī.

24. Utkhīdim gā kerā, baokan utkhī bar'ā pullī. Endrā ?—Cār.

25. Urkhō biri, khaiki kai, kirr'ō birī, ḍhirḍhirirkī bar'ī. Endr tali ?—Aṛī.

26. Khaikā kapkantī amm pajhrār'ī. Endr ?—Kulhū.

27. Cuguy-cuguy cōgnā kukk malyā phudnā-aṭkhā. Kitan nē akh'ī ?—Nāgnerr.

28. Chipichipī amm nū gisō injō upḥṛār'ī. Endr ?—Tatkhā.

29. 'Nīn isānim ra'a, ēn rājī kuddā kādan,' ennē nē ba'ī ?—Kheḍḍgaṛı cambī.

30. Bā' gahi barchan nē dhar'ā oṅgō ?—Cioc.

31. Mutthā nū sam'i, muṭṭhā nū sam'ā pullī. Endr ?—Kullā.

32. Mokhārō khāsīgahi paı ḍrū ahṛā. Adiu akhdar ?—Māsī.

1. *Translation.*—1. There were fifteen brothers with one cake. The fourteen younger brothers ate it up, then passed it on full and entire to their eldest. What is it ?—The moon.

2. A woman gives birth to one child only. Who is she ?—The plantain tree.

3. A youngster was born with four feet ; when adult, he turned a biped ; when old, he became a three-legged thing. Who is it ?—A human being.

4. Head inside, ribs outside, bowels (wrapt) upon these. What is it?—A spinning wheel.

5. Bamboo-matting below, bamboo-matting above, and between the two a kid is frisking about. What is this ?—A weaver's spool.

6. Ten crooked misshapen brothers ; they have no head, and their mouth is in their belly. What is it ?—A crab.

---

[1]. From *sobhnā*.

7 Castrated he-goats with their heads off gape skyword. What is this?—Paddy stubble.

8. Fire has broken out in one village, the smoke rises in another village and the alarm is given in a third village. What sayest thou to this? It is the hookah.

9. A man, after setting fire to his belongings, laughs (and says): 'For the nonce I shall make money.' Who is that individual?—The potter.

10. On catching sight of people, she claps her door. Who is she? —The snail.

11. When alive, one name; when killed, a lot of names. What is it?—The bamboo tree.

12. Meat inside, bowels outside. What is it?—The rice bale.

13. The thatch inside, the rafters outside. What sort of roof is this?—A leaf waterproof (layers of leaves kept in place by cross-sticks).

14. A flower droops all day; at night, it speads out. What is it?—A bamboo mat. (See note to text).

15. A certain flower opens in the rain; when the rain stops, the flower closes. What is it?—A collapsible umbrellá*

16. Millions of combs upon a tree. What are they?—The karanj leaves.

17. A youngster sinks out of sight in the early morning and re-appears at noon. What is it?—The coulter (vertical blade in front of ploughshare).

18. One takes in arms a baby-boy, he brays; one lays it down, he keeps quiet. What is it?—A drum.

19. A girl, after raking up her sweepings, takes her station at the back of the house. Who is she?—A comb.

20. A tiny fellow knocks down big, strappy, power fulmen. Who is he? —Rice beer.

21. A youngster goes about sporting a crooked switch. Who is he?—A dog.

---

*By opposition to the bamboo umbrella, which is still the normal article in backword villages.

22. A prince royal cannot bear up with the most insignificant cause of pain. What is it? The eye.

23. What is it that beats all flowers for beauty? Garment.

24. Quite alone it went; but it cannot come back alone. What is it? An arrow.

25. Dry on its way out, drenched on its way back. What is it? A water pot.

26. A waterspring out of dry wood. What is it? An oil press.

27. A mint leaf over a swaying head. Who knows what there is underneath? A cobra.

28. A broad flat fish flounders about in a few drops of water. What is it? A mango.

29. 'Stop here, I am off to see the world'; who speaks thus? A bicycle track.

30. Who can lay hold of a King's spear? Fire.

31. Held with the hand, it does not hold in the hand. What is it? An umbrella.

32. Black goat, white flesh. You know that? The urid bean.

VI. Poetry.

Oraon bards are not devoid of instinctive notions about lines, stanzas, syllabic measurement, caesura and rhymes. But all this seems to be very erratic. Thus, between the 4-line stanzas of a song, one stanza may be sandwiched comprising 6 lines, etc. The connecting thought which runs through the various stanzas of any Oraon song is extremely hard to catch—not only from the innumerable allusions made to peculiarities of domestic and tribal life—but also because the Oraon *genre* is so extremely dramatic and lyric. The eye is, at first reading, simply nonplussed by a display of flashes and a revel of colours, while the ear can make nothing of apparently disconnected bits of dialogue. A Western reader feels knocked about a little. Yes, in the case of Oraon songs, if he comes back upon the wonder perseveringly, he shall see after a time the *disiecta membra* unite into a fine picture or a really moving scene, full of authentic lyrism.

Of the six songs given by Hahn, I propose to translate and explain only one, that which he marked no. 5. Being of a character comparatively sober, it may serve as an excellent introduction to ampler acquaintance with Oraon lyrism.

A SONG ON THE RANCHI MUTINY OF 1857.

Summary.—Maṇī-sahi Jagernāth, the rājā of Chotanagpur, is too much engrossed in his pleasures, and also too desperate a coward, for taking notice of the rebellion which desolates his dominions and his people (st. 1, 12, 13, 14 15). Two disloyal zamindars, Thakur Bisnāth of Bundu-Tamar and Pandey Gangpat of Bhaunro, [1] have it all their own way (st. 1 and 20). Only the British (st. 16, 17, 18) and such able native officers as Loknāth (st. 20) will be able to stay the universal ruin.

From internal evidence (last stanza), it is found that the poem was composed between the 15th and 21st of April 1858, and, from this itself, we further realize that this song's title in Hahn's edition ('a song for the *May-June* Jatra') cannot possibly be authentic, unless indeed the poet had forgotten to alter, in view of Gangpat's recent execution, a present tense to a past one.

The stanzas marked by Hahn 6, 7 and 8 must have occupied other ranks in the original. They are printed in the present edition with the figures 16, 1 and 12, respectively.—In carrying out a few syllabic corrections in lines too long or too short, I have been guided by the principle that an illiterate coryphaeus, reciting from memory, will unconsciously introduce *padding*, or skip over some *padding* of the original text.

---

(1) Close to Dighia (Bero P. O.)

1. Rājā ho, Jagarnāth rājā,
Ninghai rājī nū laṛekā manjā !
Ninghai rājī Bhūḍū-Tamar,
Ninghai rājī nū laṛekā mañjā !

2. Hal'ū mal'ū Ṭillā pāṛū,
Ghoṛō maiyā nary'ālagdai ?
Pellō ninghai khēkhel-kiyyā*!
Ghoṛō maiyā nary'ālagdai !

3. Kaṅkgahi ghoṛō nū
Na argō, nehālū pāṛū ?
Kaṅkgahi ghoṛō nū
Pell argō, nehālū pāṛū ?

4. Kirr, Laliyā, endr kādī ?
Malā kirron, nantarā kādan.
Jūṛī jōkhas koṛā keras :
Malā kirron, nantarā kādan.

5. Ninghai pāṛkan pellō pāṛyā ;
Polloi ko, dhanāmudī pāṛū.
Pairī birī pellō pāṛyā :
Polloi ko, dhanāmudī pāṛū.

6. Balī kam'ā, ho, balī kam'ā :
Pell-eṛpā ḍanglō ra'ī.
Jōkh-eṛpā, ho, ringī-cingī :
Pell-eṛpā ḍanglō ra'ī.

7. Endrge, koi, cīkhhar cīkhar
Oṇṭā kabrā khēran argta'ādi ?
Jōkhar bhejjā mala dharnar ?
Īge kabrā khēran argta'ādi ?

8. ' Dhibā ci'ā ci'ā !'
Ningan, pello, Naipāl hō'on.
En bār manālagdan,
Ningan, pello, Naipāl hō'on.

9. Hairē, engdā Gangō pellō
Ganglā jhūṛe-jhūṛ nū ra'ī :
Ād gangelā khoyā kerā,
Gangelā jhūṛe-jhūṛ nū ra'ī

10. Ayang keccā kerā :
Bhayā, nēkan ayang ba'ot ?
Dharme tuar nanjā :
Bhayā, nēkan ayang ba'ot ?

11. Ayang-bang malkā !
Hairē, bekārekan laggī !
Hairē, endr nanot ?
Haire, bekārekan laggi !

12. Belasgahi kukk māyā
Kāṛsā jhilmilr'ālaggī.
Ceṇḍā pellō mār laucā :
Kāṛsā jhilmilr'ālaggī !

13. Kalā, budiu hō'ar barā :
Idi ganē ullā malā kālō.
Tīnā kheḍḍan ḍheṅkoy nanī,
Idi ganē ullā malā kālō.

14. Hīrī bar, koi, bannā kicrī
Ningan ambar, rijh mal laggī
Hāṛī kāl, koi, bannā kicrī :
Jhikā bilcā bar'ālaggī.

15. Bēlas sannī nū conbā rahcas :
Cōreā bongas bācr'āge.
Tangyo keccā, darā ās
Sherghatī bongas bācr'āge.

16. Ek'am Sāheb ittyas,
Panārī pargan nū bar'āldas.
Rassal Sāheb ittyas,
Panārī telengārin ondrdas.

* *Understand* : Your sweetheart (tramps) below (thee), on the ground !...

17. Kampanī Urbar gūli ambnar
Hājāribagh telcngar malyā.
Mākhābīrī gūlin ambnar ār,
Telengārin, bhaiyā rē, chek'ā.[1]

18. Telengar jiroṇg-joroṇgr'ā barcar,
Ṭikū paddā nū chauni nanjar.
Endrnā, Jagarnath-sāi belāyo,
Bongdai, kā ekhō kālagdai ?

19. Haridal Giridal irbārim
Laṛekā pariyā kecoar :
Jiyan ḍhīṭh nanā,bhaiyā rē !
Laṛekā pariyā keccar...

20. Bhaūrontā Gaṇgpat-rāi rājin
Dhīre dhīre piṭṭa' ādas :
Loknāth-sāi bhaiyā re, rājin
Dhīre dhīre sambhṛa'ādas !

TRANSLATION.

1. O King, o King Jagernāth,
In thy realm mutiny has broken out !
In the Bhundu-Tamar[2] country,
Within thy realm mutiny has broken out !

I.— Universal misery caused by the rebels.—(*a*) lovers impoverished and separated.

—2. Tilla, thou silly piper,
Mounted upon a horse, thou hummest a tune ?
Thy young-wife tramps below on the (hard) ground...!
Thou, mounted upon a horse, hummest a tune !

—3. On a wooden horse
Who'll ride[3], thou capital singer ?
Shall on a wooden horse
The girl ride, thou capital singer ?

4. Come back, Laliyā, where art thou going ?
—I won't come back, I am bound elsewhere.
A dancer of mine[4] is gone abroad :
I won't come back, I am bound elsewhere.

---

[1] *Chek'ā*, short form of the infinitival dative *chek'āge*.

[2] Bhundu, 85°38', 23°9'

[3] *I.e.*—I have no horse left for her. Her own horse has been impressed or stolen.

[4] *Lit.*—a boy-chum (of mine).

—5\. The girl has done singing to thy tune :
Thou art helpless, wealthy singer.
She sang the space of a morning.
Helpless thou art, wealthy singer.

(*b*) Village dancing-schools deserted.

6\. Make a door, friend, make a door :
The girls' hall is yawning.
The boys' is gay with arabesques :
The girls' hall is yawning.[1]

(*c*) Young men have left the country.

7\. Why, o maiden, all in tears
Doest thou sacrifice a piebald cock?
No youngsters ask thee for a dance?
Is it for this thou sacrificest a piebald cock?

(*d*) Exactions and plundering.

—8\. 'Money, money, give me money'!......
—I will take thee, sweetheart, to Nepal.
I am racked and ruined;
I will take thee, sweetheart, to Nepal[2].

(*e*) People live on grass-produce.

9\. Alas! young Gango, my daughter
Is (toiling) at Job's tears thickets :
She is gone to cut some of these (for our meal),
She is among Job's tears thickets[3].

(*f*) Orphans left uncared for.

10\. Mother is dead :
O little brother, whom shall we call mother?
God has made us orphans :
O little brother, whom shall we call mother?

[1] *ganglo* means 'ajar', but also sometimes 'wide open' or 'gaping'.—On the village institutions alluded to here, see Or. Dict., under *dhumkuryā* and *pell*.

[2] This bit of dialogue takes place between any two lovers, *not* between Tilla and Laliya once more.

[3] The proper name Gango has nothing to do with the common noun *ganglo*

11. No father, no mother!
    Alas! how sick at heart one feels!
    Alas! what shall we do?
    Alas! how sick at heart one feels!

II.—Worthlessness of King Jagernāth.

12. Upon our king's head
    The royal cap[1] sends flashes about.
    A girl in her prime has smitten him:
    The royal cap sends flashes all round.

-13. Go, bring me yonder maiden:
    With the one at my side, time won't pass gaily.
    She limps of the right foot,
    With her, time won't pass gaily.

-14. Come this way, lass, thou with the striped raiment
    Without thee I feel cheerless...
    Go that way, lass with the striped raiment:
    Scintillant earrings are coming (for thee).

15. Our King as a youngster was cooing:
    He (once) fled to Chorea[2] to make himself spruce;
    His mother died, and he...
    Took off to Sherghati[3] to put on finery.

III.—Movements of British troops.

16. An English (captain) has dropped in,
    He is coming to the Panārī pargannah[4].
    Russel Sāhib has dropped in:
    To Panārī he is marching troops.

[1] Not a *turban*, but a peculiar head-dress distinctive of Hindu rajas.
In her prime, lit. nubile.

[2] Chorea, a village north-west of Mandar.

[3] Sherghati, on the Murhar river about 20 miles south-west of Gaya, and 20 miles north of Chatra.

[4] Panārī pargannah 84°, 37′ 33′ and 23° 4′ 5′.

17. Tommies have arrived glittering in the sun,
In Tiku village they have garrisoned[1].
Why, o Jagernâth, o king,
Shouldst thou run, and whither art thou taking thyself?

IV.—Reverses and hopes.

18. The Company Directors are pouring bullets
Into the Hazaribagh sepoys.[2]
Far into the night shots are fired,
Brother, to stop them.

19. Both Haridal and Girdal
Have fallen on the field:
Hearts on high, brother!
Fallen they have on the field...

20 Gangpat-Râi of Bhaunro is having
The country butchered by inches[3].
(But) Loknath-sahi, brother, is becoming, inch by inch,
The (gentle) mainstay of our country.

The End.

[1] The insurgents, numbering 3,000 had assembled at Tuko, not far from the Bhaunro zamindari, quite close to Dighia. Pursued by the British, they pushed on to Chatra, Hazaribagh district, passing through Pandri (85° 4', 23° 31'), Balumâth (84° 59, 23° 48') and Nowadeeh (84° 58', 23° 57'). This last stage was reached on the 27th September, only five days before the tragedy came to a close.

[2] Allusion to the subsequent defeat of the 8th Native Infantry and other rebels by Major English, on the 2nd of October 1857 The action took place at Chatra, 20 mile north-west of Hazaribagh town ('Mundas and their Country', by S. C. Roy pages 232—235).

[3] Pandey Gangpat was hanged on the 21st April 1858. It was this individual who fired at the Lutheran churchtower the cannon-ball embedded in it to this day.—Lâl Loknath Sahi was deputed, under Government orders, dated 15th April 1858, to prepare a register of all bhuinhari lands "The idea that some operations were going on to protect their rights pacified the Mundas and Oraons for the moment." (Mundas and their Country, pages 269, 270)

B. & O. G. P. (Rev.) no. 4—300—3-12-1931—S. C. M. and others.